W9-BZF-996

# Curriculum Differentiation

Saint Peter's University Library
Withdrawn

SUNY Series
# FRONTIERS IN EDUCATION
*Philip G. Altbach, Editor*

The Frontiers in Education Series draws upon a range of disciplines and approaches in the analysis of contemporary educational issues and concerns. Books in the series help to reinterpret established fields of scholarship in education by encouraging the latest synthesis and research. A special focus highlights educational policy issues from a multidisciplinary perspective. The series is published in cooperation with the Graduate School of Education, State University of New York at Buffalo.

*Books in this series include:*

# *Curriculum Differentiation*
## *Interpretive Studies in*
## *U.S. Secondary Schools*

*Edited by*
Reba Page
and
Linda Valli

State University of New York Press

Published by
State University of New York Press, Albany

© 1990 State University of New York

All rights reserved

Printed in the United States of America

No part of this book may be used or reproduced
in any manner whatsoever without written permission
except in the case of brief quotations embodied in
critical articles and reviews.

For information, address State University of New York
Press, State University Plaza, Albany, N.Y. 12246

Library of Congress Cataloging-in-Publication Data

Curriculum differentiation: interpretive studies in U.S. secondary
    schools/edited by Reba Page and Linda Valli.
        p.   cm.—(SUNY series, frontiers in education)
    Includes bibliographical references (p. ).
    ISBN 0-7914-0469-2 (alk. paper).—ISBN 0-7914-0470-6 (pbk. :
alk. paper)
        1. Education, Secondary—United States—Curricula.   2. Curriculum
planning—United States.   3. High school students—United States—
Social conditions.   4. Ability grouping in education.   I. Page,
Reba Neukom.   II. Valli, Linda, 1947–      .   III. Series.
LB1628.5.C87   1990                                                    90-31585
373.19′0973—dc20                                                          CIP

10   9   8   7   6   5   4   3   2   1

# Contents

Chapter 1

# Curriculum Differentiation: An Introduction

Should U.S. secondary schools provide different courses of study to different groups of students? This theoretical question about curriculum differentiation undergirds the more specific action-questions of practitioners and policy-makers. Should college-bound students be provided college-preparatory classes and work-bound students, a vocational curriculum? Should students who are "advanced," "slow," or "handicapped," perhaps by pregnancy, be provided classes in which they can "work at their own speed" on materials suited to their "special" conditions? Should students from cultures other than those of the white, middle class mainstream be provided classes in their native languages and cultures? Or, should adolescents of all talents, needs, and aspirations study a common curriculum in preparation for participation in a democratic, pluralistic society?

These questions about the differentiation of the high school curriculum and its relation to social differentiation evoke the contradictory norms of American society. Paradoxically, the norms charge secondary schools to provide equal educational opportunities for all students while also providing a differentiated education for each. Schools are expected to bind all adolescents together in a civil democracy, to provide all with marketable skills, but to do so without infringing the unique development of any. In short, high schools must not discriminate, yet they must differentiate (Cazden 1986; Varenne 1977).

As a result of these complexities and the values they express, curriculum differentiation poses difficult, potentially volatile, dilemmas for American educators and citizens. Since the turn of the century, the possibility of accommodating an increasingly diverse student population with differentiated curricula has been one of the high school's prepotent responses (Powell, Farrar & Cohen 1985). The questions reverberate in today's revived debate about the purposes of public schooling, sparking competing calls for a core curriculum, the equitable distribution of "humanized" knowledge, and early and efficient specialization. Given high Hispanic and black birth rates and a new wave of immigrants from Southeast Asia and Latin America, the issue is to become even more highly charged in the near future.

Ironically, however, just as the topic of curriculum differentiation re-emerges as one of crucial theoretical, pedagogical, and political importance, many involved in its debate consider the issue closed. On one side, proponents regard the practice as a neutral, necessary response to "individual educational needs." Like advocates from earlier decades, they see curriculum differentiation as a realistic, efficient, or necessary response for the high school to make to an ever more diverse student population. However, at the same time, critics on the other side are equally certain that all forms of curriculum differentiation should be abolished. Progressive critics, noting that poor, minority students are often over-represented in low, special, or vocational tracks, while middle class, white students are often over-represented in high, mainstream, or academic tracks, argue that curriculum differentiation in the schools simply reproduces the unjust socioeconomic and racial differentiation in the wider society. Some even imply a conspiracy theory. More conservative critics decry a watering down of the curriculum and a loss of cultural literacy. They argue the study by all of commonly acknowledged classics.

The fervor and certainty expressed by proponents of differentiation and by their critics suggest that differentiation in schools is a simple black or white issue. Adherents on both sides presume its manifestation in schools is uniform, its effects self-evidently good (or bad), and, therefore, its practice merely a straightforward choice for educators and citizens: either an individualized or a common curriculum. However, in posing the issue as a simple choice, partisans of all persuasions ignore and cannot explain the compelling, contradictory evidence provided by their opposites: while we expect schools to individualize education, we also expect them to provide all with equal educational opportunity. Thus, like the voluminous research literature on tracking and other forms of curriculum differentiation, the present debate is riddled with internal and external contradictions, based on slight data, and represents simplistic formulations of the relationship between curricular and social differentiation.

The nine interpretive chapters in this book inform this polarized debate and recast it. Emphasizing the importance of studying educational processes as they occur in classrooms, schools, and communities, the studies portray graphically the complexity, diversity, and sociocultural contradictions with which curriculum differentiation is enacted, rather than its simplicity. They describe the informal as well as the explicit procedures through which schools value and distribute knowledge, analyze the multifaceted rather than singular meaning of differentiating practices, and interpret curriculum differentiation's intricate relationship to broader precepts of social differentiation, such as age, race, class, and gender. Simultaneously, the chapters exemplify the usefulness of interpretive studies of schooling. Because their data are specific and the connections between them are carefully analyzed, interpretive studies provide the reconceptualization of curriculum differentiation on which valid theory and excellent and equitable practice and policy depend. Both individually and as a collection, the nine chapters in this volume exemplify what and how one sees in differentiated secondary school classrooms when using an interpretive lens.

## STUDIES OF CURRICULUM DIFFERENTIATION IN THE INTERPRETIVE RESEARCH PARADIGM

Studies of schooling in the interpretive paradigm, of which the articles in this book are an extension, significantly sharpen understanding of the school's differentiating, or sorting and selecting, function. In part, they clarify persistent contradictions in traditional studies of curriculum differentiation and tracking. By looking inside the black box of schools and classrooms, they describe the processes and contexts in which curriculum differentiation produces its intended—and unintended—effects. For example, surveys provide contradictory accounts of the relationship between track placement, student ability, and sociocultural characteristics but, because they provide no information about what actually happens in schools and classrooms, the contradictions remain inexplicable. They become more understandable with interpretive documentation that demonstrates, for example, students are unable or unwilling to provide accurate survey responses for several reasons. For example, they do not know their track placement (Rosenbaum 1976), are misinformed about it (Cicourel and Kitsuse 1963), conceal it (Page 1984), or are in more than one track (Valli 1986).

Interpretive research also elaborates issues in traditional studies. Spindler and Spindler (1982) and Wilcox (1982) explore the sources and mechanisms of what Rosenthal and Jacobsen (1968) called the self-fulfilling prophecy. Rosenbaum (1976) explains the independent effect of track placement on IQ which Goldberg, Passow, and Justman (1966) demonstrated. And, Metz (1978), Swidler (1979), and Popkewitz, Tabachnick, and Wehlage (1982) show how differentiation is accomplished in a complex *interaction,* rather than in either differences between schools (Coleman 1966) or differences within schools (Jencks and Brown 1975). By focusing on *how* relationships are accomplished, interpretive studies recast simple social algorithms so that, for example, one no longer looks for teacher expectations, in and of themselves, to determine learning.

At the same time, however, interpretive research contributes much more than the clarification or fleshing out of experimental and survey research. It provides a fundamentally different way of thinking about differentiation in schools and its relationship to social differentiation.

## EXPLICATING MEANING: THE INTERPRETIVE TASK

Interpretive studies of curriculum differentiation ask what people in schoolrooms do and what they know that makes their behavior sensible (Spindler and Spindler 1987), with the goal of explicating the meaning of curriculum differentiation. A good explication makes the taken-for-granted practice of providing different courses of study to different groups of students appear strange rather than all-too-familiar. It thereby brings differentiation to consciousness so that it can be scrutinized and understood, rather than overlooked as common sense (Geertz 1973; Spindler 1982). Like anthropological accounts that "reduce the puzzlement of . . . primitive facts in faraway places," interpretive studies of schooling at home "clarify what goes on in [schools]" to help us learn about ourselves (Geertz 1973, p. 16) and to deliberate on possible actions. By contrast, traditional studies typically take at face value curriculum differentiation's inputs (e.g., track placement) and outputs (almost always academic achievement test scores). They measure relationships between placement and achievement and assert generalizations about the distribution of tracking's effects.

The interpretivist's interest in meaning provokes inquiry in three general domains: (1) the perspectives of school participants, (2) the processes in which meaning is produced and (3) the contexts in which meaning is shaped. With the domains in mind, one asks:

(1) What are the perspectives of school participants regarding the roles of the teacher and student and the nature of the curriculum in differentiated classes?

(2) Through what face-to-face processes do school participants make visible and negotiate their perspectives and, thereby, construct meaning?

(3) How is the meaning of curriculum differentiation that is constructed in a classroom linked to more stable precepts of institutional and social differentiation, such as academic ability, age, or social class?

These questions reflect assumptions about curricular and social differentiation that differ from those of survey and experimental research. Most crucial is the distinction made in interpretive research between *facts* of social and educational difference and their *meaning*. For example, differences abound: children differ in IQ, track placement, race, levels of self-esteem, and on countless other traits. However, the meaning of differences emerges only as people interpret and act on them. Thus, IQ, track level, race, self-esteem, and other traits are not automatically or inherently significant. They become important as people in classrooms *make* them important in particular ways. Handicapped students who drool are treated matter-of-factly in some classes whereas, in others, the identical behavior is stigmatized. From the interpretive perspective, then, the specific ways people understand differences are not extraneous to, or mere mediations between, inputs and outcomes. They *are* the inputs and outcomes. Understanding differentiation requires understanding its meaning.

From this fundamental distinction flow several related assumptions. First, although meaning does not inhere automatically in social or educational phenomena, neither is it simply idiosyncratic or random. Differences are not just a matter of what each person wants to believe. Rather, meaning is a *social* construction, and in two senses. First: a person's perspective is shaped by those of others with whom s/he interacts. Second, the perspectives of individuals are not created solely *in situ* but reflect broader historical and sociocultural understandings. Interpretive research attends to both aspects of socially constructed meaning. It attempts to make explicit both the creative particularity of an event as distinctive human beings speak and act about it, as well as the event's broader, more stable, representativeness as a recognizable kind of human event.

For instance, the curriculum is commonly posited as the school knowledge that an individual teacher transmits to students, with the success of all measured by students' achievement test scores. However, the curriculum that occurs in classrooms is much more inclusive than this rather technical, individualistic definition suggests, and school knowledge is shaped in significant ways by the responses, reactions and, on occasion, the counter-definitions, offered by students. Thus, a teacher may use a film with the best of pedagogical intentions—"to enhance students' knowledge of Greek mythology," as one teacher explained. But, students' knowing reactions to lugubrious, narrative intonements about "the Greek's knowledge of herbal lore," shots of nude statuary, or Zeus' assault on Leda shift the significance of the classics. Simultaneously, although student catcalls reflect the personalities and events that are specific to a particular classroom and therefore not completely predictable, they nevertheless derive from implicit age-based norms of the more stable, American, adolescent subculture, which leads us to expect sexuality as a prominent focus. Similarly, the teacher's lesson plan, although also idiosyncratic, reflects as well the acknowledged, tacit, informal norms of the faculty of the school regarding an appropriately classical curriculum.

In other words, patterns — adolescent joking, faculty cultures — mark individuals' behavior across settings. Their regularity may suggest causal "social structures." However, although such structures are taken for granted as the way things really are, they are themselves constructions, peculiar to a particular time and culture (Mehan 1978; Wehlage 1981). Rather than causing or determining people to behave in particular ways, they are resources. People use them in ways that make sense, or are understandable, given their situations. Thus, not all adolescents joke about the Greeks nor do all English teachers teach about them because, in particular times and places, participants may perceive those behaviors as culturally misguided. Interpretive studies attempt to capture both the micro and macrolevel aspects of social reality and therefore run a middle, intersubjective course between radical individualism and radical social determinism (Erikson 1986).

A second assumption of interpretive studies is that because phenomena acquire meaning as individuals actively interpret them, variation and ambiguity are predominant and valuable features of the social world (Spindler 1982). An event like lower-track placement, although it shares surface similarities with lower-track placements elsewhere, is not everywhere and at all times the same. Rather, its significance varies, since individuals differ in their perspectives, and interpretations change with time and place. Moreover, even very small variations between events, although immeasurable, may nevertheless have strong effects. For example, statistically-treated classroom observations record marked similarities between all levels of tracked classes: all are flatly enervating (Goodlad 1984; Oakes 1985). The similarities confound measurement of robust differences between tracks. However, from an interpretive perspective, precisely the proximity of gross similarities and subtle differences accounts for the stigma and persistence of some lower-track placements as much as heavy-handed differences might. Like other *caricatures,* lower-track classes derive their punch from both their similarity to and their difference from the regular classes they parody (Page 1987a). As this example suggests, the assumptions of traditional research that an educational variable, like lower-track placement, is a discrete, uniform entity may mislead. Variables in the social world are rarely so clear-cut, nor are they necessarily additive or linear in their effects. Instead, their meaning is highly indeterminate; often they interact dynamically, with some setting limits on the effect of others.

Finally, interpretive studies, if wary of the purportedly universal laws of human behavior sought in traditional research, are not merely microscopic anecdotes or, as a colleague once accused, "creative writing." They are interpretations and they have an interpretation's validity. Interpretive validity derives from the internal coherence of an account and its grounding in appropriate theory (Varenne 1983). The researcher systematically and analytically interprets for the reader the interpretations of classroom participants of events that happen. Thus, "ethnography is neither subjective nor objective . . . but mediat[es] two worlds [those of the reader and the subjects] through a third [the researcher's] (Agar 1986, p. 19). A good account refines or clarifies our understanding of the events. It does not prove or predict the world, but helps us learn about it.

Interpretive studies begin with "thick descriptions" (Geertz 1973, citing Ryle 1949). Because they are detailed, such accounts provide readers with vicarious experiences, so that events can be comprehended that one may not know firsthand or that one takes for granted (e.g., dropping out of school). Comprehension involves seeing situations that are usually stereotyped in a new, "humanized" (Agar 1986, p. 44) light. Thus, through a good interpretation, dropping out of school may emerge as a sensible, if lamentable, choice, rather than as an individual's or the system's failure. At the same time, these studies provide the "intellectual instrumentalities" (Bellack 1978, citing Dewey 1916), or concepts, with which to identify and analyze practices in one's own school or in schools described in other studies which resemble the situation treated in the interpretive study. In other words, interpretive studies do not claim to generalize from a selected sample to a population as statistical accounts do. Rather, they provide a particular way of looking at schooling: a metaphor or a model. Furthermore, analogous cases do not so much accumulate, as they systematically probe and elaborate previously accepted interpretations so that events and concepts are more incisively understood. In short, interpretive studies capture the "profundities of the world" — dropping out, stratification, school knowledge, power, equal educational opportunity — in "homely . . . ethnographic miniatures," and convey the mundane specificities with which people enact and re-create the profundities (Geertz 1973, p. 21). Such research provides the possibility for critical reflection about and conceptual clarification of curricular and social differentiation which precede informed choices in educational policy, practice, and theory.

## A DIFFERENT CONCEPTUALIZATION OF CURRICULUM DIFFERENTIATION

Interpretive studies generate a reconceptualization of curriculum differentiation. It is a sociocultural and political as well as a scholastic process (Apple 1979; Kliebard 1987). Thus, curriculum differentiation is emergent in the curriculum-in-use, rather than fixed in syllabi, state guidelines, or lesson plans. It is oblique and multifaceted, rather than straightforward or rational: in daily lessons, teachers' and students' negotiate their definitions of their roles and of knowledge (Keddie 1971) in particular institutional settings (Lesko 1988; Metz 1986; Page 1987b). In the process, not just track placement or perfunctory skills, but roles, interactional prerogatives, status, and knowledge are differentially allocated within a school and between schools.

    This conceptualization contrasts with those of traditional studies. Particularly in research grounded in educational psychology (Good and Brophy 1987), curriculum differentiation is often assumed to be neutral and strictly academic. Accordingly, when schools track, they rather passively accommodate the talents and/or interests of individual students, objectively measuring students' abilities, efficiently providing appropriate materials, and fairly testing self-evidently important outcomes, particularly academic achievement. Traditional sociological studies differ from the psychological by calling attention to the school's role in allocating resources to students with different assets and aspirations. However, they often present an equally mechanistic view of tracking. Somehow, the school order is determined by and replicates the social order. Where the social order is presumed to be meritocratic, curriculum differentiation is a functional, efficient allocation of human and curricular resources. Where the social order is irredeemably inequitable, as in revisionists' critiques (Bourdieu & Passeron 1977; Bowles & Gintis 1976), curriculum differentiation serves the interests of the powerful: lower-track students are located in lower-track classes where they receive lower-status knowledge in preparation for lower-class jobs. Therefore, traditional studies treat as self-evident or extraneous the intentions and choices of teachers or students and the relationship between curricular and social differentiation. The reconceptualized view differs from both of these in its focus on the institution of the school and of curriculum's meaning. It acknowledges that curriculum differentiation is always contextualized rather than neutral, school rhetoric to the contrary, but because of human meaning-making in a complex culture, the effects of context are not so easily predicted as macrosociological theory suggests.

Not surprisingly, given the reconceptualization of curriculum differentiation, interpretive studies not only clarify but complicate curriculum differentiation. A major confusion: the significance of the relationship between definitions of knowledge, their distribution in tracked classes and schools, and students' sociocultural characteristics. Some studies cast the issue in terms of correspondence theory: schools allocate high status knowledge to socially advantaged students who predominate in high-track classes and low-status knowledge to socially disadvantaged students who are over-represented in lower-track classes (Anyon 1981; Oakes 1985; Wilcox 1982).

However, other studies indicate the oblique relationships between track placement, valued knowledge, and social class. For example, upper-track classes are not uniformly upper-class: Rosenbaum describes a homogeneously working-class school in which working-class rather than middle-class students form the majority in upper-track classes. Nevertheless, despite their class background, students go to college. At the same time, definitions of knowledge also vary: the high-track curriculum is not uniformly "high-status," at least as defined in the liberal tradition, but may be as technical, skills-based, and instrumental as the lower-track curriculum described in other schools. Thus, Rosenbaum's upper-track students attend community colleges rather than prestigious or four-year institutions, despite their high track (Rosenbaum 1976).

Furthermore, students' reactions to school knowledge, whatever its status, is not easily predicted. The definitions of important knowledge which students bring into the classroom are grounded in cross-cutting factors of class (Willis 1977), race (Ogbu 1978), age (Everhardt 1983; Hargreaves 1967), or gender (Davies 1984), and they may not include bookish, abstract school knowledge at all. At the same time, lower-track, working class students may have *more* abstract definitions of knowledge than teachers or high-track students, yet be prevented from demonstrating them (Keddie 1971; Page 1989). Similarly, some poor, minority, lower-track children prefer or require a private, individualized, highly structured curriculum of worksheets (Furlong 1977; Metz 1978) but, elsewhere, children of comparable sociocultural status see such a curriculum as alienating (Rosenbaum 1976) or respond positively to a liberal curriculum (Heath & Branscombe 1985). The effects of differentiated curricula on students' attitudes are also puzzling. Studies report that poor, minority lower-track students in Catholic schools see tracking as helpful to a positive self-image (Valli 1986), whereas similar students in public schools feel stigmatized and suffer low self-esteem (Oakes 1985).

As interpretive studies of curriculum differentiation continue to be produced, the need grows to make sense of the contradictions. This points to the question: how do interpretive studies accumulate or generalize? Simply tallying interpretive studies, as for example, on the basis of meta-analytic categories of whether they show tracking to be deleterious or salutary, reduces the findings in a way that violates the very basis for and value of interpretive research, not to mention statistical sampling procedures. On the other hand, to say that variations between interpretive studies simply reflect different contexts — "every case is different" — produces a kind of facile relativism. A third and better tack suggests that interpretive studies generalize weakly, by analogy (Wehlage 1981). They provide both a detailed account and a conceptual framework, so that the reader is able to find cases analogous to the one reported, either in the real world or in the research corpus. Variations between sites or studies require the modification of theories about how teaching, learning, schools, and society are organized and related. In short, interpretive studies of curriculum differentiation do not accumulate in a consensus, but prompt the "refinement of the debate" (Geertz 1973, p. 29). Their value is in providing data with which to strike new metaphors for conceptualizing curriculum (Kliebard 1982), as Apple (1979) does in speaking of the politics of curriculum or Rosenbaum (1976), when he clarifies tracking as a tournament rather than a contest. The specifics of interpretive studies are the necessary bedrock for better theory.

Erickson (1986, pp. 134–39) demonstrates how contradictions in the "thick" details of interpretive studies can be compared to identify the bases for analogy and more incisive understanding of the complex relationship between curricular and cultural differentiation. He begins with two studies of differentiated curricula (i.e., Au and Mason 1981; Barnhardt 1982) which support the notion that where teachers organize lessons that are congruent with students' home cultures, achievement is enhanced. However, subtle contradictions between the two studies prompt Erickson to speculate that academic gains are achieved, not because the curriculum matches children's definitions of knowledge, but because in culturally congruent lessons students can attend less to the social dimensions of "studenting" and are therefore freed to concentrate on academics. This modification of the theory of cultural and curricular congruence then allows Erickson to incorporate even more divergent data by suggesting that culturally *incongruent* curricula, such as DISTAR's routines (i.e., Stallings and Kaskowitz 1974), may enhance the achievement of minority children because its ritualized format, which children quickly learn, provides a similar freeing of attention for academic tasks. Pushing the modification even further with new data (i.e., Kleinfeld 1979), Erickson notes that even with curricular and cultural clarity, the successful accomplishment of lessons also depends on teachers and students establishing consensus regarding their relationship and task. This shifts the metaphor for classroom interactions so that interactional interference appears not so much as a necessary outcome of cultural or curricular difference, but as a matter of politics and choice. Curriculum is a matter of negotiation and persuasion involving individuals' notions of schooling's purposes. Thus, Erickson concludes that while cultural differences may increase the risks for interactional dissonance in curricular matters, they do not require it. Applying his conclusion to curriculum differentiation: grouping may increase the risk for "trouble" between teachers and students, but only in particular contexts, where participants choose to make track placement significant in their interactions.

In interpretive analyses, the microcontexts of classrooms are regarded as different in ways that are significant for teaching and learning, and the macrocontexts of communities are regarded as important sources of differences in student and teacher characteristics. However, school-level contexts are often treated as equivalent settings and, therefore, are rather frequently overlooked as a source of contradictions. Psychologists typically control for context; social theorists often see the school as a simple transmitter of social precepts. However, curriculum theorists (Kliebard 1987; Apple 1983; Giroux 1981), as well as some sociologists (Metz 1988) and anthropologists (Hymes 1980), argue the need for institutional analyses which consider the limited autonomy of the school and the curriculum.

Thus, as Dell Hymes (1980) has evocatively suggested, we must begin to ask, what kinds of schools are there? The question challenges the presumption that schools are equivalent types without distinctive features and calls to the fore an organizational context that might explain some of the many inconsistencies that plague educational studies. At the same time, the question challenges the usefulness of traditional classifications of schools: size, location, socioeconomic resources, or sector have not proven particularly helpful in mapping schools or in identifying the sources of their diversity. Indeed, interpretive studies have made clear that formal labels such as "magnet school" or demographic facts such as "racially integrated" fail as unequivocal predictors of a school's distinctiveness.

Instead, research must consider the informal characteristics of the school organization—its culture, climate, or meaning system—as a crucial source of diversity (Jelinek, Smircich, and Hirsch 1983; Metz 1983, 1986). Then one asks not only about a school's resources, but what a school *makes* of them (Barr and Dreeben 1978, 1983), recognizing thereby that the school culture provides a context within which specific practices of educational and social differentiation are rendered meaningful. Accordingly, schools that are similar on objective, formal dimensions may have quite different identities. Two schools that take students' social characteristics into account in differentiating the curriculum may misconstrue them, so that a middle-class student body *perceived* by school personnel as working class may be provided a skills-based curriculum, while an objectively similar student body, differently defined within a different organizational culture, may be provided a liberal curriculum (Page 1987b). Similarly, a curriculum of worksheets used to provide all students with a fair chance in one school (Metz 1986) may alienate students in another institutional context (Rosenbaum and Presser 1978). With the concept of institutional culture as an important structural feature of schools, we would not expect that curriculum differentiation is everywhere the same. Instead, its meaning arises in the complexity of differentiation within a school (by track or program) and differences between schools (by culture).

This institutional question about the different types of schools also suggest an agenda for interpretive research that emphasizes comparative analyses of schools. That is, in addition to extended, systematic, individual accounts that provide valid information about schooling, interpretive studies must also begin to consider and articulate the relationship between different schools and various studies. With such an agenda, the detailed, specific portraits remain important in their own right, but, taken in toto, they emerge as well as points with which to build comprehensive schemata of curriculum differentiation and schooling. This volume contributes to such an agenda.

## THE INTERPRETIVE STUDIES

The chapters are organized roughly by unit of analysis. They move outward from microanalyses of lessons within classrooms to system-level interpretations of tracking practices across schools. This organization highlights the importance of classroom, school, and community contexts in shaping curriculum differentiation's enactments and meaning. While the chapters share the focus on institutional arrangements, they differ in the groups of actors, aspects of context, and types of schools they portray. Some emphasize teachers' and administrators' perspectives; others stress the perspectives of students in tracked classes, and in alternative programs. Although most chapters analyze public school contexts, two look within Catholic schools.

In the first chapter, Page asks what it means to be a lower-track student. Contrary to conventional wisdom, track placement does not automatically signal a clear-cut student role, that for example, lower-track students are "slow" or are uninterested in academic endeavors. Instead, as Page's analysis of processes of disagreement in one lower-track lesson illustrates, complex classroom and cultural contingencies as well as students' refusal to be predictably labelled prompt a profoundly ambiguous role. Teachers regard lower-track students as troublesome anomalies: they should be both unskilled and uninterested in academics *and* diligent and committed to study. Teachers enact such ambiguous expectations in a "relevant" curriculum: academic subjects are personalized to engage students, yet engagement is also carefully circumscribed. Thus, lessons present students with contradictory rather than consistent injunctions. Given the contradictions of "relevant" lessons, students react unpredictably to them, and thereby confirm teachers' worst fears about controlling "these kinds of kids."

Valli also looks at the meaning of lower-track placement, but in the context of a Catholic school. By comparing the school experiences of upper and lower-track students, she discovers a parallel orientation toward effort, rather than a negative, distinguishing stereotype. This emphasis is played out in classroom lessons and interactions, permeates the school's tradition and culture, and is institutionalized in school policy. Because effort is considered more important than ability, tracking is not inherently detrimental to lower-track students, as it seems to be in other schools.

While the first two chapters describe marked differences in public and Catholic schools constructions of the lower-track experience, the third chapter documents marked differences within the public sector. Investigating the college preparatory curriculum at two high schools within the same school district, Hanson finds that high-track students do not have equal access to the same knowledge and skills. The study throws in question the results of countless statistical surveys which count college-preparatory classes as uniform phenomena. Hanson's chapter also illuminates the processes through which schools fail to provide college access for even talented poor and minority upper-track students. Surprisingly, the processes contradict the high social class/high-status knowledge/high-track correlations of cultural reproduction theory.

Like Hanson, Hemmings and Metz look at curriculum differentiation across schools. However, their focus is teachers' definitions of their work and the societal, local community, and student pressures that shape them. The authors develop the construct of Real Teaching to capture teachers' sense that their work must be both socially legitimate and instructionally effective. They find tension between legitimacy and effectiveness, particularly in schools where societal and local community expectations do not match. The congruence of these two sets of expectations is instrumental in teacher's job satisfaction and in curricular differences within and between schools.

The next two chapters expand curriculum differentiation beyond its most common manifestation in American secondary schools in tracking to include its increasingly important manifestation in alternative programs. One program operates as a separate school; the other is a program within traditional high schools.

Lesko examines the formal and informal curriculum in an alternative public high school for school-age mothers. Regarded as unusually successful, the school curriculum appears different from that in traditional high schools and positive in its impact on teenage girls. However, beneath the differences are fundamental gender-based constancies with the curriculum of regular schools. In both contexts, the curriculum embodies unexamined assumptions that women need to be taken care of and a traditional view of women's work outside the home. The chapter raises the irony of an alternative school curriculum being quite similar to that of a traditional high school in its deep structure and meaning.

The following chapter gives attention to another special group of students — Hmong refugees. By comparing bilingual and mainstreaming programs in two high schools, Goldstein writes about curriculum differentiation as it occurs not only on a formal programmatic level but also, and with more import, within classrooms as participants negotiate relationships among themselves and the curriculum. Like Lesko, Goldstein discovers a curricular irony: the ESL-supported mainstreaming program, though intended to integrate bilingual students in regular classrooms, is similar to the transitional bilingual program in differentiating immigrant students from American peers. To arrive at this conclusion, Goldstein analyzes why two schools use different strategies for the same group of students, and how students interpret these strategies. Central to the analysis is the interaction of school and student cultures.

With Camarena's chapter, we move back to traditional tracking practices, but this time with a cross-sector comparison. Looking at a small sample of California schools, Camarena contrasts the different strategies public and Catholic schools use for curriculum differentiation to answer a basic and complex question: is tracking *per se* divisive? The chapter provides another strong case that tracking need not be structured to limit educational opportunities, but can be used to enhance lower-track students' success in high school and their opportunities to attend college.

The Anderson and Barr chapter takes us out of the context of schools and into a school district's central office where broad policy decisions about curriculum differentiation are made. Written from an administrative perspective, the chapter describes the slow, sometimes circuitous, path followed by the district in developing and re-thinking tracking policies. The focus is on the value-laden, conflicting beliefs which teachers, administrators and parents hold about curriculum differentiation and how those beliefs are negotiated to shape policy.

Like Anderson and Barr, Sanders argues in the next chapter that the traditional paradigm of school organization, which views tracking as a rational, necessary, bureaucratic response to student diversity, is limited in its explanatory power. Viewing tracking as an organizational strategy rather than simply as an educational treatment, Sanders proposes that curriculum differentiation is a way for teachers and administrators to organize their activities in educational environments with conflicting goals. By analyzing data from twenty-five schools, she finds three operational strategies of curriculum differentiation — linear, elective, and loosely coupled — and argues their relationship to specific organizational characteristics of schools.

In the concluding chapter, the editors, Page and Valli, review the nine interpretive studies to specify their contribution to theory, practice, and policy in regard to curriculum differentiation. Considered individually, the nine chapters provide sensitive, yet systematic, renditions of the particularity and patterns with which curriculum differentiation is enacted in a wide variety of school communities. Each chapter combines the structural analysis and narrative details without which understanding of schooling remains either formless or devoid of life. At the same time, considered as a whole, the chapters offer a body of data with which to begin a comparative, or ethnological, analysis of differentiation processes in American secondary schools. They provide examples with which to contemplate the meaning of differentiation in schools and society as it arises in the complexity of differentiation within schools and differences between them.

Chapter 2

# A *"Relevant"*[1] *Lesson: Defining the Lower-Track Student*

What does it mean to be a lower-track student? Does the role differ from the regular student's? And what factors influence its definition: students' personalities or intelligence? teachers' expectations? tracking structures? differentiated knowledge? social conditions?

These are among the grand questions of curricular theory, practice, and policy. Common responses sketch two categorical scenarios. In the most popular view, students in lower-track classrooms are academically unskilled, uninterested, or unruly. To succeed in school, they require a differentiated curriculum. Lessons should emphasize development of basic rather than higher-order skills, "relevant" rather than bookish subject matter knowledge, and structured rather than informal modes of interaction. The second sketch inverts the traditionalist's image. From a radical perspective, lower-track students are valiant, penetrating, alienated victims of an unjust system. Some studies indicate that they are disproportionately poor, male, and minority as well. Because curriculum differentiation results in stigma, mindlessness, and routine, it prompts rather than prevents school failure.

Each definition is treated as a category of integrity, stability, and power. Theorists, practitioners and policymakers rely on one or the other in distinguishing lower- and regular-track students and in prescribing remedial curricula. However, the categories often take on lives of their own. That is, they become stereotypes which persist even when they are no longer useful or they are applied in situations in which they are downright

17

erroneous. Unexamined—indeed, so much a part of the lore of schooling as to be unexaminable—they hinder the development of adequate curriculum theory and programs.

For example, the assumption that there are robust differences between regular and lower-track students veils fundamental similarities between the roles, particularly a shared subordinate status. It eventuates in real consequences: lessons that may stimulate rather than ameliorate intellectual difficulties; uniform remedial policies fraught with unintended local consequences; or theoretical inattention to differentiation *within* lower-track classes. In short, if the clear-cut, abstract definitions simplify curriculum differentiation, they also misrepresent it.

My purpose in this chapter is to reconsider the meaning of the lower-track student's role and its determinants by rendering a fine-grained, multicolored portrait of one lesson, rather than the broader, black (or white) abstraction. Although unusual, educational close-ups furnish the concrete referents with which to reconsider curriculum's grand postulates. My "thick description" (Geertz 1973) conveys some of the words one teacher and eighteen students exchanged in a lower-track English lesson. Thus, the data are limited and quite mundane. However, because they capture differentiation's processes and contexts, they allow consideration of how, when, and where it made sense (or did not) for classroom participants to produce differentiation and what they made it mean. Furthermore, although highly specific, the data also speak to other lower-track lessons. Processes I describe correspond to those in other lower-track lessons in which I observed as part of a larger ethnography in two comprehensive high schools in the midwestern, middle class city of Maplehurst (Page 1984). Theoretical constructs drawn from other studies of curriculum differentiation to interpret the data furnish a further measure of the single lesson's generalizability (Wehlage 1981).

## TEACHERS' DEFINITION OF THE LOWER-TRACK STUDENT'S ROLE

Crucial elements of the definition of the lower-track student's role are provided by teachers. In a variety of explicit and implicit ways, they signal the seriousness with which students are to regard lessons or homework, the kinds of topics appropriate for students' attention, the degree to which students will engage with and contribute ideas, the respect they will accord peers, and a host of other activities.

Central to the definition is the balance teachers stipulate between educative pursuits and social control. Because classrooms are crowded, public places (Cusick 1973; Jackson 1968), teachers must ensure that groups of students behave if individuals are to learn. At the same time, however, unyielding control can dampen academic enthusiasm and effort. Thus, teachers' juxtaposition of educative and instrumental goals is delicate as well as critical.

The balance teachers establish varies with context and provides thereby for differentiated student roles in different settings. Tracking is one important context. Both traditional and radical analyses assume a straightforward correspondence between teachers' definition of the student's role and tracking. However, tracking's influence may be considerably more complex than either a beneficent accommodation of students' needs (see Passow's review, 1988) or a simple correlation of low-track, low-expectations (Oakes 1985; Rosenthal & Jacobsen 1968). For example, Maplehurst teachers, mirroring the persistent contradictions in tracking studies, express considerable ambivalence regarding lower-track students. They lament regularly the apathy and lack of engagement of "academically unskilled" students, even as they also emphasize as a principal concern "keeping order" among the behaviorally "immature." They worry aloud that lower-track students flatly disdain academic activities, are erratic in attendance, or have the potential to drop out. Apparently, if teachers have clear misgivings about lower-track students' "acting out," they share equally clear worries about their not acting in school at all.[2]

And, the teachers' definition is compounded by students' reactions. Unlike Pygmalion, no real-life lower-track student (or regular-track student, for that matter) is abjectly docile. Moreover, in Maplehurst, lower-track students have resources with which to negotiate in the school hierarchy. The great majority are white, middle class, and score, on average, in the third rather than in the bottom quartile on standardized achievement tests. If they are not as advantaged or as skilled as some of their regular-track peers in the well-regarded Maplehurst schools, neither do they present teachers with the extreme difficulties of severely handicapped or alienated lower-track resistors in imperiled institutions (Metz 1978; Willis 1977).

In short, because balancing purposes of control and education is a dilemma, as is negotiating with students, Maplehurst teachers' definition of the lower-track student's role is not a precise correlation but a complex paradox. It challenges the conventional wisdom that the definition is simple: either a fair estimation of lower-track students' individual, principally academic, needs or a prejudiced assessment based on behavioral, track, or sociocultural characteristics. More accurately, Maplehurst professionals see lower-track students as troublesome anomalies. They speak persistently about "keeping control" of lower-track "circuses," yet control is of uncertain warrant and teachers complain that they "have to pull teeth just to get kids to participate." Teachers predict students' failure, yet they expect students to try. They anticipate students will devalue scholarship yet they insist that they care about it. Thus, if Maplehurst teachers regularly voice a stereotypical view of lower-track students as academically, socially, and behaviorally incompetent, they simultaneously express expectations that students will be engaged, will enjoy educational opportunities, and will achieve educational success.

Teachers' definition of the lower-track student functions as pedagogical lore, rather than as a rational assessment or as a knee-jerk prejudice. Informally acknowledged among faculty members, it blends both subjective and objective information about students' academic characteristics. Incorporating sociocultural and behavioral characteristics as well, it yields a free-wheeling, multidimensional, often contradictory constellation.

Teachers *use* the definition as they define, interpret, direct, and negotiate the complexities of lower-track classrooms. They express it in lower-track lessons and thereby translate a diffuse abstraction into concrete situations. Students also translate as they not only see but practice and react to teachers' designations of their intellectual and interactional prerogatives.

The translation process is visible in that most common and mundane of classroom activities: talk. Talk both exhibits and effectively maintains the "perilous despotism" (Waller 1932) of classrooms: the balance between education and order. It is a medium and means through which teachers and students present and negotiate their definitions of self, other, and school knowledge in particular institutional contexts. Classroom discourse's most common form is the recitation: a tripartite, reciprocal exchange of teacher-question, student-response, and teacher-reaction, followed by a next question (Bellack, Kliebard, Hyman, and Smith 1966; Edwards and Furlong 1978; Mehan 1979). This form persists because it provides for the orderly coverage of educational materials by twenty-five to thirty-five participants.

Classroom discourse also includes breaks in its ritualistic rhythm in the form of disagreements. Teachers regard disagreements with considerable ambivalence (Battistoni 1985). They welcome them as the epitome of intellectual and democratic exchange, yet they also fear the conflict and disorder disagreements signal, particularly when they involve lower-track adolescents whom teachers may worry are less sophisticated than adults in skills of argumentation and in knowledge about academic topics. In the examination of a single lower-track lesson below, I compare the evolution and management in it of usual classroom discourse and disagreements with talk in regular classes to trace the differentiated balance teachers define between learning and orderliness in different tracks and its implications for the student's role.

*Discourse and Disagreements in Maplehurst's Regular-Track Classes*

Talk in Maplehurst's regular-track classes in which I observed is voluminous, lively, and voiced by many classroom participants. Indeed, Maplehurst's classrooms are remarkably different from the bland, privatized educational settings described in other middle class, comprehensive high schools, where teachers and students negotiate "treaties" of low academic requirements in exchange for reasonably compliant behavior (compare Lightfoot 1983; McNeil 1986; Powell, Farrar, and Cohen 1985; Sedlak, Wheeler, Pullin, and Cusick 1986). Maplehurst's regular classes are intellectually purposive and the regular student's role is one of relaxed, yet serious, and sometimes superlative academic endeavor.

Lessons proceed in this manner because teachers structure them to promote regular students' active engagement with traditionally academic subject matter and skills. Without relinquishing their prerogatives and obligations to direct the sequence, topics, and meaning of classroom talk, teachers curb their dominance in classroom discourse and their authority over knowledge so as to encourage student contributions. Teachers expect the socially-advantaged, high-achieving, regular-track students to contribute valuable, diverse opinions in lessons that foster debate and discussion. Several emphasize the teaching of "critical thinking skills: I want them to get the facts and become aware that authorities like the press or governmental officials don't always tell all the facts, or slant the facts." Rather than perceiving disagreements as primarily disquieting events, teachers welcome them as events that "liven up the lesson," signal student involvement, and confirm the teacher's professional expertise and skill. Consequently, teachers allow discordant exchanges between students to develop. Even the teacher's authority is not immune from criticism: students may confront a teacher with the question, "Well, how do you know that?" and the query will not be regarded as impertinent.

The regular student's role is highly public as well as academic and participatory, with the result that Maplehurst's regular classes are filled with a variety of voices. Recitations and lectures, punctuated by seminar-like discussions and small-group work, are more common modes of instruction than individualized, silent seatwork. Teachers promote the public expression of students' opinions through explicit allocation of the floor to students. Two history teachers required regular-track students to

SAINT PETER'S COLLEGE LIBRARY
JERSEY CITY, NEW JERSEY 07306

begin class with presentations of extended, oral "editorials" to which peers responded directly. In a regular English class, after students read their short stories aloud to the class, the teacher referred questions about themes or characters to "the author: Is that what *you* intended?" She thereby called attention to the student's authority over knowledge.

In sum, Maplehurst teachers encourage the exchange of knowledge in their regular-track classes. In contrast to the "flatness" deemed characteristic of other secondary classrooms (Goodlad 1984; Oakes 1985; Tye 1985), Maplehurst's are lively, with regular-track students publicly engaging with and contributing to school knowledge.

*Discourse and Disagreements in Lower-Track Classes*

By contrast, when Maplehurst teachers move to their lower-track classes, talk of all kinds—recitative or disagreements—is less frequent. Anticipating "trouble" from students whom they typify as uninterested in academics and as "lacking the critical thinking skills to participate in a discussion," teachers provide "the basics" and "structure." Individualized work on noncontroversial topics — worksheets, films, and silent reading — is the most common activity and is much more common in lower-track than in regular classes. Silent seatwork constituted a major portion of all lower-track classes in which I observed and a near-invariant routine in some.

However, while Maplehurst teachers, like lower-track teachers in other schools (Metz 1978; Oakes 1985), emphasize seatwork, they also alternate individualized activities with whole-class activities. As professionals, they sense that classroom pragmatics require breaks in what can become an individualized, deadening routine. They assert that instruction in "the basics" must be "relevant" if it is to motivate. Such teacher ambivalence produces uncertain lower-track lessons which both legitimate *and* circumscribe students' engagement with school knowledge.


## MR. BRADLEY'S "RELEVANT" LESSON ABOUT GROUP COMMUNICATION

The ambiguity with which Maplehurst teachers regard lower-track students is visible in Mr. Bradley's lesson about group communication. On many counts, the lesson is well-designed. And, it expresses positive elements in the teacher's assessment of lower-track students. As it unfolds, however, it also fulfills the taken-for-granted prophecy that lower-track classes are "trouble." In short, the lesson exhibits and re-creates the lower track's troublesome anomalies.

Yet Mr. Bradley's students are neither hostile nor stupid and he is not an ogre or incompetent. The ninth grade English class in which he directs the lesson in October 1982, is an Additional Needs class. Additional Needs classes serve a small number of academically unsuccessful students who fail in Maplehurst's regular-track classes but who are ineligible for special education placement, by presenting an "adaptive" curriculum in smaller classes. Mr. Bradley's group—eighteen students, predominantly white and male with only one black and three females—is good-natured and seemingly always ready to talk. Almost all attend class regularly, make some show of completing homework, and participate obediently in daily lessons.

And, more than other lower-track teachers in Maplehurst, Mr. Bradley makes a conscious effort to encourage students' informality and loquacity. A skilled veteran of fourteen years of teaching, he expresses a rather hip style in his predilection for jeans, flannel shirts, a moustache, and an ear for the adolescent vernacular. Therefore, while distinguished from regular classes by a predominance of worksheets, films, and silent reading periods, Mr. Bradley's lower-track class includes occasional extended recitations.

Mr. Bradley's October lesson, a recitation about the "communicative power" of a group of six fictional characters, is the culminating activity of a three-week unit on group communication. The communication unit (which followed a four-week stint reading *Romeo and Juliet* and preceded a four-week unit on the mechanics of composition) taught students that various factors influence group communication: group size, the importance to discussants of the topic, whether discussants know one another, and whether the group is "cohesive; are they like the other members in the group?" Furthermore, Mr. Bradley gave the lesson a political cast. He taught that people wield "power" when they communicate in groups. Some participants "come to a group with more power," depending on their education, age, appearance, or wealth. Others "earn power" in the group, because they are experts on the topics to be discussed. Drawing on a chapter in a college speech text, "Essentials of Group Discussion," Mr. Bradley presented the ideas about group communication in a variety of modes during the three-week unit: brief lectures, films, short stories, and written worksheets.

On many counts, the lesson and the three-week unit embody a positive role for Additional Needs students. They offer serious academic content, not mindless skill-drills. They require higher-order and divergent thinking skills, not algorithmic routines. And they prompt students' active, public contributions to school knowledge, rather than their privatized compliance. However, if the lesson and unit are more imaginative and less trivial than lower-track lessons described in the literature (Oakes

1985) or than many I observed in Maplehurst's schools, students exhibit nevertheless the very academic deficiencies, obstreperous behaviors, and educational indifference that Mr. Bradley predicts and that differentiates lower-track classes from the purposive yet relaxed encounters that characterize regular-track lessons. The lesson ends in all participants' disgruntlement: despite its imagination and "relevance," students disengage, complaining that the teacher "never listens," while the teacher, despite relatively advantaged lower-track students, confirms his doubts about the efficacy of "discussions with these kinds of kids."

Mr. Bradley voices considerable ambivalence about the unit and its final lesson. Because of his interest and training in speech, Mr. Bradley is certain that "all freshmen need a unit on group communication." He is "less certain that Additional Needs students get anything out of the unit." Even though students are actively involved in the final lesson, Mr. Bradley expresses concern afterwards in an interview about both behavioral and academic discipline:

> I never know quite how far to let things go. I want them to talk about these things, but they can get out of hand so easily. Then I have to stop it---I think one of the things that I feel with them is that a lot of times you can't really get into the things that you'd like to get into, that you can teach to regular classes. Or you can't get the depth. It's kinda fun to make a connection with something that is a little bit more than just the basics in teaching, you know. And it's not often possible to do that with Additional Needs kids because they're so limited. And so you can't really dig in very deeply---What we were doing today [in the lesson to be examined here], maybe that was a mistake, I think generally, overall, those kids didn't know what they were doing.

Thus, Mr. Bradley acknowledges the dilemma all teachers face—whether regular or lower-track—in accomplishing both educative and instrumental goals. He wants students to "talk about these things," but "never knows how far to let things go." Moreover, his ambivalence about lower-track students is particularly visible: he emphasizes the importance of not letting Additional Needs students "get out of hand," as well as his lower expectations for the "depth" of students' understanding of the lesson's content.

### Setting the Stage: A Teacher's Commonsensical "Story" about Social Relationships

The dilemma surrounding the delicate balance between educative and instrumental purposes, coupled with the expectations regarding students that can skew its enactment in lower-track classrooms toward an over-emphasis on control and a de-emphasis on education, are visible in the explicit *content* of Mr. Bradley's last lesson in the communication unit. That is, Mr. Bradley signals his expectations for students in the subject matter he presents. Indeed, he seeks to motivate students by casting school knowledge in "relevant" terms.

Mr. Bradley sets the stage for the following day's recitation with a "story of six hypothetical characters: We're going to put [them] together in a group and see how they will communicate." In a lively but unrushed mode, with fluorescent lights dimmed, and making occasional notes on the softly humming overhead projector, Mr. Bradley tells the "story," while students take notes, occasionally interrupt to ask questions, or interject quips of their own.[3]

The first character, *Mike,* appears:

Mike is fourteen years old, a ninth grader at the high school . . . His father makes $90,000 a year---so he's pretty well off . . . Mike gets along with the parking lot crowd at the high school but is not a part of it [doubting noises from some students] . . . He letters in three-THREE!-sports: football, basketball, baseball. This is very unusual, but he was able to do it . . . Is he smart? He is an honor student, straight A's . . . And he's very good-looking . . . He's also the student body president . . . You might think he'd be a snob, but he's not. Kids like him. All the girls would like to have a date with him . . . Oh, yes, and he races a dirt bike in the summer time (appreciative murmurs from the boys in the class, many of whom carry cycle magazines to class).

A foil to Mike, *Ray* is a stereotype of the lower-track student:

Ray is handsome-fifteen years old. A high school dropout, but he is smart. He didn't drop out because he couldn't do the work . . . He comes from a different economic background than Mike: he has eight brothers and sisters, his dad has left home, and his mother works as a waitress, making $8,000 per year . . . Because of his family, to help out his mother, Ray has had to work part-time jobs for quite some time . . . He's been in a little trouble, here and there, suspended for this and that: drinking, or drugs, or cutting classes . . . He's having kind of a tough time of it, not because he's a *bad* kid, but because of family problems . . . He is the oldest of eight kids . . . Ray has a pretty tough life.

Mr. Bradley describes the other four characters in the fictional group in similar fashion, connecting them to Additional Needs students' experiences. *Mr. Smith* is the fifty-eight year-old principal, "a good fellow, most of the kids like him and think he's pretty fair." *Officer Bill* is a twenty-seven year-old policeman who works in the Drug and Alcohol Program at Mr. Smith's high school. He "busted" Ray on at least one occasion, "but he's not like the usual policeman who rides around in a patrol car and tells you to get out of the local Stop 'n Go—he's more like a counselor." *Leroy Johnson* is a thirty-two year-old black teacher of Ray and Mike. He has a reputation for being a "tough teacher: you have him and you work in class. It's not like this class."

The last character Mr. Bradley introduces is *Mary*. A male student wisecracks, "Virgin Mary," and the Additional Needs class dissolves in laughter. Dramatically, Mr. Bradley walks across the room, puts his hand on the student's shoulder, and quietly, but firmly, says: "Will! you! please! be! quiet! You *know* you tend to irritate me." The laughter subsides easily and the teacher continues with the "story":

> Mary is twenty-four . . . She is a secretary, makes about $12,000 a year . . . She graduated from high school, but not from Smith's high school . . . She's very good looking--this (pointing to his cartoon drawing on the overhead) is just a bad photo of her (laughter, catcalls from the students about the teacher's artistic ability and Mary's hair style) . . . She's single . . . She was an average student in high school . . . She does have two younger brothers who attend Smith's high school . . . Mary is the only person of the six in the group who doesn't know anyone else in the group before its first meeting.

After the description of Mary, Mr. Bradley explains that the group of six characters is convened to "discuss the problem of drugs and drinking going on around the high school and how to solve it." Based on his descriptions, students are to rank the six characters in terms of their communicative power.

This "story" of six characters and the recitation that followed it the next day present students with a classroom exercise in which the explicit goal is higher order thinking skills: students are to apply abstract principles of group communication in an analysis of the dynamics of the concrete if fictional group.

Furthermore, Mr. Bradley's description of the communicative behavior of the fictional group of six characters has added, personal meaning for students by virtue of its "relevance." Following common prescriptions for remedial curricula (not only in schooling's lore but in curriculum theory as well, as in Bigge 1988), Mr. Bradley's "story" parallels the particular realities of Additional Needs students in Maplehurst. Several students in Mr. Bradley's class are like Ray: they are fourteen or fifteen, have been "busted" for drugs, and have contemplated leaving school. Some belong to the "parking lot crowd" Mr. Bradley mentions, the label by which delinquent students are known. Indeed, Mr. Bradley explicitly directs students to "put yourself in the group" to determine how characters will influence one another. He admonishes them: *"Romeo and Juliet* may have seemed like it was 'out there.' This stuff is not out there; it's right here and now."

Nevertheless, if Mr. Bradley's presentation of communicative principles is designed to motivate students to *"think"* about social and communicative differences, it also maps the social world and its processes in a particular way. For example, in the teacher's account, the straight-A student, Mike, will be expected to influence the principal more than Ray, the dropout. By contrast, Ray will evoke sympathy: "He's had a tough life." Mr. Bradley does not discuss why group communication works this way. As a result, while the teacher constructs the group's characters so that stereotypical differences between them will provoke students "to bring all the things [communicative principles] into play," the academic material and the significance of its latent sociocultural assumptions are also presented as self-evident and realistic.

Students react to the lesson with interest. They accept many of the links between the lesson's formal content, their knowledge of the way the world works, and their personal school situations. As the lesson intertwines theoretical precepts about group communication with students' experiences, it forges a particularly tight relationship between curricular, cultural, and personal knowledge. Its content furnishes students an analogy: the educational and social principles that govern communication in the fictional group will govern discourse in Mr. Bradley's lower-track classroom. Thus, the "here and now" lesson's content presents real students with information not just about communication but about *their* communicative role.

*Framing the Lesson for Differences of Opinion:*
*"More Than One Right Answer"*

In addition to presenting "relevant" content, Mr. Bradley translates his definition of the lower-track student's role in the lesson's *form*. In his introduction to the recitation on the day following the "story," he states explicitly that students will participate publicly in a group discussion which will include disagreements about the relative communicative power of members of the fictional group. He sets down the ground rules for an activity in which the possibility of "several right answers" is legitimated:

> *Drinking* and *drugs* in the high school, awright? That's the topic that's going to be discussed [by the fictional group]. What I want to do--is *find out* how you ranked them ... Awright! And this is important--I *don't think*--

that there is *one*:: right answer here. As long as you can tell me *why you feel* that so-and-so might have more power than so-and-so, you, there may be *several* right answers, as long as you can back up your answer. I think in *some*:: cases--some answers are better than others, some are *more*::: right than others, but there are a lot of them that could be about the same. So. Let's take a look (1.0) and start with Mr. Green. Let's just run through your ranking. Who did you rank one, two, three, four, fi::ve, six?

However, despite the legitimation of diverse opinions and open-ended discussion, Mr. Bradley's framing move is also laced with ambiguity. On the one hand, the teacher indicates that he wants "to find out" how students rank the fictitious characters. To encourage student participation in the ensuing activity, to get it underway, and for content objectives, he emphasizes that there is no "*one* right answer." This comment forecasts the possibility of controversy and differing opinions for which Mr. Bradley insists twice that correctness will be determined by whether participants can give reasons for their opinions on the issues and "back up" their ideas. Hence, his position as teacher will ostensibly not be the traditional one of determining right and wrong answers according to an answer sheet but, instead, will involve judging students' skills of argumentation. On the other hand, Mr. Bradley also states that some answers are "more right than others." Because he does not specify how the "better answers" will be identified, he retains authority in the discussion, but he defines it so that its scope is uncertain.

The effect of the ambiguous frame, like the "relevant" content, is not immediately apparent. Only as the lesson unfolds is it given meaning. Thus, from a lesson plan, a teacher survey, or a brief observation, one might expect considerable debate as to the relative power positions of the six characters, given Mr. Bradley's legitimating frame, the controversial and "relevant" content, as well as students' active interest in the lesson. Instead of heated debate, however, in the lesson's first twenty-five minutes, usual classroom discourse prevails and there is orderly coverage of the controversial topics Mr. Bradley narrated. Direct disagreements in a lesson that is planned for them are remarkable by their *absence*.

*Establishing the Recitation: The Paradoxical Achievement of an Absence of Disagreements*

The *absence* of direct disagreements in the first half of Mr. Bradley's lesson is an *achievement* which classroom participants collaboratively produce. The absence is achieved primarily through the establishment of usual classroom discourse, as manifested in the tripartite recitation structure. Teachers pose questions to which students respond, and teachers react to their responses before posing the next question. Because teachers occupy the third, reacting position, they control both the topic and the turns of talk. However, recitations are joint constructions: if students do not participate, a recitation will flounder and the teacher will not be able to teach.

Following the opening frame and working reciprocally, Mr. Bradley and students set in motion the ritualized structure of the recitation. Mr. Bradley calls on Steve to "run through" his ranking of the six characters[4]:

```
1   Steve: Mr. Smith, Officer Bill  ⌈
2      T:                            ⌊ Mr. Smith came first. Officer
3         Bill, second. Look at your own list right now.
4   Steve: Leroy Johnson, Mary  ⌈-
5      T:                        ⌊ Leroy Johnson, Mary.
6   Steve: Mike 'n Ray.
7      T: Mike (1.0) and Ray-- last. Okay! (snaps fingers)
```

These opening lines of discourse shape (and are shaped by) the crucial, yet delicate, balance teachers and students construct between educative and instrumental goals. Mr. Bradley poses a question, to which Steve, working reflexively, matches his response: promptly, he provides the appropriate content (name of characters) in the correct form (a list) at the appropriate juncture (after the teacher's question). Reacting in a highly economical but powerful move, Mr. Bradley interrupts to link Steve's response to the lesson's purposes and to tie the opening of the recitation to its frame and its subsequent unfolding. Validating the two names Steve offers by repeating and broadcasting them (11. 2–3), Mr. Bradley simultaneously clarifies that Steve's list of names is appropriately ranked: "Mr. Smith came *first*." (my emphasis) Mr. Bradley concludes his interruption with a multi-purpose directive to the rest of the class: "Look at your *own* list right now." This brief, seven-word directive confirms that the list being offered is not the only list possible and reiterates that there may be different lists: each person in the room has her/his "*own* list." It also anticipates the future contributions of other students when Steve completes his list, and thus reminds students that this is a *class* activity. Finally, it reminds students that at present they are only to "look" at their lists, not to shout out where theirs differ from Steve's.

The familiar ping-pong pattern of classroom discourse, although collaborative, concentrates control of the lesson in the teacher's hands. In contrast to conversations between equals, which are characterized by a two-part exchange structure (Sacks 1972), classroom discourse operates to return possession of the floor to the teacher in the third, reacting move (Mehan 1979). Because teachers occupy this position, they can shape meaning, guide topic development, and direct turns at talk.

From the third position, the teacher can also manage the emergence and evolution of disagreements. The processes by which the teacher controls the occurrence of disagreements, yet retains students' active and necessary participation so that a recitation proceeds, is illustrated in the talk following Steve's list:

```
 8  T:      Mike (1.0) and Ray---last. Okay! (snaps fingers).
 9          Let's run around and get a couple more here. Yeah,
10          some, anybody, have--something different from
11          that one? Butler, yeah.
12  Butch:  Mr. Smith, Leroy Johnson, Officer Bill--
13          Mary, Mike 'n Ray.
14          (4.0)
15  T:      That's almost the same, wasn't it?
16  Butch:  Yeah, but Leroy Johnson and Officer Bill
17          are (undecipherable).
18  S:      I put Leroy Johnson
19  S:          Ray, you know-
20  T:      Okay--Here---Number one (writing on overhead
21          projector), Let's do it this way.
22          Smith--⌈(2.5)-
23  Butch:       ⌊(ya⌈wn-groan)
24  S:              ⌊Let⌈me write that down.
25  Dick:              ⌊I got something.
26  T:      Okay! Hang on. Did anybody else put--a different
27          person (snaps fingers) in the number one spot? (snaps
28          fingers)
29  Dick:   I put the cop.
30  T:      Okay, that's Officer Bill. (4.0) Awright.
```

Here, from the third position in usual classroom discourse, Mr. Bradley controls disagreements in a variety of ways. For example, he clarifies the broad topic under discussion (11. 20–21), so that trivial disagreements — whether Officer Bill is third or fourth on the list — are avoided. Second, he uses care in correcting students' answers, as when he tentatively questions Butch's alternative list (1. 15): the qualified rather than harsh correction allows the teacher to direct the lesson's meaning yet ensure students' continued participation.

Most importantly for producing an absence of disagreements, by occupying the third, reacting position, Mr. Bradley buffers students' differences from each other. When Butch proposes a ranked list of the six characters which is different from Steve's, he speaks to Mr. Bradley, not to Steve. Moreover, it is Mr. Bradley, not Steve, who reacts to Butch's list. Therefore, the usual classroom discourse structure allows for the *array* of a variety of "right answers" to a single question. Contradictory ideas — Steve's, Butch's, Dick's — can be set side by side, without calling attention to the fact of their opposition. This meets the requirements of Mr. Bradley's curious lesson in which differences of opinion are explicitly solicited but are not constructed as direct, potentially uncontrollable disagreements.

In sum, in the lesson's opening, teacher and students collaborate in the production of an orderly *array* of different ideas, rather than in direct disagreements about the controversial topic of communicative power in a fictional group discussing drugs at a high school. The orderliness results because Mr. Bradley occupies the third position: the class can express a variety of "right answers" to a single, possibly controversial, question (the teacher's educative goal) while, simultaneously, any disagreement is buffered and controlled by the teacher (the teacher's instrumental goal).

*Achieving a Classroom Disagreement: A Conflict Between the Forms of Usual Classroom Discourse and Disagreements*

Despite teachers' control of disagreement (and the wider culture's ambivalence regarding them which the control expresses), disagreements arise in high school lessons. They differentiate regular and lower-track classes in Maplehurst. Disagreements are not unusual in regular lessons in Maplehurst because teachers plan for them. Indeed, they may account for the elan of Maplehurst's regular classes and the regular student's active role.

Surprisingly, given teachers' feeling that conflict is much greater in lower-track classes, disagreements there are quite uncommon. If infrequent, however, their significance is considerable. In their evolution, they make visible the ambiguity of the students' prerogatives, students' struggles to act competently in the face of mixed messages, and the cross-purposes with which teachers and students may interpret school knowledge.

The first and the major disagreement in Mr. Bradley's lesson concerns Mary, the secretary. Voiced only after twenty-five minutes of ritualized recitation have elapsed,[5] during which time Mary is not even mentioned, the disagreement begins with four students, but eventuates in a long string of confrontations that draws in almost all other students and Mr. Bradley. It echoes through the remainder of the lesson, prompting continuing argument whenever Mary's power to influence the fictional group is broached. Indeed, it becomes part of the history of Mr. Bradley's lower-track class: in reviewing for the final examination two months later, Mary revived all the passions of the original encounter.[6]

Mary's power as a topic in Mr. Bradley's lower-track lesson with eighteen ninth graders — if not among the fictional characters — proves "surprising" to Mr. Bradley. He had anticipated that lower-track students would argue that straight-A Mike is a "goody-goody" and Ray street-smart, but he had not figured a heated, long-lived disagreement about Mary's status. The meaning of the disagreement is carried both in its substance and in the way it is negotiated by teacher and students. Through the disagreement, the Additional Needs students experience, first, that their and the teacher's perspectives on the world are not so congruent as their interest in Mr. Bradley's "relevant" story suggested. Second, students experience the profound contradictions in their communicative prerogatives: the role in Maplehurst includes only very limited participation in disagreements about school knowledge even, ironically, in a lesson that calls explicitly for such participation.

The disagreement about Mary begins when Mr. Bradley turns the class to a consideration of the secretary's ability to earn communicative power in the fictional group discussing drugs and drinking in a high school:

```
31  T:        Um. (3.0) Who haven't we talked about in terms of
32            earned power? (1.0) How about Mar⌈y?
33  Patty:                                     ⌊Mary.
34  T:        How about Mary?
35  Dick:     She ain't ⌈-(softly)
36  T:                  ⌊Where's Mary going to fit into the picture?
37  Butch:    At the end (softly).
38  T:        Where's Mary going to fit into the picture? Yeah!
39            Butch!
40  Butch:    At the e::nd.
41  T:        Why at the end? I agree with you. Tell me why.
42  Butch:    She's only ⌈a secretary-
43  Dick:                ⌊She's just a secretary.
44  Butch:                              -What's she know about this
45            problem?
46  Patty:    Yeah, but she, ⌈she's got
47  Tiffany:                 ⌊she's got⌈-
48  Patty:                             ⌊- younger brothers⌈and--
49  Tiffany:                                             ⌊- younger -
50  Patty:    -sisters that ar⌈e in school.
51  Tiffany:                  ⌊-involved in school.
```

```
52  T:        She's got two younger brothers ⌈--
53  Butch:                                   ⌊Well, she talks to them
54            everyday about it (sarcastically, to Patty and Tiffany).
55  T:        She's got two younger brothers ⌈--
56                                           ⎢She might have given them
                                             ⌊(advice)?
57  T:        Okay! Okay. Hang on. (1.0) Go ahead Louis.
```

The emergence of disagreements is difficult to predict, but their form is as recognizable as that of usual classroom discourse. An assertion prompts a counter-assertion (e.g., "no"; "yes, but") which is then followed by moves to resolve the disagreement and, eventually, by a final exiting move (whether the disagreement is resolved or not). In Mr. Bradley's lesson, Butch, supported by Dick, asserts sarcastically that Mary "is only a secretary — what's she know about this problem [of drugs in the high school]?" (11. 42–45). The boys' assertion prompts a counter-assertion by Patty, joined by Tiffany (11. 46–51). Contradicting Butch's and Dick's opinion (and, as it turned out, Mr. Bradley's, 1. 41), Patty asserts that Mary will earn power in the group, rather than occupying a position "at the end" of the group. This initial confrontation spawns a train of heated resolution moves and additional disagreements about Mary.

A noteworthy feature of direct disagreements in classrooms is that the counter-assertion, here by Patty (beginning 1. 46), is a *reacting* move. That is, a student, rather than the teacher, performs the evaluation. Patty's reaction follows the event that precipitates it — Butch's extreme answer—with no buffering move by the teacher. Consequently, the teacher's control over the direction and content of classroom talk is preempted as Patty and Tiffany take the reacting position. Structurally, direct disagreements (teacher question/student response/*student* evaluation) stand in contrast to usual classroom discourse and the merely implicit expression of disagreement through arraying of different ideas (teacher question/student response/*teacher* evaluation).

The course of a disagreement, once voiced, is mutually charted by classroom participants as they work to resolve it. In their negotiations, participants are at cross purposes on substantive issues. That is, they disagree about some topic. In addition, they may act at cross purposes within contradictory discourse structures which specify different rules for one's talk and role (Pomerantz 1978). That is, classroom participants may also differ about whether having a disagreement is their appropriate agenda.

For example, from the teacher's vantage point, students may appear "out of order" who operate within the disagreement structure and who therefore will occupy the third, reacting position. Indeed, in the third position, students *are* out-of-the-order of conventional classroom discourse and a respondent's role. Thus, when teachers say that arguments give unequal and unfair amounts of floor time to a few students, lead to "free-for-alls" and "crushed feelings," or sidetrack coverage of the lesson, their perceptions are not simply up-tight, imagined, or authoritarian personality defects. Their perceptions have a real, if largely unconscious, basis in the structure of classroom talk.

Contrarily, in the view of students operating from within a disagreement structure, students are legitimately engaging with the lesson's content because, in a disagreement, one *must* occupy the third position to make the counter-assertion. Thus, students may discount as illegitimate teachers' attempts to stop disagreements, regain control, and re-establish regular classroom discourse, as indeed such efforts are if one is operating from within a disagreement structure. From that perspective, "Teachers just don't listen to what we have to say."

The contradiction between the discourse structures resonates with teachers' differentiated expectations for regular- and lower-track students. Whereas in regular classes Maplehurst teachers promote and sustain students' public disagreement, they read similar behaviors differently in the lower-track: disagreements there are "shout-outs," "childish arguing," "trouble," or a discussion that is a "circus." Within such a context, Mr. Bradley's immediate impulse is to *stop* the disagreement between Patty/Tiffany and Butch/Dick to regain control of the situation. He interjects a reaction (1. 52), possibly a correction, to Patty's counter-assertion, noting that Mary has "got two younger brothers" and therefore may know something about the drug problem at the high school. However, even when repeated a second time (1. 55)), Mr. Bradley's interjection fails to stop the direct disagreement between the absorbed students. Finally, Mr. Bradley loudly suggests that the disagreement be set aside momentarily: "Hang on" (1. 57). However, despite these efforts to stop the disagreement, students persist in their interest in the topic of Mary's power and in Mr. Bradley's lesson:

```
58  Louis:   She isn't even in that school and she
59           doesn't have nothing to do with it and
60           that -⌈-
61  Butch:       ⌊She'⌈s got (indecipherable)
62  Louis:          -⌊and she ain't going ⌈to be talking-
63  Patty:                                 ⌊(undecipherabl⌈e)
64  Louis:                                              ⌊- to
```

65              her little brothers and stuff when, you know, every-
66              time when they ⌈-
67  Butch:             ⌊(undecipherable)
68  T:                 ⌈     (snaps fingers)
69  Louis:             -come home from school.
70  Patty:     (giggles)         ⌊
71  T:        (snaps fingers). Did you hear that?
72  Patty:     (giggles)
73  Butch:    Yeah.
74  Dick:     Yep.
75  T:        What's her only link? Probably her little brothers.
76              Is that a strong link?
77  Class:     (in unison) NOOOOOO.
78  T:        Probably not.
79  Mike:     They probably wouldn't tell her anything anyway.
80  T:        Probabl⌈y wouldn't tell her too much anyway.
81  Patty:            ⌊They're *not* going to tell her *nothing!*
82  T:        She's 10 years, what's she, 24?
83  S:        Yeah.
84  T:        So she's probably, uh, seven, eight, nine years older
85              than they are anyway. She is *not* in the high school.
86              (1.0) She, she's got a couple of things going for her,
87              but none of them are strong. She, I doubt, I agree with
88              you, I don't think she's going to earn a lot of power.
89              How many people had Mary *last* on their list? How many
90              people had Mary last on their list? Hands! (Only three
91              students raise hands.) Now that surprises me.

Here, Patty and Butch continue their interchange about Mary in illicit whispers (11. 61–72), even though the teacher has given the floor to
Louis. Mr. Bradley implicitly recognizes the operation of both the official
and the disagreement structures when he snaps his fingers at Butch and
Patty as they continue their disagreement *sotto voce* (11. 68 and 71): he
reprimands the two disputants for continuing to talk, but without inter-
rupting the usual classroom discourse structure which he has just re-
established and under which Louis has the floor.

Furthermore, as the discourse illustrates, the lower-track students
are not only "hooked" by Mary but they pursue their disagreement with
considerable skill and perseverance, notwithstanding Maplehurst lore
that disparages their ability to debate. Patty, Butch, and other students
spiritedly, not mindlessly, offer reasons for their positions and rebuttals
of those to which they are opposed. For example, Patty and Tiffany assert that Mary *will* know something about the drug and alcohol problem

through her younger brothers. Butch counters that he doubts that Mary talks to her much younger siblings about such topics (11. 53 – 54). But Patty responds that an older sister might give some occasional advice (1. 56). Thus, students follow Mr. Bradley's directions in the original framing of the lesson: using argumentation and justification of opinions, they "back up" their answers by telling him "*why* [they] *feel* that so-and-so might have more power." In contrast, Mr. Bradley often relies simply on the weight of his personal opinion to convince students of his point of view: "Still, though, Mary would be on the bottom of my list. I think Mike would be in front of her, *I* think so."

## Double Differentiation

Teachers' intuition that lower-track disagreements skew the balance between purposes of education and order so that lessons are out of control is prompted not only by the structural conflict between disagreement and usual classroom discourse forms, but by a second feature of direct disagreements: *siding.* In this phenomenon, students take sides with one or the other of the original disputants in a disagreement, so that volume and numbers, rather than argumentation, often settle disagreements. Siding may appear especially problematic to lower-track teachers because it corresponds to their perceptions that the classes are "dumping grounds for behavior problems" or classes "without positive role models." If several students join together, teachers may feel themselves out-numbered by a "negative peer group."

In the disagreement about Mary, siding occurs in the opening salvo, when Dick collaborates with Butch in his assessment of Mary's rank, even to the extent of echoing Butch's derogation of Mary: "She's only a secretary"/"She's just a secretary" (11. 42–43). In parallel fashion, Tiffany joins Patty in Mary's defense in the counter-assertion: "She's got younger brothers and—sisters that are in school"/"She's got—younger —[?]—involved in school" (11. 46–51). Siding continues through the remainder of the lesson.

Concern about the emergence of a unified group of students is reflected in Mr. Bradley's response to the disagreement between Butch/Dick and Patty/Tiffany. Rather than legitimating their difference of opinion—for example, by directing one party to state its case and the other party to listen and respond—he gives the floor to Louis, a student who was not a part of the original disagreement. Louis, however, does not deflect but extends the disagreement as he sides with the other males. He repeats Butch's earlier statement about Mary: " —and she ain't going to be talking to her little brothers and stuff when, you know, everytime when they come home from school" (11. 62–69). As students align themselves in disputes, the teacher's power to direct classroom talk and maintain order is potentially diminished.

Siding also has important ramifications for students because it affects processes of differentiation *among* students in a lower-track class. In Maplehurst, male students outnumber females by a large margin in seven of the nine lower-track classrooms I observed regularly.[7] In Mr. Bradley's class, there are fifteen boys and three girls. Because of the operation of siding, if an issue such as Mary arises, it is possible that lower-track female students will simply find themselves outnumbered, rather than out-argued. By the same token, girls (or others of minority status) who argue may appear strident or over-zealous and, therefore, be dismissed as cranks, simply because there are only a few representatives to voice their viewpoint. This is precisely what happens in Mr. Bradley's lesson. As the subject of Mary continues in renewed debates, Patty consistently but unsuccessfully carries the defense. Only once does a male student contribute an argument in favor of Mary's having power in the group. Such an imbalanced outcome is less likely in Maplehurst's regular-track classrooms where the sexes are more evenly distributed.

Furthermore, the judgment about Mary's position may be intensified for the women because of the way Mr. Bradley structures "relevance." In his "story," Mary is the only woman and she is a secretary: "she didn't fit real well [in the group] and you had to think about why she didn't." Yet the fictional group could have been equally "relevant" and illustrative of communicative dynamics had it included several women or women in a variety of occupations, such as teaching and school administration as well as secretarial work. Instead, Mr. Bradley's narrative reproduces a negative, stereotypical image of women's place in the world and provides for its continued viability in his lower-track class.

Are Patty and Tiffany, like fictional Mary, to accept a powerless position in the classroom because, as Patty eventually notes in explaining Mary's lack of power, "She's the only female." In the fiction group, gender is the factor that sets Mary apart from the other group members. She has many status-enhancing characteristics, according to the commonsensical factors enumerated in Mr. Bradley's introductory description: money, education, age, and appearance. On at least three of these, she outranks both Ray and Mike, the teen-age students. Nonetheless, Mr. Bradley's predominantly male class argues that the male adolescents have more power than a female adult. Analogously, do Butch and Dick also have more power in Mr. Bradley's classroom than Patty and Tiffany because they are in the male majority?

Here, the complexity of curriculum differentiation and its translative relationship to broader precepts of social differentiation is particularly salient. The over-representation of boys in lower-track classrooms, the discourse phenomenon of siding, and the "relevant" content conjoin to produce important differentiated meaning for the lower-track student's role in general and added impact for a particular sub-group as well. Although normatively, gender is not supposed to be a factor in one's role as a student, in this lesson it is both visible and decisive. The oblique operation of these processes suggests how other minorities — blacks, mainstreamed Special Education students, poor students, English-as-a-Second-Language students — may experience a doubly differentiated lower-track student role.

## "At the End": Concluding the Disagreement

Siding and the contradictory discourse structures of disagreement and usual classroom talk stimulate negative aspects of teachers' ambivalent expectations regarding lower-track students, and they prompt teachers to stop direct disagreements quickly so as to regain control. The intuitive reaction affects the resolution of disagreements as well. In lower-track classrooms, more than in regular-track classrooms, disagreements are resolved by the teacher. Teachers quickly stop exchanges between students, re-assert their authority in regard to the "right answer," and discredit the opinions of students' peers. By contrast, in regular classes, Maplehurst teachers not only allow disagreements to continue longer and close them with more equivocation, but they direct students to disagree directly with each other. Teachers seem to encourage and relish disagreements, interpreting them as confirmation of the intellectual rigor that they, as expert professionals, generate.

Even in lower-track classrooms, however, the teacher's strategies for managing disagreements must not be too heavy-handed. If teachers simply impose their opinions or terminate disagreements autocratically, students' willingness to participate as respondents in recitations may falter. Indeed, unilateral resolutions of disagreements often backfire and disagreements re-surface.

In Mr. Bradley's lesson, Mary persists as the major topic of dispute despite Mr. Bradley's repeated efforts to close the argument. After the initial disagreement between Butch and Patty, the class ratifies Mary's low position, seemingly to everyone's chorused satisfaction (1. 51), yet the argument breaks out anew almost immediately. In a parting shot, Mike suggests yet another reason for the side that thinks that Mary is last on the list: "They [the brothers] probably wouldn't tell her anything anyway" (11. 53 – 54). This statement is extreme in its disparagement of

Mary's influence: it is not just that Mary will not talk to her brothers after school, as Butch argued earlier (11. 25–26), but that the younger siblings will not deign to talk to Mary about "anything." Immediately, Patty offers a counter-assertion, stressing her disagreement through use of the double negative: "They're *not* going to tell her *nothing* (11. 56–57). Thus, the disagreement about Mary which Mr. Bradley had closed begins again with renewed heat.

Across the remainder of Mr. Bradley's lesson, the question of Mary's position in the group provokes four additional extended disagreement sequences. Each time, only Patty and the other two women offer reasons in defense of Mary's powerful position in the fictional group. Their isolation is visible in the last few minutes of the lesson in a final altercation about Mary. Its dynamics are telling for understanding how teachers' ambivalence comes to life in confused lessons which control students by leaving them bewildered as to their responsibilities.

The teacher asks about whether the topic of drugs in the high school is important to group participants:

```
 92 T:       Mary! (Is drug use an important topic to Mary?)
 93 Sean:    Minus.
 94 T:       Could be, very likely could be. Not involved in
 95          the problem, out of high school. Might not be
 96          important to her at all.
 97 Patty:   (softly) Yeah, but she has her brothers.
 98 T:       What?
 99 Patty:   Nothing.
100 T:       She has to - (2.5) - what?
101 Patty:   (shrugs)
102 T:       Okay. I, could be a topic, excuse me, it could
103          be interesting ⌐ - -
104 Tiffany:             └ She ⌐ could have a friend like that.
105 T:                     - - └ could be important. She
106          could have what?
107 Patty:   A friend.
108 T:       More than friends.
109 Tiffany: Brothers.
110 T:       Her brothers, who would be involved, and that might
111          might be a plus.
112 Dick:    I'll bet (softly, sarcastically).
113 Louis:   Well, why would they, uh, where do you get Mary from?
114          Why would you put her life in, in there?[8]
115 T:       Why'd I put Mary in this group? Good question. Why
116          would I put Mary in this group?
117 Mike:    I guess she's not involved with the school or nothing
```

118               or she having, no, no reason, her brothers ⌈-
119  Patty:                                              ⌊She's the *only* female.

Here, as in the initial disagreement, Patty disagrees with a negative
assessment of Mary's status. However, this time, her counter-assertion
is spoken very softly: "Yeah, but she has her brothers" (1. 97). In contrast to her earlier fervor, Patty, doing battle one last time, appears finally
to have learned her place. When Mr. Bradley asks Patty to repeat what
she says, she refuses to participate further in the discussion (11. 99 and
101). She expresses her disagreement only non-verbally, by shrugging,
twisting in her seat, and looking disgruntled.

In turn, Patty's refusal to discuss Mary upsets Mr. Bradley's ability
to go on with the lesson. He stammers and excuses himself (11. 102–03).
He allows Tiffany to interrupt with a reason why the topic of drugs could
be important to Mary: "She could have a *friend* like that [who uses
drugs]" (1. 104). Patty then re-enters the discussion (1. 107), echoing Tiffany's last defense of Mary. Possibly to secure Patty's re-engagement in
the recitation, Mr. Bradley then reverses the position he has held throughout the lesson in regard to Mary. He prompts Patty and Tiffany to suggest
that Mary's relation with her brothers *is* significant (1. 108), even stating
the importance of this relationship himself: "Her brothers, who would be
involved, and that might be a plus" (11. 110–11).

This closing interchange exemplifies the delicate balance that classroom participants produce between educational coverage and order and
its significance for lower-track students' scholastic uncertainty. Having
presented her point of view regarding Mary in four earlier major disagreement sequences only to have it overridden by the teacher and the majority
of the class, Patty makes one last, half-hearted defense and then quits.
She refuses to disagree further. At that point, the teacher finds himself
losing the participation of an active student and, simultaneously, the recitation. To allay the loss, the teacher not only invites Patty to participate,
but reverses his position relative to the disagreement's topic. That is, to
keep the recitation alive — to teach the lesson he has planned — he encourages a perspective on Mary that previously led to direct disagreement and loss of control (and that even here, "at the end," threatens to
re-erupt with Dick's disdainful reaction, "I'll bet" [1. 112]).

Thus, students participate in ambiguous interchanges. As in this lesson, they may experience rewards when they behave passively, as much
or more than when they engage actively with the lesson's subject matter.
By refusing to disagree verbally at the end of the lesson, Patty wins en-
couragement to participate as a disputant. She also wins long-sought recognition by the teacher of her substantive position on Mary's—and wom-

en's — communicative power. Other students — majority or minority — may experience similar feelings of power when they withdraw from active participation in class activities. By making teachers "pull teeth" to secure their involvement in recitations, lower-track students reassert their significance as classroom actors. Furthermore, while these processes also occur in regular classes, the dynamic is particularly charged in lower-track classes where teachers' ambiguous role definition for students promotes conditions in which participants can find themselves at cross-purposes.

This "thick description" of a lesson also unveils for consideration the taken-for-granted rationale undergirding remedial curricula. "Relevance" — in the lesson's content and form — produces some unintended consequences for the lower-track student's role, in some cases a double impact. Thus, Patty is an exemplar of the lower-track student in disagreement with teacher and peers over an issue that is not distantly academic, but that is definitive of self. Patty hears that Mary has no power because she is "only a secretary" who knows little about anything. Yet secretarial work is precisely Patty's career choice, as it is the "modal choice" of other lower-track women (Valli 1986; see also Rosenbaum 1976). Often singlehandedly, because of the over-representation of boys in the Additional Needs class and the discouragement from Mr. Bradley, Patty protests Mary's dismissal by citing sources of her strength. But Patty is also shown that she herself has little power. Like Mary in the fictional group, she is outnumbered in the real-life group. Her series of disagreements with the teacher and most of her classmates is managed in such a way that thoughtful argumentation appears futile. Eventually, Patty withdraws from the discussion and her exclusion is achieved. Yet, in an ironic twist, precisely her passivity produces salutary recognition of her ideas. Ambiguously, Patty's passive stance as a student and as a female, as much or more than her active, direct disagreement, is reinforced at the lesson's end. Male students' experiences are hardly more promising. They also can be arbitrarily closed out of serious public discourse. And, the view of social relationships that at least some brought to this classroom, if confirmed, hardly augers well for their civility.

Finally, this "thick description" of Mr. Bradley's lesson and of the anomalous role it defines for Maplehurst's lower-track students sketches curriculum differentiation's interactive variables, aperiodic processes, and multilayered contexts: defining processes in classrooms involve instructional practices (the use of public recitations or individualized seatwork), material constraints (the over-representation of males in lower-track classrooms), students' and teachers' ambiguous expectations of each other and self (shaped by the school's tracking order and by the wider social order), and the unconscious but crucial contradictions in discourse structures (usual classroom discourse and disagreements). Accordingly, curriculum differentiation is much more complicated than is implied in theories of labels or expectations, teacher power, student resistance, tracking structures, or student deficiencies and the "relevant" curriculum that will ameliorate them. Its processes will not disappear with policies that simply abolish tracking.

The power of Mr. Bradley's lesson lies in its ambiguity, not in its obviously controlled or straightforwardly educative design. In other lower-track classrooms as well, the content, form, and management of discourse combine to produce as well as to reflect a situation in which students (particularly females in this case) experience public engagement and disagreement ambivalently. That is, in a lesson with many good features, students nevertheless alternate between active participation and passive withdrawal. Therefore, lower-track students *are* "out-of-control," "not consistent," and, in teachers' definitions, annoyingly "unpredictable."

Yet students' unpredictable behavior is a response to teachers' anomalous lessons. In design and execution, Mr. Bradley calls for "more than one right answer" yet squelches all but his own. He stresses "giving reasons for opinions," but relies on his formal authority to resolve differences of opinion. He effectively, imaginatively engages students in important topics, but punishes the engagement. Indeed, ironically, *both* students' engagement in *and* their withdrawal from classroom activities confirm teachers' pedagogical lore about lower-track students: if students argue, they are "like little kids ... in shouting matches"; if they withdraw, they "don't care about ideas." In short, lower-track lessons present a very powerful Catch-22.

"At the end," then, we may well recall that Mr. Bradley is not insensitive to classroom dynamics, a rote follower of a textbook or of tracking, incompetent in subject expertise, or on a power trip. And, Maplehurst's lower-track students are not boorish louts nor are they uninterested or incompetent in dealing with academics. Further, as the many similarities in processes between regular and lower-track classes suggest, tracking alone is not an omnipotent structure that renders lessons inequitable or excellent. In contrast, then, to categorical descriptions (often embedded in pedagogical and social lore), this close-up suggests the value of rethinking assumptions such as "relevance" which guide the design of remedial curricula. John Dewey (1956, p. 23, originally published 1902) provided one alternative. Teachers, as well as theorists and policymakers, may rely too much on students' psychology. Instead, the logic of academic disciplines, "representing a given stage and phase of the development of experience," might provide a better foundation from which to understand "relevance" from the student's viewpoint.

## NOTES

1. Quotation marks denote statements by staff members and students in the Maplehurst school district. All names are pseudonyms. I also indicate some characteristics of talk, using these symbols: overlapping utterances by [brackets]; short, untimed pauses by -, slightly longer pauses by --, and timed pauses by (seconds); emphasis by underlining and greater emphasis by CAPITALS; elongated syllables by co:::lons; omissions of parts of quotations by . . . ; and descriptions regarding the situation in parentheses.

2. Maplehurst teachers' ambivalence reflects the major theme in the history of curriculum differentiation, as David Cohen recounts it (Powell, Farrar, and Cohen 1985, Chapter 5): educators lobbied for compulsory education for all children yet provided differentiated curricula because they distrusted the intellect of the masses.

3. As Keddie (1971) documents, other teachers tell "stories" in response to perceptions that lower-track students cannot think abstractly.

4. I number lines of discourse consecutively in this chapter. The segments were not consecutive as they occurred in the lesson, except where noted.

5. Two direct disagreements about other topics were voiced prior to the argument about Mary but neither developed into a disagreement sequence.

6. Walker and Adelman (1976) note the importance of ongoing, long-term observation for understanding the meaning of specific classroom events.

7. Cazden (1986) also mentions the lack of attention paid by researchers to gender differences in tracked classes. See also Rosenbaum (1976) and Valli (1986).

8. Here, a student in the class notes explicitly the oddities of Mr. Bradley's mapping of the world in the "story" of the six characters.

LINDA VALLI

Chapter 3

# A Curriculum of Effort: Tracking Students in a Catholic High School

Curriculum differentiation can be described a number of ways. In *The Shopping Mall High School,* Powell, Farrar, and Cohen (1985) use the terms horizontal and vertical curriculum. The horizontal curriculum comprises the various subjects taught for credit across and within departments: mathematics, French, Russian, English I, typing, home economics, Shakespeare, Creative Writing, the Modern Novel, and so forth. The curriculum is differentiated by subject. The more extensive the horizontal curriculum the more likely it is that students will receive school knowledge quite different from one another.

Another way of differentiating school knowledge is through the vertical curriculum: subjects are taught at various levels of difficulty. This differentiation is less apparent since courses often have the same title. For example, English I can have a section for college bound students, a section for vocational students, and a section for honors students. Topics covered within these courses are often the same, but higher-level courses generally cover more of them, in more depth, using more inquiry-oriented strategies.[1]

Horizontal and vertical curriculum describe official school knowledge. Their extent can be gleaned from course catalogues, syllabi and textbooks, which give a broad, aerial view of school knowledge. However, to get close to what is taught and learned, one needs to know the curriculum-in-use, which may or may not correspond to the image of school knowledge found in official curriculum sources. The curriculum-

in-use is the actual knowledge created in the daily interactions of students
and teachers within their specific institutional and social contexts. This
curriculum is discovered only through participation in the daily life of the
school and examination of how teachers and students derive and create
meaning within and beyond the parameters of official school knowledge.

A number of powerful concepts have emerged from studies of classroom knowledge: concepts like the witch-hunt syndrome (Henry 1963),
counter-school culture (Willis 1977), the logic of technical control (Apple
1982), and the mystification of knowledge (McNeil 1986). One particularly salient curriculum differentiation concept is that of caricature (Page
1987). In Page's study of lower-track classes in two college-preparatory
high schools, Additional Needs classes in one school were caricatures of
regular educational encounters: student-teacher relations were ironic
and aimless; the classroom climate was wildly chaotic; academic progress was the least important aspect of classroom life; and topics were selected on entertainment, not academic criteria. The lower-track curriculum in this school was a grotesque version of an academic curriculum. It
was neither the real thing nor something genuinely different, such as a
basic skills curriculum or a vocational curriculum.

These three concepts — horizontal curriculum, vertical curriculum,
and curriculum-as-caricature — provide cogent ways of seeing differentiation and of understanding how students in different tracks receive different school knowledge. They shed light on the differentiated curriculum
at the school described in this chapter. They explain certain features of
school life and, more importantly, generate a new concept: the concept
of a parallel curriculum. Through a parallel curriculum students in different tracks receive remarkably similar educations even though their academic courses never intersect.[2] In the school I analyze, the main similarity in courses, irrespective of track differentiation, is an emphasis on
effort. The importance of making an effort persists across tracks and
gives definition to the parallel curriculum.

The concepts of parallel curriculum and curriculum-of-effort
emerged from data collected during a field study of Catholic schools. The
fieldwork was part of a national survey of Catholic schools designed to
assess how effectively Catholic secondary schools serve students from
low-income families (NCEA 1986). Central Catholic was one of five
schools selected from the survey for a follow-up field study of urban
schools which seemed successful with low-income, minority students.
Selection criteria were a minimum minority enrollment of twenty percent, the principal's estimation that at least 20% of the student body came
from families with incomes below the federal poverty line, and a rela-

tively high number of teachers saying the school was particularly effective with low-income students.

A five member research team held weekly meetings during the months prior to the initial site visits in 1985 to develop focused interview protocols, a student and parent questionnaire, a stratified sampling procedure, and a daily schedule to maximize classroom observations and interviews. School documents, policies, and curriculum materials were also reviewed prior to the visits. Teams then spent a week in each of the selected schools (Bauch et al. 1985). This initial field work sparked interest in the school's tracking system. Of the five schools, Central Catholic was the most explicitly and extensively tracked. A student's track number was as public as his name. Yet student interviews failed to produce negative comments about tracking, and classroom observations of lower-track classes failed to uncover the apathy, chaos, or randomness prevalent in other schools (Oakes 1985; Page 1987; Valli 1986b).

Wanting to directly compare school experiences across tracks, four field researchers returned to Central Catholic the following year.[3] Twenty-four class sessions were selected for observation. The objective was to pair a general track class (Track III or IV) with an academic class (Track I or II). The paired classes were taught to the same grade level by the same teacher in the same academic discipline. A two or three ability group difference existed within each pair.

Team members wrote narrative accounts of paired classroom observations focusing on similarities and differences in curriculum, instruction, classroom climate and organization. They interviewed the classroom teachers, wrote personal reflections, and discussed their observations in team meetings. Most observations were audio- or videotaped. This second site visit convinced the team that curriculum differentiation at Central Catholic was quite different from that in research portraits of most public schools. This difference might help explain the positive Catholic school effect which Coleman & Hoffer (1987) and others (Camarena 1987; Greeley 1982) claim is particularly strong for low-income, minority students in general tracks in Catholic schools.


## THE PARALLEL CURRICULUM AT CENTRAL CATHOLIC

Central Catholic is a male, diocesan high school located in a large eastern city. A brochure describes it as "an American, democratic, Catholic, Liberal Arts and humanistic, urban, comprehensive high school." In its fifty year history, the school has become more exclusively urban, drawing more than 1,000 students from mostly working class families in the immediate area (NCEA 1986). The brochure emphasizes the school's urban quality: Central Catholic seeks to meet the needs of urban students, make them aware of the demands of the city, and prepare them to improve the city's quality of life.

With the possible exception of a small, neighboring Catholic school, Central Catholic serves the lowest income population of all high schools in a diocese which operates the fifth largest school system in the country. It admits all Catholic boys who apply and has the reputation of accepting students, irrespective of religion, whom other schools reject because of low academic potential. Some students enter reading at the fourth grade level. The school is also reputed to risk admitting students with a history of anti-school behavior.

In 1985, the tuition was $1,100, the standard rate for the diocese. Approximately $100,000 a year goes toward tuition assistance to 20% of the student body, but the principal expects each family to pay at least $300 a year. According to both the principal's estimate and a subsequent parent survey, about one-third of Central Catholic's students are from low-income families. About a third are minority students, mostly black; and about a fifth are non-Catholic. Fewer than 60% go to college, less than the average Catholic school but above the public school going rate (Coleman and Hoffer 1987; NCEA 1986).

According to the course catalogue, which each student receives, "all courses except Physical Education are tracked." The catalogue gives one title and description, but different track numbers, for all required courses in English, social studies, science, foreign languages, and religion. For example, all ninth graders are required to take Freshman English. The catalogue describes the course as:

> Review of grammar with emphasis on the parts of speech, verb usage and possessives. Review and development of sentence patterns and practice in composition. Reading, appreciating and writing about novels, short stories, poetry and plays. Units on speech, vocabulary and mythology.

The practice of giving courses a common title and description but different numbers gives the appearance that students are only differentiated through the vertical curriculum. In other words, the catalogue suggests that all ninth graders cover the same topics (parts of speech, verb usage, possessives, sentence patterns, vocabulary) and read the same literature (novels, short stories, poetry, plays, mythology). A reasonable presumption might be that students in lower-tracks spend more time on parts of speech, covering a novel, practicing coherent paragraph writing, and so forth. However, the catalogue gives no suggestion of the type of horizontal curriculum described shortly, in which lower-track students cover a contemporary adolescent short story while upper-track students study a Shakespearean play, even though they are enrolled in courses with the same title.

Looking beyond the course catalogue to the school at large reveals a curriculum which is both more and less differentiated than the catalogue indicates. The vertical curriculum is *more* differentiated in that it actually has seven, not four, distinct ability levels. Though the course catalogue lists four tracks for most courses, all administrators and teachers said the school actually has seven tracks. Track III, a general track enrolls the most students, over half the student population. This track has four separate sections (A, B, C, and D), which are ability grouped. Track III students can correctly identify themselves by track letter as well as number. This number of ability groupings makes Central Catholic more like large public schools than like Catholic schools, which typically have only three levels of differentiation (Lee and Bryk 1988).

The horizontal curriculum is also more differentiated than the catalogue indicates, since the school's explicit policy is to use different textbooks for each ability level. Thus, covering different content is more likely than if all sections of a course used the same text. Adding to the horizontal differentiation is a school policy that Track III and IV students take one less course a semester than Track I and II students. Students in the two academic tracks receive more knowledge since they take more courses and, according to all school members, cover more material per course. The knowledge they receive is also of "higher status": Shakespeare vs. adolescent short stories.

Differentiating both the horizontal and the vertical curriculum to such a degree requires considerable school effort. Because track placement is the administration's and not the student's decision, as it is in many public schools (Camarena 1987; Lee and Bryk 1988), student records have to be evaluated for initial placement and reviewed for potential movement to a different track. Using different texts for each track also requires additional planning time and effort for the faculty. As interviews and classroom observations confirmed, Track III does not simply receive Track II's former lectures, assignments, and exams. Teachers construct different lessons for different tracks of the same course.

But, Central Catholic's official curriculum is also *less* differentiated than one would presume from this analysis. First, Track IV, the lowest track, is virtually eliminated by junior year. By the end of their freshman year, half the Track IV students have moved into Track III. By their junior year, only three Track IV sections remain: in English, social studies, and

Table I: Program of Studies

| | Track I | Track II | Track III | Track IV |
|---|---|---|---|---|
| 9th Grade | Freshman English<br>Western Culture<br>Identity/Sacraments<br>Honors Algebra<br>Physical Science<br>Foreign Language I<br>Physical Education | Freshman English<br>Western Culture<br>Identity/Sacraments<br>Algebra<br>Physical Science<br>Foreign Language I<br>Physical Education | Freshman English<br>Western Culture<br>Identity/Sacraments<br>Introductory Algebra I<br>Physical Science<br>Physical Education | Freshman English<br>Western Culture<br>Identity/Sacraments<br>Modern Mathematics<br>Reading<br>Physical Education |
| 10th Grade | Sophomore English<br>Regional Studies<br>Old/New Testament<br>Geometry A<br>BSCS Biology<br>Foreign Language II<br>Typing I | Sophomore English<br>Regional Studies<br>Old/New Testament<br>Geometry B<br>BSCS Biology<br>Foreign Language II<br>Typing I | Sophomore English<br>Regional Studies<br>Old/New Testament<br>Introductory Algebra II<br>Biology C<br>Typing I | Sophomore English<br>Regional Studies<br>Old/New Testament<br>Applied Mathematics<br>Biology D<br>Remedial Reading |
| 11th Grade | Junior English<br>U.S. Cultures<br>Morality/Church<br>Algebra/Trigonometry (Elective)<br>Chemistry Study (Elective)<br>Foreign Language III (Elective) | Junior English<br>U.S. Cultures<br>Morality/Church<br>Algebra II<br>Chemistry BC<br>Foreign Language III (Elective) | Junior English<br>U.S. Cultures<br>Morality/Church<br>Foreign Language I<br>Geometry C (Elective)<br>Chemistry BC (Elective) | Junior English<br>U.S. Cultures<br>Chemistry D<br>(Remaining courses are in Track III) |
| 12th Grade | Senior English<br>Christian Marriage<br>Art/Music Appreciation<br>Consumer Economics<br>Social Studies AP (Elective)<br>AP Calculus (Elective)<br>Physics (Elective) | Senior English<br>Christian Marriage<br>Art/Music Appreciation<br>Consumer Economics<br>Psych/Soc Elective<br>Trigonometry/Elementary Functions (Elective)<br>Elective | Senior English<br>Christian Marriage<br>Art/Music Appreciation<br>Foreign Language II<br>Consumer Economics<br>Youth and Law Elective | (No Senior Level Track IV Courses) |

chemistry. Moreover, unlike schools in which students may fulfill the English requirement through a remedial reading class, at Central Catholic, reading is taken in addition to, not in place of English. Like students in the academic tracks (I and II), all general track students (III and IV) are required to take an academic curriculum: two years of a foreign language, four years of English, a year each of Western Culture, Regional Studies and U.S. Cultures, a year each of Physical Science and Biology, and two years of mathematics.[4] Algebra I, Algebra II and Geometry are offered at the Track III level; general math is offered only for Track IV students. Like their peers in higher tracks, all Track IV students eventually study a foreign language: two years of French, Spanish, or Russian. All students take typing and art or music appreciation. And eventually, all do read Shakespeare.

Thus, in spite of a seven track, ability-grouped system of differentiation, with different texts used in different tracks, lower-track students follow a course of study parallel to their upper-track counterparts. Their horizontal curriculum is not as extensive, but the gaps between the layers of the vertical curriculum are relatively small.

Why then, does Central Catholic go to such lengths to place students into a finely differentiated curriculum while simultaneously going to such lengths to create similarities between the tracks? Why not two or three tracks rather than seven? Why not eliminate the vertical curriculum entirely and offer options only through the horizontal curriculum? The answer lies, in part, in the central lesson the school teaches—that each student is worth the school's best effort at a suitable and challenging education and that each student in turn has an obligation to put forth his best effort to succeed. This lesson is taught across the horizontal and vertical curricula, is embodied in and undergirds the school culture, is communicated through classroom interactions, and is institutionalized in school policies.

Viewed in this way, tracking becomes not simply an organizational solution or an instructional strategy, but a symbolic system as well. It embodies cultural meanings about society, schools, and students. Those meanings, however, are not the same in all schools, but are profoundly influenced by context (Cohen 1969; Metz 1986).[5] If Central Catholic is an unusually successful school with low-achieving students, its success lies not in the tracking system per se, but in the lesson of effort the system conveys to its students. At Central Catholic, the primary meaning of "tracking" was not sending students along different paths, often with little guidance, but rather following and monitoring them, working hard to promote their best effort.

## THE PARALLEL CURRICULUM: CURRICULUM-AS-EFFORT

Two recitation/discussion segments of ninth grade English classes taught on the same day by the same teacher illustrate critical features of Central Catholic's parallel curriculum. The first lesson is taught to the highest track, and is part of a review of Shakespeare's *Julius Caesar*. The teacher having just presented the definition of a Shakespearean tragedy, comments on the first characteristic: a hero with a tragic flaw. In the following exchange, he asks students to consider the meaning of "tragic flaw" and to determine the "tragic hero":

> T: Whoever that person is somehow has a weakness or flaw which causes him to make a fatal mistake . . . Now, take that definition and I'm going to ask you a question. In terms of the tragic hero and in terms of what happened to him, who is at fault. Take a look at what we just said now. If we have a tragic hero, who is at fault for the end that comes . . . ?

> S: Himself.

> T: Okay. That's important. He himself is going to be responsible for what happens. Why is that? He is going to be responsible for his own death. Somehow he is going to be responsible for it. Mike.

> S: . . . (inaudible) . . .

> T: Okay. He has some weakness. Now that weakness in most of Shakespeare's plays is basically a good point that he has to excess. It's not that he's bad; it's not that he's evil, most of the time. He's a decent person except that somewhere in his character he has this trait in excess. Now think about Shakespeare's characters. I'm gonna ask you if you had to pick out the heros from Julius Caesar . . . who would you begin to pick?

> (After a lengthy discussion, two are left: Brutus and Caesar).

> T: Let's take a look at Caesar first. If we had to list his tragic flaw . . . if we look at the play until his death at the end, what seems to be his flaw? Remember Brutus's speech.

> (Clarifying discussion about physical disabilities, mental problems, and character flaws).

> T: Brutus accuses him of it constantly. We have to see whether Brutus was right or not. As a matter of fact, when Anthony gives his speech, the line that comes over and over and over again is . . .

> S: That Caesar was ambitious . . .

> T: Now. Ambition by itself. Is it a positive or negative trait?

S: Positive.

T: Positive trait. It's good to be ambitious. If you're not ambitious, what happens to you?

S: You go nowhere.

T: You go no place at all. You end up hanging out on street corners, with nothing to do, for excitement you shoot out busted windows. (Laughter). Anything like that happens. Ambition is a good trait . . .

The second lesson is from the lowest track freshman English class, called Track IV, but seven ability levels below Track I. In this lesson, the same teacher introduces a popular adolescent short story from the literature book.

T: Before we start, let me ask a couple questions. If you say someone is a loser . . . if you point to someone and simply say, "He's a loser" . . . I'm not talking about an athletic contest or something . . . If somebody says, "Do you know so and so?" and you say, "Yeah, he's a real loser," what do you mean? . . .

(Guided discussion elicits phrases like being out of a job, "hanging out" on the corner, hasn't done anything outstanding, nothing is going his way, poor, on drugs, a waste, and has "dug a hole" for himself).

T: . . . You have on p. 291 the picture of a loser. Now, we're gonna take this story of a kid who's a loser. You can be classified as a loser by two people . . . by two groups of people. You can be classified a loser by . . .

S: Others?

T: Okay . . . by other people. That's not too bad . . . Who is the worst possible person who can classify you as a loser?

Ss: A better person? Parents? Family? Another loser? Yourself?

T: Yourself. What happens when you finally come to the conclusion that you're a loser? I mean . . . when you condemn yourself . . . that you've reached the bottom? We're gonna go through the story of a kid who has reached the point where he's classified himself as a loser. We're gonna read the first few paragraphs to get started . . .

(Students read a few paragraphs aloud. Teacher interrupts to comment, question on meaning)

T: . . . What happens if you sit around thinking that someday everything will clear up? It doesn't. It's like looking at that test grade. If it's a 90, it's not gonna change. If it's a 70, it's not gonna change . . . If it's a 60, it's not gonna change. You can't sit around. What do you have to do? If you want to make a change, what do you have to do?

S:   You have to work for it.

T:   You have to get up and work for it. You can't sit around and wait for it
     to happen. It doesn't happen. You can't sit around hoping to be a better
     baseball player, a better basketball player. It doesn't work. You can't
     sit around hoping to be a better student . . . and he's about to find it out.
     Pick it up, Steve.

     (Steve reads. Teacher stops students to emphasize theme of loser . . .
     of waiting around for something to happen).

T:   Yeah, up to this time he's been blaming what?

Ss:  His size, his bad complexion, that fact that he was young . . .

T:   So, it's not what that makes you a loser?

S:   Appearance.

T:   Right, physical appearance. It's something else that does it to you.

In both classes, Brother Michael emphasizes qualities of the main
character. For Track I students, those qualities are leadership and ambition—good and noble traits if not held in excess. If you are not ambitious
you go nowhere; you end up on the street corner shooting out windows.
This mini-sermon is directed to students who, like Julius Caesar, are ambitious and potential leaders, who would never be a Street Corner Society
(Whyte 1943). In this interpretation, the shooting-out-windows reference
is more a characteristic of what "the others" are like—those who go to
the neighboring public school, or maybe even those in Track IV.

In the Track IV class, Brother Michael also emphasizes the qualities
of the central character. But in this case the character is not a leader. He
has no ambition. He is, in fact, like the students in Track IV, a loser. He
does not succeed because he waits for things to change and blames external circumstances for his predicament. This interpretation is reminiscent
of the curriculum-as-caricature construct. Only in this case, the remedial
track is an inversion rather than an imitation of the academic track. The
main character, with whom Track IV students can identify, is an isolate
instead of a leader, offers excuses instead of possessing ambition, and will
be a failure rather than a success.

But another interpretation is possible: that both English classes
teach basically the same lesson—ambition is good and success is possible, but only if you do not hang out on street corners, only if you do not
see yourself as a loser, blaming others and outside forces for your failure.
In Brother Michael's view, both characters, and students in both tracks,
are equally responsible for what happens to them. This second interpre-

tation makes the Track IV curriculum experience analogous to Track I's. It is a parallel curriculum. Both groups of students are warned about the street corner; both are encouraged to be ambitious, make the effort, and believe in themselves. This interpretation of Brother Michael's classes as a curriculum-of-effort is more plausible than the caricature interpretation because it is reflected in and supported by Central Catholic's school culture, classroom interactions, and institutional policies.

## School Culture

Much has been written about the family or community atmosphere of Catholic schools (Bryk and Driscoll 1988; Coleman and Hoffer 1987; Lesko 1988; NCEA 1986). The phrase "persons-in-community" is sometimes used to capture the Catholic school's mission to promote human dignity and build community (Lesko 1988). At Central Catholic, school family is a literal construct. The school, which opened in 1916, has been staffed by the same community of religious brothers since 1926. The brothers still comprise 25% of the total faculty. Half of these religious brothers are themselves graduates of the school, as are 25% of the lay faculty.[6] Since a number of faculty members are women, the percentage of eligible faculty alumni is even higher. Like the students, many faculty members have brothers and/or fathers who graduated from the school. Ninety percent of the faculty graduated from one of the local archdiocesan high schools and over 50% have been at the school fifteen years or longer. This common history enables the faculty to develop an unusually strong shared culture or "shared set of meanings" about their role in educating these young men (Metz, 1986, p. 53). In a very concrete sense, Central Catholic is a neighborhood, community school with a family tradition and faculty who identify strongly with their urban students. In one teacher's words, it is "not a 'we-them' situation."

The school is deliberately organized to promote school success, particularly for the young men in the general curriculum tracks, who do not know much of it. The orientation toward curriculum-as-effort is pervasive, stable, and highly respected. In a group interview, parent after parent told stories about their children and others' who succeeded at Central Catholic only if they put forth the effort. The stories always contained elements of the faculty's personal knowledge of and concern for individual students: teachers determined to push students and not let them slide by.

One story in particular was told with such significance that it bordered on myth, intended to "persuade the audience that the events are to be read in a certain way" (Lesko 1988, p. 24). This was the story of Tom Sullivan, who graduated with one of the parents' sons. When Tom's mother died, he went to live with the religious brothers in order to "prepare himself better . . . he knew that if he was here he would get that kind of preparation . . . they took him under wing and prepared him . . . gave him all this time." Tom graduated at the head of his class, attended Princeton, and was an outstanding student.

This story was told with pride by a parent who "was never blessed with anything [a son] higher than Track III" and, in the 1950s, had himself been thrown out of Central Catholic. Another father had the same respectful tone when he told about his son flunking out. While commenting that students who disrupt class and don't try to learn will be put out, he remarked . . . "For instance, I am the president of the Father's Club. My kid flunked out. Being the president of the Father's Club and raising money, you've got no weight! . . . They tell you this . . . 'If you are paying your hard-earned money to send your son here, we are not going to let this boy disrupt the class. He's going'."

One father admitted being upset initially with a faculty member who failed his son and thereby deprived him of the opportunity to play the last football game of the season. The parent recalled the teacher's remarks at the time:

> Basically, he just failed by one point. It would have been very easy to pass him, and I have passed other kids who I see are really trying hard. They come to me after school and tell me they have a problem. I try to help them. But your son's attitude is 'Leave me alone; don't bother me; you're wasting my time.' That's the reason I didn't want to give him that one point . . . you can't let this kid con everyone and get away with it.

The father asserted that the experience *evenutally* changed his son's attitude: "He realized he had to do what was expected of him to get the grade he deserved. In other words, he had to earn it."

One parent talked about a brother from the school coming over to his house to see his son, whom the brother had flunked a few years before. Another mentioned calling a brother at 4:00 in the morning to see his son who was in the hospital and "in a little trouble with the law." The brother arrived at the jail at 6:30 a.m. A mother who was a single working parent spoke of the assurance she felt about her son attending Central Catholic:

> I never had any worry of him ever trying to cut a class or cutting a day from school. Because if he was a little late and wasn't there by a certain hour or time, right away they would call . . .

This personal orientation, or in one parent's words "extreme interest," toward students supports a curriculum-of-effort. As Wehlage, Stone, and Kliebard (1980, p. 358) discovered in their study of drop-outs, problem students often "equate 'strictness' with 'caring'." Faculty can push students to work academically because they themselves exert the same effort: they give students reason to believe they genuinely care about their personal growth and well-being. Effort is not reserved for crises or for exceptional students, but is part of Central Catholic's regular routine. Teachers and students interact naturally and comfortably with each other in classrooms, halls, the gym, the parking lot. They meet before, during and after school, vigorously competing against each other in pick-up basketball games, working together everyday to clean the lunchroom, painting classrooms together over the summer. Faculty personally contribute to the cost of student trophies and they attend student dances. Students personalize detention, calling it "sitting for Brother James." Nowhere did we observe the type of distanced student-teacher relations found in other urban high school ethnographies (Cusick 1973; Metz 1978; Willis 1977).

Effort was also expended on matters beyond the school's walls. When racial tension flared in the neighborhood, the principal walked the streets, addressing parents and graduates by name in attempts to quell the conflict. This sense of community responsibility seemed to infect students. Central Catholic boys were notorious for their generosity. Although one of the poorest schools in the diocese, Central Catholic regularly contributed the most to charitable ventures like Mission Bowl and Breadbasketball. In contrast to the coercive, self-serving spirit of money-raising at the all boy's Catholic school portrayed in the recent film, "The Chocolate War," the spirit at Central Catholic was one of genuine giving. "We learn that we have responsibilities to other people ... That's a big thing here, helping other people."

Mr. Dunagon, a first year teacher, favorably contrasted his experience at Central Catholic to his prior experience in two other Catholic schools. He used expressions like "doors being held open for me here that were never opened before," "kids saying hello who don't even know me," "students calling me by name." He spoke of positive faculty-student relations:

There seems to be a high percentage of involvement in activities by the faculty. More than any other school I've been in ... You can go out at four o'clock and you'll still see cars ... at other schools by 2:30 it looks like a wasteland ... There's general interest here, by presence and a lot of talking about it. It doesn't seem to be a totally book-oriented, faculty-student relationship.

Private interviews with students support Mr. Dunagon's comments. Students talk about teachers who help students try harder, spend time with them in activities, have personal relationships with them, talk to them "like you're a normal person, not a child." They speak of teacher availability for both academic and personal problems: "If you're having troubles at home or anything . . . you can go and talk to the student counselor."

> All the teachers are available to talk to . . . Brother Stephan in the hallway. I myself didn't even realize it; it's true. He's like a counselor. Like all your teachers are like counselors. They care for you.

Personal, respectful relations help students translate the faculty's "extreme interest" in them as caring, not bossing. They know that many of the faculty have been at the school for years, that many sat, as students, in their very seats. They also know that teachers are not assigned to Central Catholic by the diocese, but choose to teach in this increasingly inner-city school.

## Classroom Interactions

Classroom observations indicate that while teachers' relations with students are personal, the personal never substitutes for classroom instruction, as Cusick (1983) found it did in studies of three public high schools. A therapeutic curriculum (Page, in press; Powell, Farrar, and Cohen 1985) rarely replaces Central Catholic's curriculum-of-effort. The faculty are not just friends, counselors, and basketball competitors. They are teachers determined to make lower-track classes as educationally rigorous as upper-track classes. In fact, the educational experience of the general track parallels the academic to such an degree that the word "general" is something of a misnomer.[7] Although the content is clearly different, the pace often slower, and textbooks at lower reading levels, an academic curriculum is always the focus of classroom interactions.

Of the twelve classes observed during the first site visit, observers judged six to have high student engagement in instruction, four medium-high, and two medium. Engagement levels are not associated with track, but with the classroom activity structure. All of the high- and medium-high classes have some teacher lecture or demonstration and some discussion, recitation, written assignment, oral reading or verbal practice. Contrary to other descriptions of remedial or lower-track courses (Metz 1978; Oakes 1985; Page 1987), the remedial reading teacher began the lesson with whole group instruction before moving into written work. Engagement was high and students stayed on task during practice time. The two classes with the lowest level of engagement were Track II and IV 9th grade religion—the only two classes with no direct instruction. Students did "quiet reading" and written work for the entire period.

During the second site visit, classroom observations took place on the senior's second-to-last day of school. Yet fieldnotes are filled with comments like "wasted no time" and "worked from bell to bell." Even lower-track teachers continued to present new information. In religion, Track IV seniors learned about prenuptial instruction and investigation. Mr. DiCosta walked Track IV biology students through an introduction to DNA by breaking the word down and linking it to terms previously studied: nucleus; glucose and ribose; de- and oxygen. Drawing on their personal knowledge of the Boy Scout Code and Morse code to explain the function of DNA, he continued to introduce new terms: nucliotides, cydocine, helix, and so forth. Throughout the period, Mr. DiCosta monitored student understanding with questions like, "What are the pairs? Are you following me? Does that make sense? What if you used a rubber ladder and started twisting?"

For a 7th period Track IV U.S. Cultures class, observer fieldnotes reflect amazement at student behavior. Although the teacher was detained about five minutes, the juniors waited quietly. Once class began, teacher and students remained on task, mapping the progress of World War II. The teacher seemed authoritarian to the observer, but students were neither intimidated nor uncomfortable. The frequently wrong responses were corrected with comments such as, "What you say is correct, but let's separate scientific and military contributions to the war effort." No hostile or negative interactions occurred, possibly because students believed this teacher was "seriously attempting to help them academically" (Metz 1986).

In a junior level Track III American literature course, Mr. Williams engaged students in a discussion of Poe's "The Black Cat." Claiming that he spent considerably more time selecting interesting, relevant literature for lower-track classes, he nonetheless selected classics. The next assigned reading was Shirley Jackson's, "The Lottery." Like Mr. DiCosta, Mr. Williams worked hard to connect new knowledge to students' personal knowledge. He also connected this psychological thriller to the larger theme of the personal struggle between good and evil. In doing so, he risked making himself and students vulnerable by personalizing the danger of carrying grudges. Mr. Williams recalled recently letting David—a student in the class—experience his anger, then telling him to let it go, to cool off, to realize the incident was not worth continuing to be upset about. He publicly asked David if he had let go of those feelings and waited for an answer before bringing the discussion back to the suppression of emotion in "The Black Cat."

As in Brother Martin's class, Mr. Williams' effort is not directed primarily to abstract book knowledge, but to self knowledge and larger moral issues. At Central Catholic, the curriculum-of-effort is not simply the effort teachers and students put into good grades and academic success, but the effort needed to take responsibility for oneself, to become more self-aware, and to work for others. Students do not reject teacher efforts in this regard as moralizing and intrusiveness because teachers do not present themselves as apart from or superior to students. Although personal relations do not substitute for educational encounters, the definition of an educated person is deeply personal; it embodies both intellectual and moral development.

This is not to say that all Central Catholic teachers like being assigned the lower tracks. Like public school teachers with lower-track assignments, they say it is more difficult, that they have to provide more examples and more detail. One teacher said he sometimes gets so frustrated he could grab students and shout, "How can you be so stupid?" The principal himself, who was teaching Track III, said he could not believe anyone could have lower ability. But the dominant discourse is quite different. Teachers talk about "structuring for success" in general classes . . . "It's harder, it takes more time and energy . . . you have to do more things to keep the interest going." Contrary to findings from public schools (Rosenbaum 1980), Central Catholic teachers devote more time and enthusiasm to lower-track than to upper-track classes. In addition to spending more time preparing, they give second chances on failed tests, offer extra help, and run tutoring sessions. Ninth grade Track IVs who arrive at Central Catholic "with a chip on their shoulder" . . . "bragging about their problems" are quickly known:

> . . . when they get in, there's only twenty kids . . . they get an awful lot of individual attention. Their homework is checked every night, more frequent quizzes. Kids get called on all the time . . . For the first time these kids are on a level of their own . . . the goal we are asking for is attainable all of a sudden.

To the teachers, Central Catholic exists for the general track students, who make up the majority of the student body. Teachers believe that if the school is not there for hard-to-teach students, it should close its doors.

The genuine faculty concern and involvement is not lost on students. Like students elsewhere, Central Catholic's lower-track students appreciate teachers who "cared enough to maintain high expectations" and used a structured teaching approach (Wehlage, Stone, and Kliebard 1980, p. 358). They quickly spot teachers whom they say "are only there for the paycheck" and contrast them to the majority. "They really do care, you know. It's not that you do well, it's that you try" ... "from my own experience, the school is there for you. But if you fall back and don't do your work, they will tell you so" ... "They don't want you to do well for themselves, but for you" ... "The goal (of the school) is that if you have a problem, anytime, even at night, they will help you." While in the classroom teachers are characterized by students as being "all work," their relation to students is considerably more expansive.

### Institutional Policies

Central Catholic's orientation toward reciprocal effort, transmitted through the general culture of the school and visible in teacher-student classroom interactions, is institutionalized in official school policies and practices. These policies deal with student-teacher ratios, teaching assignments, textbooks, changes in track assignment, failing grades, and honors. Each demonstrates school commitment to providing low-achieving as well as high-achieving students opportunities for school success.

The student/staff ratio at Central Catholic (including administrators and counselors) is 21:1. The student/teacher ratio, however, is not uniform across tracks. The ratio for Tracks I and II is 38:1, Track III is 30:1 and Track IV is a low 20:1. As a result of faculty meetings and discussions, the school established a policy of reducing the student/teacher ratio in lower-track classes so teachers can spend more time with each student. It is not viewed as compensation for being assigned the "troublemakers." As one teacher metioned, a 20:1 ratio enables a teacher to call on every student at least once each class period and to give each student a lot of attention. No Track IV student can go through a day overlooked. The smaller ratio helps teachers structure classes more: give more frequent quizzes, check nightly homework, and "run-off" more materials. Though they describe these efforts as "draining," the teachers believe it helps students develop study habits and expend more effort on learning.

Similarly, the school's policy about teaching assignments allocates scarce resources to the lower-tracks and stands in sharp contrast to the way teachers are assigned in other schools (Finley 1984). Lower-track assignments do not generate ill-will; are not negotiated away; and are not given to the newest, least-qualified and least-powerful members of the faculty. Nor is teacher status linked to upper-track assignments. Working through department chairpersons, Central Catholic administrators recruit those considered to be the best teachers for lower-track classes. In addition to recruiting their best teachers, most department chairs assign themselves to those classes. The principal, who has a masters degree in chemistry and traditionally taught Track I Honors Chemistry, assigned himself to a lower Track III junior math class. The culture of the school encourages dedication to the lower-track. As the head of the foreign language department said, "I think these kids [low-achieving] are more worth teaching because of the difficult time, academically, they have. It's great, a great experience."

The policy, mentioned earlier, of using different texts for each of the seven tracks creates considerable differentiation in the vertical curriculum. However, like the decision to separate Track III students into four sections, it was done with the intent of giving more attention to the general track student. The faculty and administration decided they had not paid enough attention to this group. They did not want to officially add Tracks 5, 6, and 7 for fear those numbers might harm students' self esteem. Instead, they divided within the track and asked departments to select a different text for each section, reasoning that using the same text promotes covering the same content in the same way, regardless of students' ability or background knowledge.

The experience of success is also promoted by moving students out of, and the eventual elimination of, Track IV. Persistent effort is made to move students up tracks. Students with an 88 average are eligible to move up a track and those who average below 80 can be moved down. These students are discussed by their teachers and administrators before any decision is made. As in other schools (Rosenbaum 1980), there is more downward movement in the two academic tracks: 15% to 5%. This means that in terms of course enrollment, students' curriculum experience becomes less differentiated over time; fewer students were in either extreme, Track I or Track IV. And, according to the students we interviewed, more often than not, the decision not to move up a track is made "informally" by their deliberate choice to keep their averages down. Students sometimes reject a higher class placement because they do not want to work that hard. But faculty, who know the students well, are alert to these attempts, tell them they were lazy, that they need to put forth more effort, and place them in a higher track anyway.

Receiving an honors pass is also a way of experiencing success and, unlike many tracking systems, enables general track students to receive honors. Both students and faculty describe the tracking system as a means of low-ability students to receive recognition for their efforts. Honors are awarded by track, so students compete with students of like ability. In this system, talent is not rewarded; effort is. Students receive first honors when they achieve an average of 90 with no grade lower than 85. Second honors are awarded to students with an average of 85 and no score under 75.

The school's emphasis on effort is assisted by an archdiocesan policy that no student fail because of ability. A student who fails three courses in a year is supposed to be dismissed for academic reasons. But students and faculty say this only happens when all school efforts fail to get the student to apply himself. Tracking is viewed by students as one school effort to keep them from failing courses too difficult for them. According to a history teacher, Track IV students fail less frequently than other students because the structured classes force them to do more. Some teachers pass students if they do their homework but fail quizzes, but automatically fail students if they neglect a certain amount of homework. This focus on effort is not lost on students. As one student said, " . . . it's not that you do well, it's that you try. As long as you're trying, and you do your best, it doesn't matter if you're doing well . . . They won't fail a student if he's trying as hard as he can. That's not the job here to fail kids. They want them to learn."


## DISCUSSION

Certain practices are associated with Catholic schools' positive effect on low-achieving students. Compared to public schools, Catholic schools require more homework, more academic track placement, more academic courses, more frequent preparedness for class, higher levels of engagement in classroom activities, and closer monitoring of students and faculty (Camarena 1987). While these practices typify Central Catholic, they alone do not explain Central Catholic's success. They do not explain why teachers set high expectations or how they maintain high standards. They do not explain what prompts students to be engaged in academic work or to accept the standards teachers set.

This paper explains student success in terms of a particular type of parallel curriculum which has both formal and informal features. At the formal level, the lower-track curriculum is similar to the upper-track in academic focus and instructional quality. The horizontal curriculum is relatively short and the vertical curriculum has relatively thin layers. Students in the general track take academic courses. At the informal level, the general track curriculum is also analogous to the academic track. It is devoid of aimless and ironic relations, characterized instead by an emphasis on effort, with teachers structuring for success and putting forth the effort to promote school success. Numerous policies reinforce and facilitate this curriculum, as do the tradition and culture of the school.

Unlike schools where the lower-track is regarded as a dumping ground for society's losers, Central Catholic has no losers. Students know that their teachers are committed to helping even the slowest among them, and that they do not equate talent or rank-in-class with moral worth. Central Catholic's tracking system is only one expression of this commitment. The seven-layered tracking system is not essential, but the meaning communicated to students through the differentiated curriculum is. Instead of expressing a school culture where students are left alone to fail (Powell, Farrar, and Cohen 1985, p. 191), tracking symbolizes faculty interest and concern. Students are, quite literally, "tracked" in the classroom and beyond: teachers follow and pursue them. Faculty check Track IV homework everyday, call homes on unexcused absences, suspend students from football games for not putting forth academic effort, visit students in jail, and invite them off racially tense streets and into their homes. Ability grouping is only one means of tracking students; it embodies the school's effort to help all students succeed. Thus, the emphasis on effort at Central Catholic does not absolve faculty of responsibility for student learning. Students do not have the sole responsibility for expending effort. On the contrary, the curriculum-of-effort institutionalizes a way of caring for the street-corner kid.

## CONCLUSION

Schools would be ill-advised to model Central Catholic's curriculum-of-effort by adopting its horizontal and vertical tracking system. As indicated in this analysis, the meaning, not the structure, of differentiation was essential in creating a particular track experience. Importing practices across schools does little to make schools similar to one another, since the meaning of those practices is bound up in a school's own history, tradition, and culture.

School policies and practices do, however, embody and reflect school culture. Central Catholic's curriculum-of-effort would not survive without its institutionalized policies and practices. Tracking students' successes, failures, choices, excuses, and frustrations through consistent practices reveals to students the school's effort on their behalf.

# NOTES

1. Rosenbaum's (1980) concepts of curriculum grouping and ability grouping are roughly analogous to horizontal and vertical curriculum. However, curriculum grouping specifically refers to college preparatory, general, and vocational tracks, whereas the horizontal curriculum does not. A college preparatory school would have a horizontal curriculum but not curriculum grouping. Central Catholic grouped officially by ability but not by curriculum.

2. "Remarkably similar" is meant in a comparative sense — compared to the "remarkably dissimilar" education students in schools like the Shopping Mall High School receive.

3. This research was supported in part by the National Catholic Education Association and by a Research Grant-in-Aid from the Catholic Univeristy of America. Pseudonyms are used throughout the paper. I would like to thank members of both research teams and graduate assistants who assisted with the analysis: Patricia A. Bauch, Irene Blum, Laurence Ogle, Thomas Small, Nancy E. Taylor, Helen Wallace, and Delores Westerman.

4. These requirements are considerably higher than state requirements reported by Boyer (1983) for the years 1972 and 1980. Lee and Bryk (1988) also report that Catholic school students, particularly those in the general track, take a greater number of academic courses than their public school counterparts.

5. See Cohen (1969) for a discussion about the relation between symbolic forms and functions. Cohen argues that forms and function can change independently and that the same cultural form need not perform the same function or have the same meaing.

6. Greeley (1982) provides a related discussion of religious ownership of Catholic schools. Although the diocese owned Central Catholic, the religious community which operated it was a powerful influence.

7. See Lee and Bryk (1988) for a discussion of the "constrained curriculum structure" in Catholic schools and Wehlage, Stone and Kliebard (1980) for a description of LaSalle High School's general track curriculum which is similar in rigor to Central Catholic's.

SUSAN HANSON

Chapter 4

# The College-Preparatory Curriculum Across Schools: Access to Similar Learning Opportunities?

The high school academic curriculum is once again in the forefront of American discourse on public schooling (Boyer 1983; Goodlad 1984; National Commission on Excellence in Education 1983; Sizer 1984). Policymakers and educators suggest that focusing on college preparation is a first step toward improving the quality of secondary schooling. They presume a rigorous academic program with expanded course requirements and more hours in school will not only better prepare the college bound, but is likely to improve the quality of education for all high school students.

Proponents of such efforts assume that the college-preparatory curriculum is a uniform phenomena with high standards. But, can we really accept this general notion of the college-preparatory curriculum? Our perception of college-preparatory classes has been colored by the voluminous research literature on tracking which documents substantially different learning environments for students in different curriculum tracks. The most academic track, usually referred to as the college-preparatory track, is repeatedly portrayed in tracking studies in relatively glowing terms (see Rosenbaum 1980 for a good review of this literature). It is more intellectually stimulating and demands more self-initiative than general, vocational, or remedial curricular tracks. Differences in teacher behavior toward students, the content and form of school work, performance standards, and the general learning environment consistently favor the highest or most academic track (Metz 1978; Morgan 1977; Oakes 1985; Schwartz 1981).

Hence, the presumption of a superior, uniform college-preparatory track is challenged by studies which analyze school knowledge as a social construct. It can be affected by the social class and/or ethnicity of communities (Apple 1979; Bourdieu and Passeron 1977; McNeil 1986). A few studies (e.g., Rutter 1979; Oakes 1985; Page 1987) explore the way knowledge in schools is distributed horizontally. They provide examples of differences in curriculum's meanings based on the shared beliefs and assumptions of school participants.

Moreover, we know that poor and minority students are over represented in many low-track classes, but we have little information about the experiences in high-track classes of bright ethnic minority and poor students. The intuitive model presumes they enroll in college-preparatory classes of uniformly high quality: mere enrollment in high-track classes provides equal access to high-status knowledge (i.e., classical, academic topics and higher-order thinking skills). However, when high-track classes in a homogeneous working class school are populated by working class students, the relationship between track placement and knowledge may not be as predictable as the tracking literature suggests.

Are presumptions of a uniform, high-quality, liberal curriculum in high-track classes accurate? This chapter compares the classroom opportunities offered to students enrolled in the highest track classes at two high schools. Because the student bodies differ in socioeconomic characteristics, the study also informs our understanding of the processes through which social class affects high-track classes. The study looks beyond quantitative measures of school resources or individual transcripts to investigate the actual substance of educational programs. Rather than asking whether students have equality of access to college-preparatory programs, the study addresses the complex question of why students enrolled in ostensibly similar curriculum programs may not have access to the same knowledge and skills.


## METHODOLOGY

This study describes how one curricular program takes on different meanings in two high schools. It compares the shared assumptions and beliefs of school participants in two schools to make the different emphasis understandable.

Ethnographic data collection and educational connoisseurship techniques were used to develop this comparative case study. To focus on the academic experiences of students enrolled in college-preparatory classes, I attended three consecutive classes at each of two high schools between twelve and fifteen times (i.e., a total of at least 240 classroom hours) during the 1983 – 84 school year. Sitting in a student seat toward the back of the room. I took field notes on everything related to the question, "What classroom practices characterize the curriculum in operation?" In addition to audiotaped notes, my written notes included the nature and length of the tasks assigned, students' and teachers' activities, and the questions asked by both teachers and students.

Five sophomore students intending to go to a four-year college were shadowed at each school. The pool of student names came from the enrollment sheets of the one honors class offered at each school for sophomore students. To ensure that I would observe classes really intended for students going on to a four year college (rather than a junior college), students who attended several classes together, including the honors class, were selected. Initial interviews with the students verified that each had an interest in attending a four year college. Most had qualified for the gifted program, and each had already passed the high school competency exam needed for graduation.

In addition to classroom observations, both semi-structured, formal interviews and informal conversations in hallways and at lunch helped clarify my observations and elicit personal information about the participants' perspective of the educational experience. Teacher interviews focused on curriculum goals and procedures and attitudes about the school and the students. Six students at each school were asked to describe their educational aspirations, to recall their experiences and perceptions of each class, and to discuss their afternoon activities, particularly homework procedures. Four administrators were also interviewed to learn more about the school organizations and tracking procedures. Many documents relevant to the curriculum were collected, including class syllabi, tests, samples of student work, student transcripts, and district curriculum guides.

This chapter begins with a brief description of the culture and environment at each high school. "Thick descriptions" (Geertz 1973) of two of the four classes observed are then presented. Concrete examples from Geometry and English illustrate the processes through which one curriculum track can take on different identities. Using cultural reproduction theory as a basis for interpretation, the differences and similarities in the learning opportunities presented to the students of the two schools are

discussed in the last section. The shared perceptions of the participants
at each school regarding the knowledge and skills necessary to prepare
high-track students for college become the basis for differentiation between the schools. The study contributes to our understanding of how the
college-preparatory curriculum is contextualized in school to meet the
perceived needs of students with different sociocultural characteristics.


## THE HIGH SCHOOL SETTINGS

This study was confined to one school district to control for variance in
district curriculum policy. The school district selected had to be large
enough that it contained both an upper middle-class and a working-class
population, yet attendance had to be segregated enough that working-
class students would not be under-represented in high-track classes.
Franklin Unified School District, having seven high schools and no buss-
ing, met this criteria. Its two high schools with the most extreme differences in socioeconomic level, Thomas and Rosemead, were selected for
the study.[1]

### The Suburban High School

Thomas High School is located ten miles from an urban center in a rapidly growing area. Ninety-one percent of the people living in this community are white and most are employed in white collar professions such
as engineering or upper level management. As one approaches Thomas
Valley, symbols of upper middle-class suburban life are apparent. Large
shopping centers become more prevalent; billboards advertise computers
and swimming pool equipment; and roads are dominated by imported
minivans and compacts. A lone fruit stand and grazing horses remind one
that this was an agricultural area which is rapidly being developed for
commuters looking for more reasonably priced homes. During week days
the neighborhoods are very quiet while children go to school and parents
work.

   Thomas High School opened in 1967 and in 1983 the enrollment to-
taled 1877. The wider Franklin community has a high regard for the education Thomas High provides, and families want to move into its attendance area. A self-evaluation report explains that most of the parents in
this community are college educated and expect their children to attend
college. Thirteen National Merit semifinalists and advanced placement
offerings in four subjects are offered as evidence of how well this school
is meeting the needs of bright students. Approximately 80% of the grad-

uates enter higher education and 45% go on to a four-year college or university. While the school has had to deal with severe budget cuts in the last few years, it has maintained the resources needed to enrich the students education with community support. In 1984, fifteen computers obtained through donations and fundraisings were used in five computer programming classes; parent volunteers kept the library open at lunch and after school.

Since almost all students take college-preparatory classes at Thomas, there is no single cohort of college-bound students at Thomas. In looking for students who took classes together, only three sophomore students took honors English and had at least two additional classes together. These students, along with two others who were in two of the same classes, were shadowed. All came from Anglo families in which at least the fathers had white collar occupations.

*The Urban High School*

Rosemead High School, located in the downtown area, was established in 1867 as the first high school in the area. In 1983, the student enrollment was 1185, with a gradually declining population in each successive grade, influenced by the drop out rate. During recent years, the attendance area has been experiencing an increase in minority populations. In December 1982, 59% of the students were Hispanic, 21% were Pacific Asian Islander, and 15% were white. The school must not only serve a large number of students who speak little or no English, but it must also serve a highly mobile population, with approximately 1300 student registrations and checkouts per year.

Most of the housing near Rosemead is old. It provides some of the cheapest housing available in the city. Small houses, light industry, boarded up buildings, automobile repair garages, and small "mercados" surround the school. The parents have a range of occupations, with the greatest majority classified as blue collar. The high school serves a population having a wide range of skills and aspirations, from students who are deficient in basic reading and math skills, to students dropping out to work on assembly lines, to students intending to seek a four-year college education after graduation.

Although the past few years have seen an increase in the number of students pursuing further education after high school, there are few advanced college-preparatory courses offered (i.e., one physics, one chemistry, and one calculus class), and no Advanced Placement classes. Yet, the best students at the school continually receive scholarship money to attend well-known colleges and universities. From the most recent senior class of about two hundred students, approximately ten students went on to a four-year college.

The school has tried unsuccessfully for years to increase its parent participation. Five to six years ago the school stopped having open houses because "no one came except the parents of kids who were doing well."

Curriculum tracking was clearly evident at Rosemead High at the time of this study. Many students taking honors English were in several classes together, and had become an identifiable group of individuals encouraged to take the most advanced courses in the school. The five students selected for this study were all bilingual and two had been born outside the United States.

## FOUR HIGH-TRACK CLASSES

Being assigned to high-track classes in and of itself does not ensure particular learning opportunities. Even when the form and content of the curriculum is specified by a district or department, individual teachers make decisions regarding the delivery of the curriculum which affect what students actually learn in school. This section begins to compare upper-track classes at the two schools by looking at the explicit content, assignments, and pedagogy used in two core sophomore classes: Geometry and English.[2]

### Rosemead High School

#### Urban Geometry

The scope and sequence of geometry is standardized across the Franklin School District. Regardless of the school a student attends, the title of the course appears on transcripts as "Geometry." And in fact, in many ways the two geometry classes I observed were quite similar. Teachers covered the same concepts; the general sequence of activities in both classes was teacher explanation, followed by students working on identical tasks; and the same number of tests (six) was given to students at both schools. In other ways, however, the two geometry classes couldn't have been more different.

Mrs. Webb, along with the one other teacher at Rosemead who had a college degree in mathematics, was automatically assigned the college-preparatory math courses. Mrs. Webb had taught at the junior high level for thirteen years and was pleased to finally receive her transfer request to the high school level. In addition to Geometry, she taught lower-track math classes.

Mrs. Webb had always taught in inner city schools and was proud of her skill at running classes at the students' pace. She reported this made it difficult for her to plan a particular day's content ahead of time. Rather, she followed a sequence of activities that aligned itself with the students' progress.

No, there is no syllabus, I teach a concept. I do problems on the concept, and then I do a test.

The students verified this, saying that except on test days which were announced about a week ahead of time, they did not know what activities they would be doing in class. Class time was spent either in direct instruction, writing homework solutions on the board, or doing individual work. Sometimes the assigned problems were new ones, other times they were problems which had been assigned for homework but few people had done.

Records of the problems Mrs. Webb assigned repeatedly show her assigning only the first few problems in each chapter. She explained that this was due to many students having trouble solving even these easiest problems. Homework was assigned in this class five of my sixteen visits (i.e., 31% of the visits). They usually consisted of the first two to four proofs in a problem set.

Mrs. Webb used humor as a vehicle for keeping the class under control and encouraging students to pay attention. She did it in such a way though that it was obvious that her expectations of these students were not very high. When someone reported a correct answer, she often responded, "I see you have been doing your homework!" with a sense of amazement in her voice. Rather than reprimand students for moaning at the mention of a homework assignment, Mrs. Webb quipped, "I'm only going to give you the ones to fill in." But even when the homework was easy, many students soon found they could get by without doing it because it was seldom collected the next day. In fact, if enough students didn't do it, extra time was provided. Because Mrs. Webb had taught in inner city schools for years, she prided herself on how to make lessons easier when students were having trouble. However, as she went over and over the same concepts, she lost the attention of many of the brightest students in the class. Three of my students were in the back of the room and spent a great deal of time joking and drawing pictures for each other.

Most of the students observed at Rosemead did quite well in geometry at the beginning of the semester. In fact, some of them found that they could get by without doing much work or being very attentive. As the semester progressed though, all five of the students (three of whom had always gotten ''A's'' in math) found themselves struggling to understand the work. Here are a couple of representative reactions to the class:

> My worst class is geometry because I don't understand it. Math was not a difficult subject until geometry came along . . . No I don't do my homework because I don't understand it really . . . No, I don't get help at home . . . No, I haven't tried to get help from the teacher at lunch.

> My worst class is geometry . . . No, I don't have a book, but you don't really need the book much anyway, except for studying . . . There's really not much homework in there . . . Most of it you can do in class when she goes over the problems . . . If you don't do your homework, it shows up in your grade, but it doesn't matter. I don't care about my grade in there . . . I don't like geometry. More than half of it is liking the class.

### Urban English

American Literature is a semester-long honors English course specifically designed for the brightest sophomore students attending Rosemead. The class was designed years ago by Mrs. Gold and is intended to provide a broad knowledge and appreciation of American Literature for college-bound students. The curriculum stressed critical thinking, independence, and self-expression. As a class the students read four novels (e.g., *Farewell to Arms, Washington Square*), a play, and several short stories and poems. The students were also asked to read four novels on their own and to select a time period in American literature about which to write a term paper. The course had a reputation for being quite rigorous and the students were rewarded with extra units on their transcript for their efforts.

   This course provided Mrs. Gold an opportunity to share some of her favorite literature, while encouraging the students to improve their writing skills and involve themselves in critical thinking. She also felt that this class had an especially important role to play at Rosemead High. She explained:

> '' . . . This class is here because these kids don't get this in their homes. If they're going to compete with others later, they need this — This literary background is taken for granted by others.''

   Signs posted around her room and on her door reveal her aspirations for the students she teaches: ''Do you know about Harvard?'' and ''Education, if it is true to itself, involves thinking, feeling, and being.''

The atmosphere of this class made it apparent that it was an elite class. Only students who had a good command of English were permitted to take honors English, and having been together the previous year, students were close friends. All the students were attentive in this class and there was little need for discipline. Students sat near their friends, and if they arrived to class a few minutes late it wasn't challenged. If this wasn't enough to remind the students of their special status, Mrs. Gold regularly made comments to them such as:

> You are my bright and shining. Some of you may go on to Harvard or Brown, or other good schools . . . When this class falls apart, I really get worried.

Mrs. Gold conducted the class like a college course. There were two major types of class periods: lectures and discussions. Class time was spent reading and/or discussing the readings, listening and taking notes on lectures, working on assignments, or taking a unit exam. There were no regular spelling or vocabulary tests, and the students did not regularly receive instruction in grammar or writing.

Mrs. Gold's enthusiasm for American Literature was evident in both her lectures and her class discussions with the students. She encouraged students to reflect on how literary authors influence our culture and how the characters and plot may relate to personal experience. Despite her good intentions, the class discussions did not go well. The students appeared captivated, but when Mrs. Gold asked for comments, they seemed at a loss for what to say. When asked why the intended discussions were more of a monologue, Mrs. Gold suggested that students had not kept up with the reading, or simply did not possess the necessary background knowledge to understand what they had read.

Although this class was intended to be rigorous, Mrs. Gold was admittedly lax about due dates. She gave the students time after assignments were due to work on them in class, defending her actions in the following way:

> "Students sometimes have ideas for papers afterward. They need time to think about what they have read . . . I used to have due dates, but no one turned anything in, so I gave in and ended due dates."

What was important to Mrs. Gold was that students complete a minimum amount of work by the end of the semester. She admitted that if the students even read two of the four novels assigned, they could receive an "A" in the class. Two of the five students shadowed received a "D" in this course because they did very little work outside of class.

Regardless of the grade students received in American Literature, they unanimously found it worth taking and spoke of the class in positive terms. Student comments suggest that while Mrs. Gold was unable to teach good study habits, she had achieved her goal of enlightening the students.

> "It's a good class . . . You can read a book and not know the meaning, just know the plot and the setting. She talks about what the book teaches you and how it relates to life and to reality. She knows a lot."

> "I like Mrs. Gold's class. She makes you think . . . about everything . . . I got a "B" in English last year and a "D" this year . . . I got a "D" because that's what I earned . . . I'd rather fail in that class and learn a lot, than get an "A" in a regular class and not learn anything."

## Thomas High School

### Suburban Mathematics

All of the mathematics teachers at Thomas have college degrees in mathematics and Mr. Ford was just one of several teachers teaching college-preparatory math. Mr. Ford requested a transfer to Thomas High five years ago because of its fine reputation.

The most outstanding features of Mr. Ford's class were its clearly defined expectations and orderly procedures. Rules were posted on the bulletin board, one handout explained how student notebooks were to be organized, another specified homework assignments for several upcoming weeks, and there was an elaborate point system. Students not only earned points for right answers on tests and homework assignments, but also for keeping a neat notebook and an up-to-date record of accumulated points. All expectations were clearly specified. Students could lose points by talking or by forgetting to bring supplies to class. Up to ten extra credit points per month could be earned for good attendance and bringing the right supplies to class.

Approximately the first twenty minutes of class were spent answering questions regarding the previous night's homework, then concepts used in the upcoming assignment were taught. This was followed by ten to fifteen minutes of free time in which students could begin the next assignment, get individual help from the teacher, or chat quietly. The teacher presumed that students did their homework and could provide answers upon request. When Mr. Ford realized on occasion that many student had not even tried to do their work, he urged students to try again that night, but continued the syllabus as planned.

One of the choices teachers make that affects the learning opportunities of students is which problems they assign. Mr. Ford chose to use the fastest pace suggested by the textbook because "the kids seem to be able to handle it." Homework was assigned *every* night at the suburban school, including Friday (i.e., 100% of the visits). A typical assignment was all the odd problems presented in a section (about ten). They usually consisted of short answer questions and two to three proofs.

While the Rosemead and Thomas geometry classes began with the same content and roughly the same pace, by January the students attending the suburban school were not only ahead in the number of topics presented, but they also had covered their textbook more thoroughly. For example, students at both schools began studying postulates of congruency and quadrilaterals at essentially the same time. However, as the school year progressed, students at the suburban school gradually pulled ahead of the students at the urban school and eventually went on to more advanced topics. They studied the Pythagorean theorem a month before the urban students and went on to Introductory Trigonometry, which urban students never encountered.

All of the students in Mr. Ford's geometry class appeared to conform to his expectations. Even one student talking to his neighbor when the teacher was talking was quite noticeable. Mr. Ford was usually quick to notice these instances and would calmly say something. Without enthusiasm, most students paid polite attention; they took notes as requested; they did their assignments; and they usually responded to the teacher's questions with correct answers. Interviews with the students revealed that while some found the class more difficult than others, all felt that the class was acceptable.

> Geometry is probably my easiest class. Yes we have homework everyday, on weekends too.

> It's a pretty tough class. I had trouble in Algebra last year too. I do as much homework as I can. The rest of it he usually goes over in class. The teacher is real good at explaining things. The class is pretty straightforward. You can look ahead on the homework sheet and know what to expect.

### Suburban English

The content of sophomore English at Thomas High is standardized, but the teachers have some autonomy in deciding how the course is organized and presented. It includes a little of everything: short stories, novels, nonfiction, poetry, plays, expository writing, spelling, vocabulary, and grammar instruction. Ms. Myers spends alternate months focusing on literature and grammar, interspersed with writing instruction every two to three weeks.

The content and instruction reflected a concern that students be prepared to do well on college admission examinations. The students read two books and several nonfiction essays in class, and were required to read two novels on their own. The students were assigned Greek and Latin roots of vocabulary words each week. Instruction, even literature, was presented with an instrumental orientation. Reading assignments focused on learning literary terms and the emphasis in writing was on the development of technique.

Whatever Ms. Myers assigned, even if it was something as nebulous as "to study," she expected it to be done thoroughly and on time. When she told students "to study the grammar unit tonight," she was quite explicit about her expectations:

> "If I said to you, 'Give me the principal parts of the verb, *to speak*' . . . You have to know them inside and out, upside down, every which way . . . I expect you to be able to spew the words back to me as fast as you know your own address and phone number . . . It's easy if you study it. You must take the time to do it."

Outside of class Ms. Myers was eager to talk about educational issues. She admitted that she felt the students "don't appreciate the quality education they are receiving." For her, school was a battleground in which it was her duty to see that the students learned their lessons. When students didn't comply, a phone call home usually got at least temporary results.

Four of the five students found Ms. Myers class relatively easy and were striving to get an "A." They found the expectations straightforward enough, did their assignments, and volunteered answers to the teacher's questions.

> It's not really that complicated . . . The hardest part of the class is probably paragraph technique.

> The class is not that hard. You have to do the homework or you won't do well on the tests.

### The Explicit Curriculum Compared

An examination of specific features of the curriculum and of instructional practices used by teachers in four college-preparatory classes at two high schools suggests that there were many differences in the knowledge offered to students enrolled in these classes. The findings demonstrate the need for investigations of curricular equity to move not only beyond the names of the classes listed on transcripts, but even beyond the instructional objectives specified for each class.

A close look at the two geometry classes reveals concrete differences which would not be apparent on transcripts and which provide different learning experiences for students. In brief, the classes use different textbooks which influence the nature of assigned topics and problems; teachers require different amounts of homework; and they explain how to work problems with different facility.

A comparison of the content and procedures of two English classes offered also shows how dissimilar two high-track courses can be, even in one school district. The teachers clearly had different ideas about what should be taught to their bright sophomore students, and they consistently translated their goals into different types of assignments. Both classwork and homework in English at the suburban school emphasized the development of specific skills. Both classwork and homework in English at the urban school encouraged students to read broadly and spend time thinking and analyzing their thoughts. While the students in both English classes were explicitly being prepared for college, the knowledge emphasized, the nature of the assignments, and teacher expectations about completing those assignments were strikingly different.

## THE MEANING OF COLLEGE PREPARATION AT TWO HIGH SCHOOLS

Differences in explicit knowledge offered to students is only a first step toward understanding why many bright students enrolled in high-track classes are not equally well-prepared for college. An investigation of the learning opportunities presented to students in college-preparatory classes would not be complete without examining the implicit ideas and values transmitted to the students through the tasks they are assigned. Here, concepts from cultural reproduction theory are used to compare the two schools. Teachers' differential portraits of students' futures, differences in what teachers perceive as valued knowledge, and differences in the community-school relationship at the two schools are compared.

Cultural reproduction theorists (e.g., Apple 1979; Bourdieu and Passeron 1977; and Young 1971) have argued that students of different social and economic backgrounds are likely to be exposed to qualitatively different types of educational programs because the way in which knowledge is selected, distributed, and evaluated in schools gives some students access to more power in society. Just as schools cannot be analyzed as institutions removed from the socioeconomic context in which they are situated, neither can a particular curriculum track be understood without placing it in the wider social context in which it is situated.

### Planning for the Future

"College-preparatory" suggests preparation for a particular future—attending a college or university after high school. In each of the classes I observed, teachers informed students of ways in which the curriculum prepared them for a future. The teachers had various conceptions of the knowledge and skills that best prepare students for a successful academic future. This affected what they stressed in the curriculum.

The definition of any curriculum is not simply a matter of stating its content and objectives, but is also partly determined by the context of the institution in which it is presented. Using cultural reproduction theory for interpretation, we would expect to find teachers at both schools socializing students for roles and values which are relatively similar to their parents and the community in which they live. At the upper and middle-class school where 80% of the graduates enter higher education, we should expect to find teachers encouraging their students to have high academic standards and take responsibility for their own work. Teachers of working class students might be expected to accept relatively lower standards and provide external modes of motivation and control. Teachers' treatment of the curriculum was not this straightforward.

In all of the classes observed,[3] teachers informed students of ways in which the curriculum they were teaching related to students' futures. But, the teachers at the two schools related their present activities to the future in different ways and to different extents. At the suburban school, teachers often linked specific assignments with future consequences. Both the geometry teacher and the English teacher reminded the students to "Look at the finished house down the road" to see how the little things like homework and grammar exercises add up. Throughout the field notes are teacher foreshadowings: "Tomorrow be prepared to do . . . "; "Next week there will be a test on . . . "; and "Our next unit will cover . . . " Not only were the value of current tasks related to upcoming tests, but they were also related to the college entrance exams which the students were expected to take in two years.

The students at the suburban school were repeatedly reminded about the importance of planning for the future. The geometry teacher urged students to think about whether they wanted a career such as engineering which required preparation in mathematics. He suggested, "If you have overall plans, and it might not be bad to have overall plans . . . " Similarly, a poster on the English teacher's blackboard read, "If you don't know where you're going, you'll probably end up somewhere else." By continually stressing to students the importance of the future, the teachers at the suburban school supported and emphasized long term goals for the students in ways that affected their reactions to present school activities.

While tests were mentioned in advance by the teachers at both schools, they were mentioned about 50% less often by the teachers at the urban school. The greatest contrast between the two schools in regard to testing was the number of times in which preparation for the SAT was mentioned by the teachers. During approximately fourteen class periods spread over the school year, the SAT was *never* mentioned by the teachers at the urban school, while suburban students were reminded of its importance six times. It appears that the teachers at the urban school did not place the same emphasis on preparation for college-entrance exams that the teachers at the upper middle-class suburban school did. That the importance of the tests was apparent to students at the suburban school is evidenced by the frequent unsolicited questions they asked about them.

While the English teachers at both schools delivered many future oriented messages to the students, the messages had different purposes behind them, depending upon the type of students the teachers saw themselves serving. The urban teacher, Mrs. Gold, wanted her students to understand that attending one of the major universities around the country was a possibility. She regularly made comments to this effect: "We want to get some of these kids into good colleges"; "If they're going to compete with others later, they need that which is taken for granted by others." What appeared to be most important to her in preparing students for a college future was literary exposure, not specific instruction in vocabulary or grammar skills. While the experiences Mrs. Gold offered in honors English were clearly intended to help prepare students for college, Mrs. Gold seldom saw a relationship between this preparation and the necessity to teach specific skills and disciplined study habits.

Thus, being assigned to upper-track classes is not in and of itself the decisive factor in how teachers view their students. Teachers' perceptions of the educational needs of their students are not based simply upon track level, individual expectations, or socioeconomic level of the students, but also reflect the institutional norms of a school. At the urban school the student body was quite varied in both its aspirations and abilities. Accordingly, there was little consistency in teacher expectations across the classes observed.

Shadowing students attending the urban school in three consecutive periods made it apparent that they attended a series of classes in which there was no consistent vision of what school was all about. Whereas in English they were expected to aspire to go to Harvard, in Geometry the same students were made to feel that they were incapable of thinking logically:

" ... The problem is these kids don't know how to think logically. It's not in their background ... "

Each teacher's presentation of the curriculum was affected by his or her conception of what the future held for those students, and this varied considerably based upon his or her image of what the future held for this "type" of student.

While the teachers at the suburban school exhibited some variation in their student expectations, there was more continuity across classes. The common faculty theme of the curriculum translated into practice was that college preparation is a particularly important, if not the most important, function of high school. This consistently articulated purpose for high school gave coherence to the tasks assigned and the study habits emphasized at the suburban high school.

Teachers transmit a complex set of values and attitudes which surround the content offered to students. By consistently reminding students to look ahead toward the future, teachers at the suburban school socialized students to deal with the present in such a way that they often thought of the value of present tasks in terms of meeting one goal—that of being accepted to a good college. The teachers at the urban school did not share a common vision. Thus, they did not place the same emphasis on preparation for college entrance exams and the development of disciplined study habits that the teachers at the suburban school did.

### The Knowledge People Care About

The curricula these teachers taught and the ways they presented them reflect the types of knowledge and knowing perceived as important for college bound students. This section discusses ways in which community context can affect the knowledge emphasized in high-track classes. What we normally regard as high status knowledge according to reproduction theory (i.e., higher order thinking, creativity, classical academic topics) is not necessarily what high-track classes offer.

Two sophomore English classes are both considered college-preparatory yet, the teachers have different perceptions of the knowledge their students need for success. In all of the classes observed at the suburban school, there was an emphasis on learning specific skills. The knowledge emphasized was technical, in the sense that it could be concretely identified and broken into small increments or steps. Even literary analysis and writing were taught as step-by-step procedures that eventually made up a coherent whole. Knowledge was generally presented in a predictable routine and students were expected to learn that knowledge in the same general way: by organizing their thoughts, planning their actions, and presenting the material according to specifications.

To encourage learning, the importance of tests and term papers was emphasized, and grades in each class were based upon clearly defined criteria measured by the accumulation of "points" for each student. Consequently, students were usually graded on things that can be easily measured. Even writing skill was evaluated on the student's ability to write a paragraph which used a particular progression of sentences.

The writing assignments at the urban school were not nearly as concrete as those assigned at the suburban school. In English the students were simply told to "explain what you learned from the book you read . . . how it relates to you and your life." Fewer specific guidelines were given and more creativity was encouraged. Students were graded more on what they said, with only a few notations regarding spelling and grammar.

The enormous difference in the assignments across classes at the two schools suggests that the types of knowledge emphasized were different. At the urban school the students were encouraged to develop personal opinions and express ideas rather than just provide factual information. These students were not taken step-by-step through a series of stages to develop their writing.

The reasons why knowledge was offered in such a structured way to the suburban students and not the urban students are complex. The Franklin schools contradict intuitive notions about the relationship between curriculum and social differentiation, in which one would expect technical skills to be taught to working-class students. Instead, at the suburban school Ms. Myers explained, "Doing things by the rules fits me and the kids. They like knowing what to do and what is expected." In all of the classes observed at the suburban school, teachers based their grades on a point system. Teachers reported that not only do points make it easier to decide borderline grades, but points also make it easier to justify grades to students and parents.

Such comments provide a glimpse as to why a college-preparatory curriculum may emphasize different tasks and skills at different schools. To understand why curricula is operationalized in a particular way, we must look beyond its classroom delivery and learn about the interactive nature of a school and the community it serves. Like many teachers at Thomas, Ms. Myers is from an upper middle-class background and finds it easy to identify with both the parents and students in the community in which she teaches. In suburban communities where parents are highly in-volved in their children's education, teachers quickly learn that they are accountable not only to the students and administrators, but also to par-ents. As one teacher simply explained, "I like being able to say, 'This is why your child's grade is low.' "

In contrast, urban teachers respond to the needs of their hetero-geneous community by attending to individual differences. The grading systems used by the teachers were more flexible than they were at the suburban school. Most teachers preferred to consider many factors other than test scores in determining final grades. A vice principal explained, "There is very little parent contact here so the school can pretty much do as it wants." So few parents showed up at open house each year that the school had even abolished this community outreach effort. Few teachers at the urban school needed to concern themselves with community re-action to teaching and grading procedures in the way that the teachers at the suburban school did.

The consequences of emphasizing different types of knowledge to students with comparable mental abilities can only be speculated. Stu-dents at the urban school were encouraged to think on their own, yet they appeared to be provided with few skills with which to organize their thoughts. While the skills needed to complete the activities in the subur-ban school were equivalent in difficulty or surpassed those needed at the urban school, the suburban school did not always demand the use of higher cognitive levels in their activities. While technical preparation may be appropriate for acceptance to college, a pressing concern is how well this type of preparation prepares students for the long range future. The upper middle-class students can write grammatically correct sen-tences, but will they have anything interesting to say? They have learned to do "selective listening" to perform well on exams, but can they recall the major message of the lecture even a year later? In short, the suburban students taking a college-preparatory curriculum were taught the skills to survive foremost as students, a short-lived occupation at best.

The students enrolled in college-preparatory programs are likely to be the pool of people from which the next generation of lawyers, doctors, politicians, and engineers will come. There are a rich array of educational trade-offs in the types of knowledge offered at these two schools. Can the working-class students perform well enough on the college entrance ex-ams to be accepted to a good college? Will the upper middle-class stu-dents be able to perform adequately when they encounter problems, ei-ther in graduate school or on the job, for which there are no rules?

Cultural reproduction theory is useful, but limited, in interpreting these findings. According to Apple (1979), "high status knowledge" in our society consists of knowledge emphasized in upper middle-class schools. This knowledge directly contributes to the legitimation and perpetuation of ideologies and practices of a stratified society. The knowledge and ideas emphasized at the upper middle-class school will, by definition, be the knowledge that the privileged sector of a society values and allocates as college-preparatory. While intuition suggests that higher order thinking skills should be considered high-status knowledge, the data in this research document that in a suburban school, an instrumental college-preparatory education was implemented. It emphasized facts and skills and encouraged students to plan present education in future terms. In short, a high-track curriculum can be as technical and instrumental as the low-track curriculum described in other schools (Metz 1978; Oakes 1985).

Cultural reproduction theory is limited because it does not consider community context. High status knowledge is not a unidimensional category across settings. This study provides evidence that the knowledge emphasized by teachers in high-track classes is strongly influenced by what teachers perceive as the community's high standards for the students they are teaching.

High schools with working-class populations may be at a disadvantage in preparing students for college, partly because the curriculum they offer does not reflect upper middle-class thinking about the skills that are most important to prepare students for college. The content of some of the urban school classes can be compared with elective courses, popular in the late 1960s and early 1970s which emphasized higher-order thinking skills and encouraged self-motivation and creativity. The more traditional basic skills emphasis, popular during the early 1980s in upper middle-class schools, was not predominant in the college-preparatory classes at the urban high school. Consequently, working-class students observed in this study did not receive as many opportunities as the upper middle-class students to learn the knowledge and skills necessary for success on college entrance exams.

## THE IMPORTANCE OF CONSISTENCY

This paper contrasts several dimensions of the curriculum and its contexts which affect access to knowledge. It provides concrete examples of the "ideas" or "cultural capital" that are transmitted in upper middle-class and working-class schools. Differences surrounding the delivery of the curriculum at the two schools suggest the complexity of providing both a quality education and access to equal learning opportunities. The implication of both is that even if the classes observed at the two high schools provided equivalent enrollments in high-track classes, this in itself would not be enough to ensure equal access to knowledge. School knowledge must be embedded in a way of life that supports high standards and a clear vision of what students in that community need to learn.

Not only access to explicit knowledge gives the dominant group in society an advantage, but access to a shared academic tradition that is perceived as valuable in the community. The difference in the consistency of what was regarded as important both within and across the classes observed was striking. The values communicated by the teachers at the suburban school through their organization and emphasis on particular features of the curriculum created a pattern which permeated the daily curriculum across classes. The consistency of values transmitted across classes may have served to heighten the learning opportunities for students attending the upper middle-class school.

The image of the students held by the teachers at the urban school varied considerably. High-track students were perceived as a significant minority in relation to students enrolled in general education and vocational education tracks. High-track students were intelligent, but they were still part of an urban, principally working class community. Teachers did not agree that most of these students would go on to a four-year college and their major priority was not always preparing the students to do so. The Geometry teacher taught math to students in all tracks and one of her major concerns was keeping her students enrolled in classes and doing some work. In contrast, the English teacher taught a variety of specialized classes, such as journalism and religion and saw herself as subject matter specialist. Both teachers had difficulty delivering curriculum to college-bound students because in the context of Rosemead, such students were an anomaly.

At both schools, teachers expected students taking college-preparatory classes to adopt good study habits. While teachers at both schools assigned homework along with relatively long-term, open-ended assignments which required students to pace themselves, assignments were followed up in surprisingly different ways. At the suburban school, teacher expectations were explicitly defined and students were regularly reminded of the importance of studying and completing assignments on time in each class. Lectures similar to the following one were a common occurrence for students attending the suburban school:

> "How many of you spent at least 30 minutes reviewing your vocabulary last night? . . . I see the majority of you didn't. When you don't do well on the test, you'll know why. Somewhere along the line, you have a responsibility toward yourselves . . . "

In contrast, students at the urban school were left to themselves to select strategies for successfully completing assignments. Teachers displayed lax standards in the amount and quality of work that they actually expected. The English teacher said that although she had asked students to read four books, two would be adequate. She announced that work would be accepted late — even weeks late, with no repercussions. Her concessions to the students demonstrate the interactive nature through which the meaning of the college-preparatory track is produced.

At the suburban school, teachers responded to students not completing their assignments with clear repercussions. One teacher announced that points would be taken off for each day that papers were late, and another teacher made a phone call home for repeated failure to complete homework on time. The teachers at the suburban school knew they had the backing of parents when it came to academic matters. They heard from students how important grades were at home and they heard directly from parents when the curriculum did not appear appropriate. One teacher explained:

> "The parents care about their kids learning at Thomas, maybe not for the right reasons, but they do care. The parents worked hard in school and it paid off. The kids look at school as a means of making money. School is the meal ticket for the future. The parents are very clear about what they want—for their kids to get into a good college . . . "

Teachers I spoke with had been attracted to teaching at Thomas High because they admired the strong academic emphasis of this school. Both teachers and parents seemed to feel a great responsibility for doing everything possible to make acceptance at college a likelihood for their students. They took actions which gradually served to develop the internalized set of values in the students which were compatible with the goals of the school and the community. This consistency in goals and expectations both across classes and outside of school resulted in a clear message to the students about why they were in school.

The message delivered to the students at Rosemead High School was not nearly so clear or consistent, even for those students enrolled in the college-preparatory curriculum. There was not one common theme that gave coherency to the curriculum, just as there was not one acceptable future in the minds of teachers and parents. Hence, there was great variety in the classroom experiences offered to students taking the high-track classes at the urban school. In comparison with the suburban students, these students were at a disadvantage in receiving learning opportunities that encouraged a "way of life" designed to ensure later school success.

Bourdieu and Passeron (1977), Apple (1979), and Willis (1977) argue that cultural capital ensures the school success of children of society's dominant groups. This study makes that assertion more understandable by documenting the existence of variation within the college-preparatory curriculum at two high schools. It is not just the opportunity to learn high-status facts and skills that gives the upper middle-class students an advantage over working-class students in preparing for college. The consistency between community and school goals and expectations in support of high academic standards seen at the suburban school contributes to student achievement by providing a context in which school goals are valuable.

## IMPLICATIONS

Variations in the learning opportunities offered to the two groups of students — similar because they were enrolled in the highest track classes available to them at their school, but different in terms of socioeconomic class and ethnicity — are striking in this study. The findings demonstrate that the college-preparatory curriculum track is not a uniform phenomenon. Although it may look on paper as if students attending different high schools are receiving equal educational opportunities, an examination of the operational curriculum and institutional culture may show significant differences. The way the college-preparatory curriculum (or any curriculum for that matter) is enacted involves a complex relationship between curriculum goals and contextual characteristics of the school, including its social class and valued knowledge.

These findings have several implications for practice. First, enrolling students in college preparatory or honors classes and telling them that they are capable of going on to college is not enough to ensure equal opportunities or success. The ways that teachers follow up assignments and the amount and clarity of the directions provided may be as important as the content of the tasks assigned. Especially in schools with varied student populations, teachers teaching different subjects in the same curriculum track should reach consensus regarding expectations and standards that are expected at different track levels so students can experience consistency from class to class. It is not simply the amount of content covered or access to particular topics that ensures equal opportunities in the future. The knowledge offered by schools must include a way of life and high standards that are supported by the school.

For upper middle-class students the data collected suggest that teachers, parents, and students should take care not to lose sight of what education is all about. External standards set by universities and college boards, along with pressure from parents have a strong influence on students and everyone may lose sight of the real purpose of school. These findings also have implications for the criteria which colleges and universities use for their admittance. This criteria has an indirect, but significant effect on the types of knowledge that are emphasized in the college preparatory curriculum. Finally, these findings have implications for colleges and university administrators. High school transcripts with simply the name of classes on them do not provide enough information regarding the substance of the curriculum that students received, and more information should be sought.

## NOTES

1. All names used in this report are pseudonyms.

2. Geometry and English were two of four observed classes. Social studies and Drivers Education, each taught for half of the observation period, were also observed. A complete report of this study can be found in Hanson, 1985.

3. A total of eight classes were observed for this study, but only details about four classes are reported here. When I state "all classes," I am referring to all eight of the classes observed.

ANNETTE HEMMINGS AND MARY HAYWOOD METZ

Chapter 5

# Real Teaching: How High School Teachers Negotiate Societal, Local Community, and Student Pressures When They Define Their Work[1]

High school teachers across the nation have a great deal of informal free-dom to define their work. Isolated in their classrooms, most of them have the autonomy to determine many if not most of their classroom aims and practices (Meyer & Rowan 1978; Weick 1976). However, the research we report here indicates high school teachers' autonomy is constrained by societal and local community expectations for secondary schooling and by students' abilities, interests and other characteristics. Most of the teachers in our sample responded to these constraints by defining the teaching task in ways that they and people they served would view as Real Teaching. Real Teaching was, first of all, socially legitimate; it recognized, and attempted to meet, public expectations for secondary school-ing. Presenting socially legitimate curricula was not, however, enough to cause most of our sample teachers to view their efforts as Real Teaching. For teachers, Real Teaching almost always included effective teaching. It was teaching that effectively ensured that the socially legitimate curric-ulum presented in class was actually learned by students. Effective teaching was a major component of Real Teaching that was woven into the concept by teachers themselves.[2]

Nearly every one of our sample teachers felt some pressure from the media, educational reformers, national politicians and other representatives of the public-at-large to take certain expectations for schooling into account in forming and pursuing their classroom objectives. They also experienced pressure from parents and other representatives of the local public to define their work a particular way. Teachers often felt, in other words, that they were being asked to meet two distinct sets of public expectations—one set being "societal" expectations, the other being local community expectations. Teachers believed, moreover, that they had an obligation to address one or both sets of expectations. To do otherwise might mean that their definitions of teaching would not be viewed as legitimate.

Meeting societal expectations for schooling meant, for most of our sample teachers, transmitting standard content and mainstream cultural traits. Meeting local expectations meant reinforcing—or compensating for—what teachers perceived to be the sociocultural characteristics of the local people they served. In most of the schools we studied, teachers managed to define their work in ways that both recognized and reconciled these expectations. However, in a few schools, particularly those serving the urban poor, meeting one or both sets of expectations proved extremely difficult. In these schools, teachers were often not able to come to an agreement about what they could or should be teaching. Such disagreements, along with other factors, fostered the rise of conflicting definitions of teaching.

While it was evident that public expectations shaped teachers' work definitions, it was students who clearly had the greatest impact on teachers' immediate aims and practices. Students' ability to learn grade-level content strongly influenced teachers' decisions about what and how much material they presented in class. Students also influenced teachers' decisions about which teaching methods they should adopt. Since effective teaching was for them an important component of Real Teaching, most teachers did their best to find methods that would ensure that most of their students were actually learning the material they presented. Teachers discovered, however, that there was a tension between socially legitimate and effective teaching. In schools where teachers were working with students who were highly motivated, this tension was relatively easy to resolve. Teachers generally had little or no trouble finding effective ways to ensure that their students were learning the material they presented. The reverse was true for teachers who headed classrooms full of alienated or uninterested students. In these classrooms, teachers often found that presenting socially legitimate curriculum made effective teaching more difficult and vice versa. Teachers working in a few of the schools we studied entered into conflict with one another over their differing views of the best ways to ensure the learning of legitimate school knowledge.

As an abstract ideal, Real Teaching was teaching that fulfilled public expectations for secondary schooling and ensured student learning. However when this ideal was translated by teachers into concrete aims and practices, Real Teaching proved to be a highly amorphous concept that was capable of assuming a variety of forms. Curricula and teaching methods were differentiated between schools because teachers felt they should tailor their definitions to fit not only societal expectations but also local expectations and student characteristics. Real Teaching, in other words, differed between schools because public expectations and student traits differed between towns.[3]

Our research also revealed that teachers' level of job satisfaction was directly linked to their ability to practice what they eventually determined to be Real Teaching. The most satisfied teachers in our sample were those who felt they were effectively transmitting socially legitimate knowledge and skills. Those who were not able to practice Real Teaching were often discontent or close to despair.

In the sections below, we examine in more detail how societal and local community expectations for secondary schooling and student characteristics affected the way our sample teachers defined their work. We also discuss how local community and student pressures led both to curriculum differentiation between schools and to conflicts between teachers. Finally, we look at the intimate relationship between Real Teaching and job satisfaction.

## METHODOLOGY

Our research was carried out during the 1986/87 academic school year. We[4] studied eight "ordinary" high schools — schools sharing organizational features commonly found in high schools across the country. In all these schools, students were required to pass similar courses before they could graduate. Teachers taught one or two subject areas to four or five classes of twenty to thirty-five students.

Because we were interested in how local community life styles shaped teachers' aims and practices, we chose schools that served populations with different sociocultural characteristics. For the sake of brevity, this chapter describes, analyzes, and compares three of these high schools. The names of informants and schools in this account have all been changed. Maple Heights High, the first of these schools, enrolled adolescents who were growing up in a suburban community inhabited by white, middle-class families. Quincy High was located in a working-class town called Silas. Most of the employed adults living in Silas were laborers or craftsmen who had never attended college. Ulysses S. Grant High was an urban school serving large numbers of low-income students, many of whom were black.

We spent a little more than two weeks in each school observing classes and interviewing teachers. We began our visits by talking to the principal and collecting statistics and other information about the school. We then followed the schedules of low-, regular- and high-ability students. After observing these students' classes for four days, we selected eight teachers to observe in more depth. Nearly all of the sixty-four teachers we selected for further observation were teaching standard academic subjects such as English, algebra, biology, and United States history. We observed each of these teachers' classes for a day and conducted long, open-ended interviews with them. We also conducted shorter interviews with other teachers and counselors.[5] The sixty-four long interviews and most of the short ones were tape recorded.

The descriptions presented in this paper are based, for the most part, on fieldnotes and interviews conducted with teachers who allowed us to spend a day with them. While our fieldwork in each school was too brief to be genuinely ethnographic, the design did allow us to compare the experiences of teachers working in schools serving different sociocultural groups. It also enabled us to view, albeit briefly, the subtle but powerful effects of social and cultural differences on high school teaching.

## DEFINING REAL TEACHING

Most of our sample teachers began the process of defining their work by adopting one or more general instructional goals. Many of these goals grew out of administrators' or teachers' perceptions of what the public-at-large wanted them to accomplish in their classrooms. A number of these perceptions could be traced to well-established American cultural beliefs while others were shaped by the media, national interest groups, and other ''societal'' agenda setters.

At the time of our study, there were a number of groups with vested interests in secondary education that were putting a great deal of pressure on public high schools to reform their programs. Colleges, politicians, businesses and other groups recommended, among other things, that high schools raise their academic standards, focus more attention on traditional or standard content and place more emphasis on the knowledge and skills needed to succeed in college or the workplace (Adler 1982; Bennett 1988; Boyer,1983; The College Board Equality Project 1983; Hirsch 1987; The National Commission on Excellence in Education 1983). State legislatures, local school boards, and school administrators across the nation felt they ought to take these recommendations seriously. Lawmakers passed new laws designed to "raise standards" and school boards and administrators pressured teachers to address "society's" current expectations for secondary schooling.

Many of our sample teachers were among those who found themselves being pressured by administrators to spend less time on what one teacher called "warm and fuzzy" curriculum—curriculum that focuses on personal development, creative expression, or interpersonal skills—and more time on standard academic content and the kinds of information young Americans need to take on legitimate adult occupations and roles. Most of these teachers came to believe, as a result, that teaching standard content and preparing students for future occupations and roles should be their most important general goals. These two goals were, in fact, the ones that sample teachers were the most likely to cite as their most important ends.

Teachers' general goals were quite broad. Most teachers found that they had to translate these goals into more specific aims. They had to make decisions about the specific kinds and amounts of standard content, occupational knowledge and other curriculum material they would teach their students. They had to decide, in other words, how to differentiate the curriculum.

Societal expectations for schooling not only gave rise to teachers' general goals, they also guided teachers' decisions about how to differentiate the curriculum. The way curricula came to be differentiated was also shaped by teachers' perceptions of local community characteristics. Because many teachers felt somewhat obligated to fulfill local expectations, i.e., to reinforce local life styles, most made an effort to tailor curriculum to fit the particular communities they served. They used their perceptions of prevalent adult life styles to help them decide *which* adult jobs and roles they would prepare students for and *what* and *how much* standard content they would present.

Teachers, however, only reinforced local adult life styles if they judged them to be socially legitimate. Teachers who worked for families whom they thought were embracing self-defeating or illegitimate ways of life often made an effort to compensate for rather than to reinforce their students' background.

Teachers took student characteristics as well as local community life styles into account when they translated their general goals into specific aims. Most assessed students' abilities, interests, and some of their other traits and then used these assessments to help them determine what and how much information to teach. Teachers judged students the same way they judged the communities they came from: they reinforced what they felt were students' legitimate traits and tried to alter or eliminate the "illegitimate" ones.

Once teachers determined what they would teach, the next step was to decide how they would teach. Almost all of our teachers tried to find effective ways to ensure that most of the teenagers in their classes were actually learning the socially legitimate knowledge they selected. This was much easier for some teachers to accomplish than for others. In some of the schools we visited, especially those serving middle-class populations, teachers said their students "aimed to please" and that they had, as a result, little or no trouble finding ways to ensure learning. In other schools, particularly those serving the urban poor, teachers felt they were working with students who "lacked important skills" or "did not care about education." Many of the teachers employed in these schools had trouble finding effective ways to instill what they felt was legitimate information.

Using Maple Heights, Quincy, and Ulysses S. Grant High Schools as examples, the rest of this chapter describes how teachers working for socially and culturally diverse communities defined their work. These descriptions include examples of the way teachers in these schools differentiated the curriculum. Also examined are some of the conflicts over curriculum and teaching methods that arose between faculty members. Finally, these descriptions look at the joys and sorrows experienced by teachers as they attempted to define their work in ways that they and others agree is Real Teaching.

## MAPLE HEIGHTS HIGH SCHOOL

Maple Heights is a suburban community located near a large midwestern city. It had, at the time of our study, a well-educated adult population. Sixty-five percent of the population had attended college. Over a third of the community's employed adults were teachers, professors, lawyers, and other workers whose jobs required college credentials. Local inhabitants and outsiders often described Maple Heights as a "professional" community.

Maple Heights was also white and middle-class. There were about 15,000 people living in the community and only 3% of the population was nonwhite. The average household income was $24,000—a figure slightly above the national median.

The public high school, Maple Heights High, enrolled about 750 students, 10% of whom were black. Most of the minority students attending the school were bused in from the city. There were approximately forty-five faculty members.

## How Maple Heights' Teachers Defined Their Work

The principal at Maple Heights High encouraged faculty members to acknowledge current societal expectations for secondary schooling. He wanted Maple Heights to exemplify society's current image of the "good" high school so he pressured teachers to "beef up" standards, present a great deal of standard content, and teach students the knowledge and skills needed to do well in college.

Teachers were also pressured by parents and other local people to fulfill local community expectations for schooling. Most found the task of reconciling societal and local expectations to be relatively easy. It was easy because these two sets of expectations turned out to be virtually the same. Because societal and local expectations were so similar, teachers at Maple Heights were able to come to a consensus about what would constitute "socially legitimate" curricula at their school.

Almost every teacher at Maple Heights believed they were serving a community that valued formal education and the professions. One teacher said that the community "genuinely admired the academic life" and that the families they served wanted children to learn what they needed to know "to go to college and become professionals."

Maple Heights' teachers were responsive to the town's well-educated parents, who, in turn, were quick to complain if they did not like something. Perhaps more important, most teachers lived in Maple Heights and had close relationships with many of the local people. Because of these ties, teachers came to identify with the town's dominant way of life. This identification caused many teachers to reinforce their conception of Maple Heights' "legitimate" life styles.

Administrative and parental pressures along with their own ties to the community caused many Maple Heights' teachers to translate the general goal of preparing students for adulthood into the specific aim of preparing students for higher education and professional jobs. Most teachers at Maple Heights pursued this aim whether, as one teacher said, students were "qualified" for college or not.

Mr. Fields, a math teacher, prepared students for higher education by presenting information and creating classroom environments that were similar to those found on college campuses. In his regular- and advanced-level math classes, he taught content that he thought students had to have in order to master college level mathematics. He conveyed this and other information in ways commonly used by college instructors. He spent most of the time in class lecturing, and be expected, and generally got, his students to sit quietly, take notes, and ask questions when they did not understand something. Like college students, his students were required to do their homework after class and on their own. If they needed help, it was the students' responsibility to seek it.

Maple Heights teachers also tried to teach students the styles of thought and discourse needed to obtain professional positions. They strongly encouraged their students to adopt a posture towards knowledge and problem solving that is commonly expressed by academics, lawyers, and other professionals. They tried to teach students to be what one teacher called "independent thinkers"; they wanted them to be able to question intelligently the claims put forth by others, utilize and build upon existing knowledge, and solve difficult problems.

Ms. Jarecki, a social studies teacher, encouraged her students to be independent thinkers by facilitating a number of lively classroom debates about important social and political issues. Students were asked to take a stand on these issues and to use sound reasoning and valid evidence to defend their positions. Mr. Horace taught his students to "think like scientists" by having them conduct numerous experiments from which they had to draw their own conclusions and back up their contentions by using other scientists' findings.

Maple Heights' teachers also wanted students to adopt some of the work habits they thought they would need to do well in college. Ms. Trimble, for example, wanted her students to get used to reading . . .

> . . . forty to fifty pages an evening on a regular basis. They will have to be able to read in increments like that when they go to college.

In addition to teaching students the habits of mind and skills needed to become college-educated professionals, Maple Heights' teachers also taught a great deal of standard curricular content. Covering "everything" was the way most teachers at the school translated into specific aims the general goal of teaching standard content. Teachers not only attempted to teach students the "basic" or fundamental facts and concepts they thought every high school student should know, they also expected students to grasp a great deal of advanced material.

At times, the aim of transmitting a great deal of standard content conflicted with the aim of teaching students the skills they need to be successful college students and professionals. Ms. Tudor, a history teacher, complained about having to sacrifice "wonderful" discussions and other efforts to teach important skills because of all the standard content she had to teach.

I have to teach five thousand years of European history in one semester. I mean it's ridiculous. I have to eliminate all the wonderful discussions we ought to be having. There's no way [I can both convey information and conduct discussions] in the short period of time I have. I can't even take a week off to show them how to do library research.

Students also influenced Maple Heights teachers' specific aims — and many of their practices. Most teachers at Maple Heights regarded their regular- and advanced-level students as very able; they felt that these students had the background and skills needed to master grade-level material. Teachers also felt that most of these students were "serious;" that they were willing to learn the socially legitimate content teachers wanted to teach.

Teachers found, however, that they had to earn students' respect before students were willing to learn the material that was presented in class. Many teachers told us that Maple Heights' students were "bright" and "well-informed" and that they expected teachers to know a great deal more about their subjects than students did. Earning students' respect took some effort.

According to teachers, students constantly tested their knowledge. They tried to trip up teachers by asking questions to which they knew the answers, double-checking facts presented in class, or bringing in contradictory information. Teachers responded to students' challenges by talking about information that was not in students' textbooks, spending their evenings working out every problem in the book, discussing current advances in their disciplines, and otherwise doing their best both to feed and to impress the young lions who sat in their dens.

If they managed to earn students' respect, teachers found that their classes became more tame and willing to "please." Earning students' respect gave teachers the freedom to select whatever practices they thought would best fulfill their aims. Teachers who wanted to convey a great deal of content could choose to spend the entire period lecturing with few disruptions. Teachers who wanted to conduct stimulating discussions could do so without any fear that students would use the time to joke or chat with their friends. Once students were tamed, in other words, lecturing, discussions, and many other teaching methods became effective means for ensuring that the material teachers presented was actually being learned.

There was a small minority of students at Maple Heights who were especially difficult to tame. Most of these students were enrolled in lower-level classes and many had little or no interest in going to college or becoming professionals. For these students, the "socially legitimate" curriculum they encountered in class was often "ineffective." It attracted so little interest that teachers were often forced to present alternative material or search for innovative teaching methods that would encourage students to learn at least some of the information society and the local community wanted them to know.

Most teachers at Maple Heights taught an essentially college-preparatory curriculum. Teachers selected it because they believed that it met both societal and local community expectations for schooling. They perceived it to be the most socially legitimate material they could present. Maple Heights' teachers also managed to be effective. Most were able to win students' respect and this respect greatly enhanced teachers' ability to make sure that learning was actually taking place. Teachers at the school who presented college-preparatory curriculum and effectively ensured learning felt they were practicing Real Teaching. Those who were not able to present such curriculum or who were not very effective in doing so felt inadequate or uncomfortable about what was happening in their classrooms. Practicing Real Teaching turned out to be very important. Those who felt they were engaged in Real Teaching were more likely than those who did not to invest long hours and concentrated effort in their teaching. Teachers' commitment to their work was, in other words, greatly enhanced by their ability to practice what they deemed to be Real Teaching.

## QUINCY HIGH SCHOOL

Silas is a town located in the Midwest. When we visited Silas, the population was about 85,000. Most inhabitants were white; less than 14% of Silas's total population was black.

A large proportion of Silas's employed adults were laborers and skilled craftsmen who earned a living in one of the town's many industries. Others were clerks or held similar positions in the service sector. Only 21% of the community's working adults were professionals or managers. Silas was, in short, a working-class town.

Silas was also less enamored with the "academic life" than Maple Heights. Most of the townspeople over the age of twenty-five had graduated from high school, but fewer than 30% of the adult population had gone to college.

Quincy High was one of Silas's three public high schools. The school served approximately 1,500 students, 80% of whom were white. About 120 teachers were hired to work with these students.

*How Quincy Teachers Defined Their Work*

Most Quincy teachers, like Maple Heights' teachers, believed that most of their students would be following the same paths as their parents. However, the paths that Quincy teachers thought their students would follow were different from those that Maple Heights' students were expected to travel. Most Quincy teachers believed that their students would end their formal educations after high school and get blue- or pink-collar jobs. This belief affected the curriculum teachers selected for these students.

The school board put some pressure on Quincy teachers to raise standards, emphasize college preparatory curricula and otherwise address current societal expectations for schooling. Much of this pressure was, however, ignored. Teachers at Quincy thought that "practical" curriculum — curriculum that prepared students for working-class jobs and "everyday life" — was in many ways more relevant for students than the more abstract kinds of content included in college-preparatory curricula. Most believed that this was the sort of curriculum that parents and students wanted. Many Quincy teachers felt obliged, as a result, to focus more attention on reinforcing local community life styles than on fulfilling societal expectations for secondary schooling.

Ms. Taranto, a science teacher, was one of the teachers we observed who was determined to make her subject "as practical as [she] can." According to her,

science more than anything else can lead people into ways to practically solve other kinds of problems that turn up in their lives.

We observed students in Ms. Taranto's and other science teachers' classes learning how to work through many of the "everyday" problems they will encounter after taking on adult responsibilities. In one of Mr. Almond's regular science classes, for example, students were asked to determine which of six different candy bars was the best buy. Students were told to measure and weigh the candy bars in order to calculate the candy bars' cost per kilogram. When students wrote up their results, Mr. Almond asked them to come up with factors other than cost per kilogram that might be taken into consideration when deciding whether or not a candy bar is a good buy.

Many Quincy teachers also wanted students to learn how to "behave"; they wanted students to learn how to obey without question those in authority and to work quietly at required tasks. Teachers in many regular- and lower-level classes expected their students to remain silently on-task unless they were given permission to speak. Some of these teachers were noticeably upset when their students failed to meet this expectation. One teacher spent five minutes angrily chastising her students for engaging in informal conversations while she was handing back assignments. Another one was quite embarrassed when two of his students began to talk quietly to one another after he assigned some seatwork. He quickly admonished the students and apologized to us after class for not having kept them under better control. In these and many other teachers' classes, we rarely if ever observed the kinds of lively debates or unabashed challenges to teachers' knowledge that were so common at Maple Heights. Questioning teachers' authority and contributing to knowledge was discouraged rather than encouraged at Quincy.

For many Quincy teachers, teaching standard content meant transmitting moderately-difficult or concrete facts and what some teachers called "basic" academic skills. Requiring students to memorize simple facts often took precedence over teaching students complex knowledge and critical thinking skills. In one regular-level English class, we observed a teacher spending most of the class period conducting a recitation designed to find out if students knew the sequence of events, names of characters, and other concrete facts about a story they were asked to read. The teacher said later that he rarely explored an assigned story's symbolism. He felt that it was much more important that students remember names and the events of a plot than it was for them to discern a literary work's deeper meaning. The head of the English department concurred. Focusing on symbolism and other kinds of abstractions was, in his estimation, "elitist" and a waste of time. According to him, Quincy students were much better off learning "basic" literacy skills—skills that would allow them to read and comprehend newspapers, service manuals, and similar kinds of daily reading material.

Not all of the teachers working at Quincy emphasized "practical" knowledge and "basic" skills. Some were determined to teach abstract or complex facts, concepts, and theories. This stance was most commonly adopted by teachers who were assigned upper-level courses but there were a few regular-level teachers who also adopted this posture. Such a stance was generally tolerated in Quincy's upper-tracks; it appeared to be much less acceptable in regular-level courses. Regular-level teachers who tried to teach advanced content were often pressured by colleagues and students to adopt different approaches.

Ms. Havlichek was a teacher who tried to teach her regular-level economics classes abstract concepts and theories but gave up after deciding she was not being very "realistic." She said that pressure from students (they were "turned off" by her approach) and colleagues (they thought she was "going overboard") caused her to conclude that she was spending too much time on content that students really did not need. She stopped lecturing about economic theory and began to teach what she thought was more relevant information. Among other things, she had her classes set up and run mock businesses, investigate different kinds of credit, and learn how to apply for and interview for jobs.

Ms. Havlichek was an example of the way students shaped Quincy teachers' decisions about what to teach. In part because they were "turned off" by abstract knowledge, Ms. Havlichek felt she ought to present different kinds of information. Students seemed, in other words, to view practical curricula as more legitimate than college-preparatory curricula.

Students also affected the kinds of classroom practices Ms. Havlichek and her colleagues adopted. Students' reactions to different methods of teaching were used by teachers to determine which practices most effectively ensured learning. Science teachers, for example, found that asking students to weigh candy bars and to conduct similar kinds of "experiments" was an effective way both of conveying practical information and controlling behavior. It was thought by teachers to be more effective than, for instance, lecturing. Teachers said that students "fall asleep" or become disruptive if a lot of class time is taken up with lectures. Because students were not very willing to sit through long lectures, the practice came to be viewed by Quincy teachers as a relatively ineffective teaching strategy.

Recitations were also quite common. They were certainly more common than the intellectually stimulating discussions we observed at Maple Heights. Teachers in regular- or lower-level classes who tried to engage students in lively debates often met with resistance. During the days when Ms. Havlichek was not being very "realistic," students joked or talked with their friends whenever she tried to prompt a discussion.

Quincy's regular- and lower-track students were the most compliant when teachers defined their work a certain way. Most were willing to go along with teachers who emphasized practical knowledge and basic skills and who kept them busy with hands-on activities, seatwork, or recitations. Students often became inattentive or disruptive, however, when teachers attempted to deviate from this more "practical" definition of the teaching task. Since teachers understood Real Teaching to include effective teaching, Quincy teachers often adopted a practical curriculum because it enhanced students' engagement. Students in this and other schools simply refused to learn what they felt was illegitimate or irrelevant knowledge.

Quincy teachers were, for the most part satisfied with and committed to their work. Like Maple Heights teachers, most of the people who taught at Quincy lived in Silas and embraced many of the community's values. They considered the way of life adopted by Silasians to be socially legitimate and they had, as a result, little or no qualms about reinforcing community culture.

However, a number of teachers at Quincy were not entirely satisfied with the way teaching came to be defined at the school. Teachers, like Ms. Havlichek, who wanted their students to break out of Silas's working-class milieu felt they were teaching students useful information and skills but they also felt they could do "so much more for the kids" if only they could figure out how. These teachers had somewhat ambivalent feelings about what they were doing; they felt they were practicing Real Teaching because they presented legitimate curriculum and were more or less effective but it was not the kind of Real Teaching they would have preferred.

At Quincy, in short, practical curricula designed to help students take on their parents' working-class life styles superseded most other kinds of curricula. Because they felt community life styles were legitimate, most Quincy teachers considered the practical curriculum they presented as legitimate. This type of curriculum would not have been viewed as socially legitimate at Maple Heights primarily because it would not have met local expectations; it would not have reinforced the dominant way of life embraced by many members of the local community. Meeting local expectations was important for both faculties. Fulfilling these expectations was, in fact, thought by many teachers to be more important than fulfilling societal ones. Teachers at Quincy tended to ignore societal expectations and yet most felt they were teaching socially acceptable material simply because what they taught fulfilled local demands.

Quincy teachers also adopted practical curriculum because it was effective. Students were much more likely to learn and obey if teachers presented content in a manner that they found acceptable. By adopting a practical curriculum, teachers were able to minimize the tension between socially legitimate and effective teaching.

## ULYSSES S. GRANT HIGH SCHOOL

The City is the core of a large metropolitan area with a population of over one million people. The City itself had over 650,000 people living within its borders. About 27% of The City's inhabitants were nonwhite.

Like Silas, The City was a blue-collar community. Most of the community's employed adults had not gone to college and were earning a living in one of many industries. The City was also home to a significant number of people who were unemployed or underemployed. About 20% of the families who resided in The City lived below the poverty line. The vast majority of the poor were black.

Ulysses S. Grant High was one of a dozen public high schools serving The City's children. For many years, the school served the working-class families who lived in surrounding neighborhoods. Most but not all of these families were white. During the seventies, demographic shifts and a court-ordered desegregation plan forced Grant to accept a much larger number of minority students. When we visited the school, a little over half of the 1,600 students who attended Grant were black. A large proportion of these students lived in some of the most impoverished neighborhoods in The City. There were about 120 teachers employed at Grant.

## How Grant Teachers Defined Their Work

At Maple Heights and Quincy, most teachers shared ideas about what and how to teach their students. This was not the case at Grant. Grant teachers failed to forge an agreement about the form Real Teaching should take in their school. One reason for this was that some teachers at Grant were more willing to reinforce local life styles than others. This led to disputes between teachers over what kinds of curriculum ought to be taught. Another source of faculty conflict was students. Many Grant students lacked the knowledge and skills needed to master grade-level work and were alienated from the schooling process. They were, as a result, extremely difficult to teach. Teachers had a hard time finding teaching methods that were both effective and acceptable to all teachers. The result of Grant teachers' disputes over curriculum and teaching methods was the emergence of conflicting definitions of teaching.

One of the definitions of Real Teaching that emerged at Grant was developed by white, middle-class teachers. Most of these teachers had little or no contact with the poor black families living in The City; they were both physically and culturally removed from the black neighborhoods they served. These teachers' perceptions of their black students' background were largely shaped by television, friends, and other secondhand sources. Many of their perceptions were exaggerated or distorted views of the way life was really lived by The City's black population. They were also quite negative. Mr. Simon, one of these teachers, claimed he was working for families who "do not value education" and who embrace illicit or illegitimate life styles. He summarized many of his white colleagues' perceptions of the black people they served when he said that Grant's minority students lived in . . .

... high crime areas. There is dope, prostitution, child molestation, rape, beatings ... everything you would imagine about the inner city.

He and many of the other white teachers in the school refused to reinforce the way of life they thought students led. They sought to prepare students for the future by compensating for the past. They wanted students to give up their home cultures and to adopt the mainstream cultural traits they thought necessary to assume middle-class jobs.

Mr. Simon and many other white teachers did their best to purge students of their "bad" traits and to replace them with "good" traits. They tried, among other things, to stop students from expressing themselves in black and other non-standard English dialects. Students were "corrected" every time they spoke or wrote the non-standard English teachers considered to be illegitimate. Many of the teachers also did their best to discourage students from adopting what they believed to be their parents' self-defeating life styles. One teacher, Mr. Harris, spent an entire class period lecturing students about the evils of teenage pregnancy and the virtues of raising children in two-parent homes. Such moralizing was common in these teachers' classes.

Most of these teachers also wanted to convey grade-level standard content. Their teaching would not be Real unless they fulfilled what they felt was one of society's most important expectations. Mr. Norton verbalized this expectation when he said "society conceives the purpose of school" and that purpose is to teach students "the material" — grade-level standard content.

Teaching Grant students grade-level content presented serious difficulties, however. Many of the students enrolled at Grant were so far behind academically that teachers were forced to re-teach the knowledge and skills normally taught in elementary school. Mr. Simon had to show his algebra students how to add and subtract decimals and perform other elementary calculations before he could even begin to teach them the material in their textbooks. He and many of his colleagues resented this. Time spent on content that students should have learned before coming to high school meant, for these teachers, less time spent on information that they believed to be more publicly acceptable.

Many of the white teachers at Grant felt that giving students seatwork was to abandon their teaching responsibilities. They wanted to lecture, facilitate discussions, and adopt other practices that required teachers and students to take an active role in the educational process.

Grant students did not, however, respond to such teaching methods the way teachers hoped they would. When Ms. Yertle tried to conduct a discussion in her history class, most of her students refused to participate. This and similar responses to her approach were a source of great frustration for Ms. Yertle. She said, "It's like you want to create something with your hands and you don't have any dough to create it with." Students in most of Mr. Simon's classes tended to act up whenever he spent more than ten minutes lecturing. He scolded students, evicted them from class, and otherwise attempted to curb disruptive behavior, but he often met with limited success. Many Grant students simply did not like his — or many of his white colleagues' — moralistic, forceful brand of teaching.

Other teachers at Grant were much more knowledgeable about and sympathetic towards the poor black families they were serving. Most of these teachers were blacks who shared similar backgrounds with their students or who had formed relationships with The City's black people. They both knew and embraced many aspects of local black culture and they tended to reinforce it.

Ms. Herst was one of these teachers. Instead of discouraging the use of black English, she indirectly condoned the language's use by speaking it during informal conversations with many of her students. Rather than lecture to students about the evils of teenage pregnancy, she gave them lots of informal advice about how to cope with unreliable partners and single-parenthood. In short, she supported much of her black students' way of life rather than condemned it.

Ms. Herst spent a lot of time in her regular-level English classes on elementary school content. She did not pay nearly as much attention to society's expectation that teachers convey grade-level content as did many of the other teachers at Grant. Effectively teaching the elementary knowledge many students lacked was enough to make her feel she was practicing Real Teaching. This teacher also assigned a lot of seatwork. Ms. Herst was convinced that seatwork was the most effective way to teach her students. It kept them both quiet and busy.

Students liked Ms. Herst and they were relatively well-behaved when they were in her classroom. She paid a price for her students' affection and compliance, however. She sacrificed a great deal of grade-level content and many of the cultural understandings students need to negotiate mainstream American life. This sacrifice did not seem to bother Ms. Herst very much. She was quite sure she was teaching in a manner that was best for her students.

There was a great deal of conflict at Grant between teachers like Ms. Herst, who buttressed students' home culture, and teachers like Mr. Simon who viewed local black culture as illegitimate. Ms. Herst and several of her close associates complained about white teachers who were "mean" to students and who "talked too much in class." Mr. Simon and his associates complained about black teachers who spoke black dialect during the school day, assigned too much seatwork, or "gave in to students too much." These two groups of teachers were firmly entrenched and were a long way from creating some sort of workable compromise.

Ms. Thompson was a teacher who did compromise. She was a black, middle-class woman who used her knowledge both of local black culture and of middle-class life styles to pave a path between life in The City's most impoverished neighborhoods and life in mainstream America. She knew where her students were coming from and she had strong convictions about where she wanted them to go.

Ms. Thompson's definition of Real Teaching was, in many respects, a synthesis of definitions developed by her more ethnocentric colleagues. She did not condemn local black culture but neither did she completely reinforce it. Rather, she used aspects of black culture to lure students into learning the grade-level content and cultural traits needed to go to college or get good jobs. She adopted many of the special glances, tones of voice, and other techniques used by students' parents to instill knowledge or win compliance. The result was that students saw her as firm rather than "mean" and as sympathetic rather than moralistic. Students were more willing to learn standard content and the knowledge needed to succeed in college because they felt that she not only understood them but that she cared about them as well.

There were, in short, a number of conflicts between Grant teachers over what and how students ought to be taught. The definitions of Real Teaching that Grant teachers developed often undercut rather than supported one another. Teachers' inability to come up with a definition of teaching that everyone was willing to share exacerbated students' disengagement from the schooling process. Grant students sensed the discord between teachers and responded by siding with some teachers and rejecting others or by refusing to participate in the schooling process altogether. Grant was a good illustration of how important it is for teachers to come to a consensus about the form Real Teaching should take in their school. It also showed how difficult it can be to form such a consensus.

## CONCLUSION

The high school teachers we studied taught us a number of important lessons. They taught us that Real Teaching is a delicate balance between societal expectations that young Americans master common bodies of knowledge and community expectations that children follow local norms and other cultural understandings. It is also a style of teaching that accomodates student characteristics. Real Teaching, in short, recognizes societal expectations for formal schooling, local culture, and students' ability and willingness to learn school knowledge.

We also learned that teachers working in schools that serve well-educated, middle-class families found it much easier than teachers employed in working- and lower-class high schools to incorporate societal expectations, local culture and student characteristics into their definitions of teaching. It was easier for these teachers both to develop and to implement a workable definition of Real Teaching because they worked in a context where there was a great deal of continuity between societal, community, and student understandings of what and how teachers should teach. In other contexts, there was notable conflict between these understandings. Developing a viable definition of Real Teaching in these contexts was, as a result, often difficult.

An important implication of what our teachers taught us is that schools are not alike; they are as diverse as the groups of people they serve. The view that schools are similar underlies many of the educational reforms recently generated by national interest groups. Such an assumption is implied in reforms that promote a single model of schooling to be adopted by every American high school. Our findings suggest that such models will not work in every school and that they may, in fact, exacerbate rather than solve the problems that plague many schools that serve working- and lower-class families.

The policymakers who design reform programs based on a single model of schooling tend to ignore the fact that the essentially middle-class models of schooling they promote may be and often are rejected by working- and lower-class people. While policymakers may ignore this fact, the teachers who work with working- and lower-class families usually find that they must deal with this reality if they want to teach effectively. Many of these teachers are forced to acknowledge that not everyone in this country flourishes in schools that adopt traditional, mainstream models of teaching and learning. In order to be successful, a number of teachers employed in working- or lower-class schools find that they have to adopt different, "non-traditional" models of Real Teaching; they have to find alternative ways to pass on common bodies of knowledge, satisfy the local community and stimulate student interest in the learning process.

Many teachers in our sample who served working- and lower-class families came to realize, sometimes painfully, that broadening the occupational and cultural horizons of their students required compromise; it involved making concessions to local culture. These teachers found that many members of the communities they served were either unaware of opportunities outside of their local experience or were convinced that lucrative adult occupations were not available to them. These teachers also learned that many of the adults they worked for have direct social interactions only with other members of the community. These people, as a result, often did not learn to appreciate much of the dominant culture. They were also skeptical of the value of the intellectual and artistic works included in school curricula. A few of these teachers found out that incorporating local culture into their approaches was among the best ways to lead students to middle-class occupations and wider points of view. Ignoring local culture and imposing a new one usually did not work.

Policies that seek to develop a single model for high school education also tend to be insensitive to the fact that students are active participants in their schools. Students can and do decide to reject educational approaches they do not find acceptable. It has to be understood that students hold veto power over all educational policies. Teachers in the working- and lower-class schools who tried to follow national recommendations often found that their students refused to cooperate. Many of these teachers accepted what they believed to be policymakers' "legitimate" view of schooling and rejected what they thought were students' "illegitimate" perspectives on the matter. Students resented teachers who refused to recognize their points of view. Intense conflict often emerged in classrooms where teachers and students rejected each others' perspectives. In most of these classrooms no one won and just about everyone lost.

Policymakers have, in short, to recognize that communities and their schools are not identical. They have to realize that teachers—all teachers —must reconcile societal, local community, and student understandings of the schooling process if they want to ensure learning. They must view teachers as cultural brokers — as individuals who negotiate productive settlements between societal, community and student understandings about what and how knowledge should be taught in schools. Such an image of teachers should lead to policies that foster the development and increase the number of faculty members who, like Ms. Thompson, use local culture to build bridges between lower- and middle-class life styles. Policies could be designed to help teachers like Ms. Havlichek to find workable strategies to broaden their students' horizons. Such policies would be, in any case, much more "realistic" than those that refuse to acknowledge our country's social and cultural diversity.

## NOTES

1. The research on which this chapter is based was supported by the National Center on Effective Secondary Schools at the Wisconsin Center on Education Research and Improvement which is supported by a grant from the Office of Educational Research and Improvement Grant #G – 00869007. Any opinion, findings and conclusions expressed in this chapter are those of the authors and do not reflect the views of the Office of Educational Research and Improvement, or the United States Department of Education.

Additional support was provided by a grant from The Spencer Foundation. This grant enabled us to re-analyze our data, reconsider our findings and to write this chapter and other works presenting the final results of our research.

An earlier version of this chapter was presented at the annual meeting of the American Educational Research Association, April 1988 in New Orleans, LA.

2. It should be noted that none of the teachers in our sample actually used the phrase "Real Teaching" when we spoke with them.

3. There was marked formal standardization in our sample schools. National expectations for curriculum, school organizational structure and daily routine were so strong that our schools looked superficially alike; the same schedules, the same courses and even many of the same books were adopted across schools. We came to speak of these nationally sanctioned patterns as Real School (Metz, forthcoming).

In some of the schools we studied, teachers had trouble reconciling the unvarying patterns of Real School with the variable characteristics of local communities and students. This was especially true in schools serving working- or lower-class families. Many teachers found that they had to alter or give up crucial aspects of Real School in order to meet local expectations for schooling or to ensure student learning. Real School was seen by many of these teachers as unrealistic. It sometimes came into significant conflict with their notions of Real Teaching.

4. In addition to the authors of this chapter, Dr. Nancy Lesko, a staff researcher at the University of Wisconsin-Madison's National Center on Effective Secondary Schools, and Alexander K. Tyree, Jr., a staff assistant at the Center, were members of the research team that collected the data on which this chapter is based.

5. We conducted eighty such interviews with other teachers and counselors. Professor Richard Rossmiller and staff assistant Jeffrey Jacobson, members of a separate research team from the Center, interviewed and observed principals and other administrators in our sample schools.

Chapter 6

# Curriculum Differentiation as Social Redemption: The Case of School-Aged Mothers

This paper examines the curriculum in use in an award-winning alternative high school for teenage mothers, a school perceived locally and nationally as an exemplary program.[1] The school's positive effects are evidenced in its students' high graduation rate, positive self-esteem displayed in interviews, and the formulation of occupational plans for post-secondary training. Given the defeatism of the general public discourse around the 'problem of teenage pregnancy,' and the lackluster records of many programs for school-aged mothers, this acclaimed school in its eighteenth year is cause for optimism for those concerned with the education of all youth.

The accolades for Bright Prospects School[2] invite an examination of its practices. This essay describes these practices and policies, but also searches for the reasons that they are widely heralded as a positive response to the problem of teenage pregnancy. The conception of the inquiry into the curriculum in these terms — what positive things does Bright Prospects do — and what are the bases of such widespread agreement that they are positive practices—necessitates an examination of the discursive context in which a school for pregnant girls is located. That is, an examination of Bright Prospects' practices and acclaimed successes necessitates both an examination of the popular discourse around teenage pregnancy, which is a discourse about young women, sexuality, and

single motherhood, and an examination of the specific educational practices at Bright Prospects. In this way, schooling practices, and in particular curricula, are seen as parts of broader social discourses (Foucault
[1970], 1973; Henriques et al. 1984).

To suggest that curriculum is part of wider social discourse is a refor-
mulation of some standard theoretical and methodological propositions.
Anthropologists of education hold as axiomatic that the context of behavior is central to its meaning (Geertz 1973; Spindler 1982); studies of
schools have examined such contexts as the micro-environments of
classroom conversation (Page 1987), geographic-cultural community
contexts (Erickson and Mohatt 1982), cultural theme contexts (Varenne
1977; Lesko 1988) and the history of social groups and institutions as context (Ogbu 1987; Precourt, 1982). Critical sociologists of education likewise establish a connection between schools and society; materialist
analyses describe schools as "reproducing" or "reflecting" the socioeconomic order (Apple and Weis 1983; Valli 1986). However well-in-
tended these studies have been, many of them merely "graft on context"
to studies of school practices (Walkerdine 1988). Context, whether economic, cultural, or institutional, often remains tangential to the central
findings of studies of schools.

Recent theoretical and empirical work critically examines the separation of 'context' and 'text' (as well as, the subject/object, mind/body,
self/other, and male/female dichotomies). Studies informed by Foucaul-
tian, psychoanalytical, and semiotic perspectives attempt to expose
the distinctions between context and text as illusory (Harding 1986;
MacCannell and MacCannell 1982). Piercean semiotics establishes the
integral importance of context in his tripartite definition of understanding. His interpretant is the social context as it is brought in to produce
meaning in a particular situation. From an historical perspective, Foucault addresses the connections between social institutions, such as the
family, the legal system, the education system, language, general social
practices, and conceptions of the self. He uses the term 'discourse' to refer to the organization of knowledge and power and their relationship
with social practices, institutions and conceptions of the self. Discursive
analysis seeks linkages among the domains of social life which usually remain separated and hierarchical.

Post-structuralist perspectives attempt to examine the meaning of
social practices as 'texts' by integrating form, content and understanding, the latter of which is the experiences the people doing the understanding bring to bear upon the social practice. From both semiotic and
genealogical perspectives, the context (the set of experiences which inform the interpretation of individuals within specific circumstances) is integral to the understanding, or meaning, of social practices.

The curricular thrust of an alternative school for teenage mothers closely parallels major themes in the broader discourse of the problem of teenage pregnancy as presented in publications such as *Time* magazine, booklets from the Children's Defense Fund and the Alan Guttmacher Institute. These publications present teenage mothers as problematic because these young women are irresponsible, likely to be bad mothers, and unlikely to be self-sufficient. In a socio-moral sense, these problems, or 'sins' make them a difficulty for themselves and for society.

The meaning of the school curriculum, as articulated by representative students of Bright Prospects School, is expressed in the same terms. Bright Prospects helps them to become responsible, to be good mothers, and to strive for self-sufficiency. The curriculum of Bright Prospects School helps teenage mothers *redeem* themselves, or deliver themselves from the position of their former sinful, or problematic, status (Rains 1971). Thus, the analysis of this paper locates the curricular thrust of a school for teenage mothers within the established themes of the media construction of the problem of teenage pregnancy. The girls confess their sins in numerous panels which the school presents for different audiences; during these panels the girls explain how the school helped them to reform and, thus, *redeem* themselves. This close relationship between the problems of teenage pregnancy and the understandings that young mothers at Bright Prospects have of changes in themselves suggests that the meaning of curriculum can only be understood as part of a broader social discourse on teenage pregnancy.

The data from Bright Prospects School were gathered during four weeks of participant-observation spread across a school year. The analysis includes data gathered through observation of classes, interviews of staff and students, examination of curricular materials, and the viewing of a videotape of a student panel discussion.

## THE DISCOURSE AROUND TEENAGE PREGNANCY

The image of a young girl with swollen belly dominates the discourse on teenage pregnancy. The *Time* (Dec. 9, 1985) cover presents her, the problem that "rends the social fabric." Her form is exaggerated against a spare background; she stands sideways, so her fully pregnant, fully sexual body is accentuated. Her ripe body is juxtaposed with her child's face. Whispy blond hair touches her shoulders. Two things stand out through juxtaposition: the face of a child and the mature, sexual body. Just as the images of an American flag being burned, a helmeted cop beating a defenseless protester, a President being shot are all images of 'disorder' signalling 'alarm,' so does the face of a child with a pregnant body signal danger. Her face communicates sadness, pessimism, and confusion. Her face forecasts uncertainty, uncomprehendingness and resignation—her face communicates the consequences of her irresponsible sexuality. This pregnant girl is exposed: her swollen belly identifies her as a sexual child having a child.

The alarming imagery of the *Time* cover is echoed in other media presentations. A Harris poll (November 1985) found that 84% of American adults regard teenage pregnancy as a national problem. Even the 1987 State of the Union Address acknowledged the national significance of the problem. But it is necessary to look closer at the discussion of the problem in order to gain an understanding of possible different meanings of this problem.

On closer examination, the *Time* article and reports from the Children's Defense Fund and the Alan Guttmacher Institute, which has compiled much of the statistics on this topic, discuss the problem of teenage pregnancy through three sub-themes: sexual irresponsibility, bad mothering, and hopelessness.

## 1. Sexual irresponsibility

An eighteen-year-old's comments set off in a box in the *Time* article exemplify the lack of seriousness: "I was going to have an abortion, but I spent the money on clothes." A seventeen-year-old remarked, "I had birth control pills in my drawer. I just didn't take them." The *Time* article portrays girls as either lacking knowledge about reproduction, overly casual about their actions, or blinded by the glamour of out-of-wedlock births to Hollywood stars. Teenage girls are portrayed as unable or unwilling to think about their futures. Given the 'obvious' (from a middle-class adult perspective) reasons for postponing sexual relations or using contraception (e.g. truncation of education, likelihood of being poor, likelihood of teenage marriages ending in divorce), the failure to postpone or use contraception can only be read as pathology or stupidity. A researcher for the Rockefeller Foundation shook her head about why lower-class girls do not think about their futures:

> Middle-class girls tend not to have babies because Mother would kill them if they did. [For lower socioeconomic groups] it's the big shoulder shrug. They don't get abortions. They don't use contraception. It's just not that important; they don't have a sense of the future (*Time* 1985, p. 87).

Lower-class girls are portrayed as alien beings who are unable to think about the future, which is one hallmark of the middle-class.

## 2. Likely to be bad mothers

This second theme in the discourse on teenage pregnancy is largely implicit in the statement of the problem. Younger teenagers are more likely to have babies with physical problems, such as low birthweight babies, "a category that puts an infant in danger of serious mental, physical, and developmental problems that may require costly and possibly even lifelong medical care" (*Time* 1985, p. 79). Teenage girls are less likely to have prenatal care, which may affect the baby adversely, for example, through poor nutrition. Statistics regarding the low level of education of teenage mothers provide further evidence that these girls will be unprepared to properly care for themselves, the fetus, and, later, the child.

*Time* chronicles the mothering of Desiree Bell, who at fifteen resented her first son.

> I used to punch myself in the stomach . . . The first year I wouldn't play with him. He didn't talk until he was nearly two . . . I would say I traumatized my own son (1985, p. 87).

The article alleges that young mothers are attached to their children until the care conflicts with their desires to have fun or date.

Once again, teenage mothers are portrayed as delinquent, as improper mothers. It appears to be only common sense that any mother who cares about her baby would seek medical care early. A mother who really cared about her child would act differently, more responsibly, not placing the unborn child at risk of physical problems nor placing her own pleasure before the care of her child. Teenage mothers are portrayed as likely to be delinquent mothers for they fail to place the care of their children as their highest priority.

## 3. Emotionally disabled: worthlessness and despair

In discussing the spread of high school health clinics which distribute birth control (with parental permission), the *Time* authors write:

> For all their apparent success, in-school clinics do not necessarily get at the emotional wellsprings of teenage pregnancy: the sense of hopelessness and resignation felt by many underprivileged girls . . . [The true root of the teenage pregnancy problems] may be a sense of worthlessness and despair (1985, p. 90).

This third theme suggests that an 'emotional disability' of hopelessness for a decent future leads to pregnancy. Having hope in a better future, i.e. striving for upward mobility, is directly connected to economic self-sufficiency. The emotional antecedents of self-sufficiency are seen as a hope in one's future, a belief that good things are attained through hard work. If these girls are without belief in their futures, then no hard work to achieve the aims will be forthcoming. The young women are not directly attacked as 'laggards,'' but are portrayed as emotionally sick and, thereby, unable to strive for self-sufficiency with its economic and moral rewards.

The "true root" of teenage pregnancy as a sense of having no worthwhile future prefaces the discussion of the costs of teenage pregnancy for taxpayers. These uneducated, unmarried young women will become dependents of the state. *Time* announced: "It has been estimated that overall, the U.S. spends $8.6 billion on income support for teenagers who are pregnant or have given birth" (1985, p. 87). One of many Children's Defense Fund booklets on teenage pregnancy is entitled "Model Programs: Preventing Adolescent Pregnancy and Building Youth Self-Sufficiency" and echoes the self-sufficiency theme in its title and in its choice of model programs. Thus, the third theme describes teenage mothers as social problems because they are emotionally disabled, or hopeless of better futures. As a consequence, society will have to support many of these girls and their children through welfare. Their lack of self-sufficiency is their third deviant characteristic.

In this brief analysis of documents on the problem of teenage pregnancy, three themes recur. First, teenage pregnancy is a problem because young women are sexually irresponsible; they fail to rationally plan for their futures. Second, teenagers are likely to be bad mothers, failing to seek prenatal care and later abusing or neglecting their children. Third, teenagers who choose to bear and keep a child are unlikely to be hardworking, upwardly mobile women and unlikely to become self-sufficient, thereby needing public assistance. These themes are strong and recurrent in the media presentations and in foundation reports on the problem of teenage pregnancy. These three themes also provide the framework for measuring progress in a program for school-aged mothers. 'Success' for teenage mothers at Bright Prospects School falls exactly within these three themes, as successful students and mothers demonstrate their redemption from their previous deviancy of sexual irresponsibility, bad mothering, and hopelessness.

## INTERPRETING THE DISCOURSE AROUND
## TEENAGE PREGNANCY

The seeming 'naturalness' of the problem of teenage pregnancy is called into question by the actual decline in the number of births to women under the age of twenty in the 1980s. "Birth rates for all but the very youngest teens, those younger than fifteen have dropped significantly since 1970" (Children's Defense Fund 1986, p. 3). The Children's Defense Fund (1985, p. 3) gives the following figures:

TOTAL NUMBER OF BIRTHS TO WOMEN UNDER 20

| 1950 | 425,000 |
|------|---------|
| 1960 | 594,000 |
| 1970 | 656,000 |
| 1980 | 562,330 |
| 1982 | 522,981 |
| 1983 | 499,038 |

Given the actual decline in numbers of births to teenagers, the construction of the public problem of teenage pregnancy in the mid-1980s must be understood by examining problems in other realms of social life. The crisis of teenage pregnancy can be understood as symbolically representing broader social issues and conflicts. Such an analysis draws upon work in symbolic anthropology and sociology and, specifically, the sociology of culture (e.g., Turner 1969; Douglas 1966; Geertz 1973; Gusfield [1963] 1986; Luker 1984). This perspective views public problems as struggles over meanings, resources, behavior, and values. Public problems, such as drunk-driving, abortion, or teenage pregnancy, are arenas for contesting sets of meanings and values. The winners of the public policy struggles attain some amount of cultural legitimacy of their views and values. Resources, real and symbolic, are controlled by the winners.

Gusfield's ([1963] 1986) study of the temperance movement exemplifies how a public problem is, in part, a struggle between groups over definitions of leisure, over their political statuses, and over attempts to define and control the proper and expected way of life. Gusfield views the rise of the temperance movement and prohibition in the late 1800s and early 1900s not as a response to the increase of alcohol use (hard alcohol use was declining), but, rather, as a response to the social disorder associated with the influx of immigrants to urban areas. Rural Protestant

Americans were alarmed at the behavior and attitudes of Irish, Italian, and Jewish (to name only three major groups) newcomers. Gusfield interprets prohibition as part of a symbolic and moral crusade to establish teetotaling WASP behavior and values as superior. Similarly, Luker (1984) analyzes the abortion debate as a conflict between competing conceptions of the family and motherhood. The problem of teenage pregnancy can also be investigated from this sociology of a public problem perspective. In Gusfield's view, all public problems are issues of competing meanings and social control attendant with definitions. The construction of teenage pregnancy as a social problem can be examined as part of a social contest over meanings, values, legitimacy, and power.

## *Birth Rates and Human Capital*

The modal teenage mother is from a lower-class background and gives birth against a backdrop of a declining middle-class birthrate (Furstenberg, Brooks-Gunn, and Morgan 1987; *Education Week* 1986). Case studies like that of Furstenberg, Brooks-Gunn, and Morgan (1987) show that all of the 300 teenage mothers to give birth in a Baltimore hospital in the study year were poor, although only one-fourth were on welfare. Publications on teenage pregnancy stress the likelihood of future economic difficulties, but omit the girls' current economic situations. The effect is to give the picture that these girls will fail to be upwardly mobile due to their own irresponsible sexual behavior. A special issue of *Education Week,* titled "Here They Come, Ready or Not" (May 1986) on the changing demographics of the school-aged population in the next twenty years proclaimed, "A country without a middle-class majority will simply not be the America we have known." If the middle-class is losing its numerical dominance, the socio-moral discourse of teenage pregnancy is an attempt to reduce the rate at which lower-class women are having children at the same time as it reasserts the importance of rational life planning, delayed gratification, and enduring marriages. Economically secure persons whose lives have been cautiously guided by these values are alarmed at the apparent disregard of the rationality of delaying motherhood. The alarm is couched in the rhetoric of caring for the teenagers' futures. Gusfield's analysis suggests that their own status is being cared for.

The socio-economic rationality of delaying parenthood is grounded, in part, upon two Malthusian assumptions: "overpopulation causes poverty, and individual failings in the form of lack of restraint cause overpopulation" (Gordon 1976, p. 76). Both of these views are important for understanding how pregnant teenagers are viewed. Pregnant teenagers are both troubled people (e.g. "emotionally disabled") and teenage motherhood makes trouble for others (e.g. taxpayers, schools, social services). People who have accumulated some economic stability and persons whose economic well-being appears connected to rational planning, self-restraint, and future-orientation (i.e., the middle classes) fear overpopulation for its perceived detrimental effects on national wealth.

The construction of teenage pregnancy as a problem affirms the continuance of the superiority of middle-class norms of responsibility and rationality and the economic rewards of a secure income in return for postponement of parenthood. Thus, teenage pregnancy becomes a piece of the social logic that understands poverty to be the result of inferior values and desires among the poor. The individual young person gains by her educational and occupational attainment (though to a diminishing rate and with greater uncertainty in the 1980s), but also supports a set of real and symbolic power relations in society. When a young person delays parenthood, she or he 'says' that such rational decisions are part of the differentiations that legitimate the middle-class person's better moral and economic position. The maintenance of a norm of behavior that defines teenage parenthood as deviant, irresponsible, or even irrational communicates and reestablishes the superiority of middle-class norms and values.

## Young, Sexual Women

However, to read the discourse on the crisis of teenage pregnancy as only a class issue is insufficient; the problem is signified by young women who are pregnant or with young children. Girls of different colors, shapes, ages with babies in their arms or on their laps stare out from the pages of *Time*. Young females *embody* the problem, literally and figuratively. Young women with extended bellies or small children both represent and are the problem of sexual irresponsibility and failure to delay motherhood. Female images are consistently used to represent a situation that invariably involves both men and women. Of what import is the fact that generally only young women's images and words are involved in a description of the 'problem' of teenage pregnancy?

The crisis of teenage pregnancy makes sexually active young women a societal issue. Historically, women's proper behavior is to be virginal or sexually passive (Weedon 1987; Foucault 1980). The teenage girls who discuss explicit participation in decisions to become sexually active violate accepted norms to be sexually subordinate to male desires and choices (Kaplan 1986). *Time* declares, "American adolescents are far more sexually active than they used to be . . . No one wants to be a virgin" (1985, p. 81). Teenage girls violate the norm to be virginal, to be passive sexually, and when pregnant, to get married, put the child up for adoption, or have an abortion.

Furthermore, pregnant teenagers, already identified as lower-class[3] raise questions about the health of the American population, its stamina, and its ability to dominate the world politically and economically (Weedon 1987; Foucault 1980; Gordon 1976). Women's bodies are symbolically and materially related to a nation's population and the health of that population (Turner 1984). In this light the issues of economic competitiveness and industrial viability as articulated, for example, in the National Commission on Excellence's report, "A Nation at Risk," are linked with human capital concerns, such as the quality of human resources produced by lower-class teenage mothers. Historical and sociological studies (e.g. Turner 1984; Gordon 1976; Foucault 1981) directly connect concerns about female sexuality and progeny with eugenics and the concern for the vitality of the social body. Women's bodies and their offspring are objects of the patriarchal state's policy-making and policing. With these associations, women's sexuality and procreative activity rightfully fall within the purview of national and economic interests.

At another level, there is a hystericization (Foucault 1980) around the image and reality of pregnant teenagers that may outstrip the long-term effects of early childbearing (Furstenberg, Brooks-Gunn and Morgan 1987). The body is a location for the exercise of will over desire (Turner 1984). When the media portraits suggest that women's desire is overpowering the social will, a sense of disorder is triggered (Smith-Rosenberg 1985). A response to greater social freedom for women can be the discovery of a new form of female pathology (Smith-Rosenberg 1985). A diagnosis of emotionally disabled young women appears after a period of increased sexual and social freedom for women.

Given that the number of teenage pregnancies is declining, this section suggested a symbolic accounting for the construction of teenage pregnancy as a serious problem at this historical moment. The construction of teenage pregnancy as a social problem represents and expresses the uncertainty of economically well-off Americans regarding their own position vis-á-vis increasing numbers of immigrants and minorities in a shrinking economy, as well as concern for the U.S. economic viability. In light of some progress on women's rights and movement into the public world, the problem of adolescent women being seen as out of control (emotionally and sexually) may be part of a backlash attempt to return women to the constraints of marriage and child-centered thinking. Given these different strands, it is no surprise that teenage pregnancy explodes across the media, gripping adults with its provoking imagery and polysemic symbolism.

This brief investigation into the discourse around teenage pregnancy is the prelude to an inquiry into the curriculum of an alternative school for teenage mothers. The following section examines how the school curriculum, as experienced and articulated by successful students, manifests the same three major themes as did the broader public discourse; that is, successful students describe themselves as sexually responsible, good mothers, or with bright futures. Public panel discussions provide the forum for girls to recount their former wildness, declare their new selves, and communicate their maturity and responsibility. Thus, the Bright Prospects program succeeds in helping deviant, pregnant girls to redeem themselves; panel discussions provide the forum for students to confess and renounce their former identities and to be applauded as newly-born successful students and good mothers.

## Bright Prospects School

Given the theme of rationally delaying parenthood in the discourse on the problem of teenage pregnancy, it follows that most educational programs aim to prevent pregnancy through delaying sexual activity and/or using contraceptives (Children's Defense Fund 1986). Bright Prospects stands out because it is a school for young mothers, not just a program for girls while they are pregnant. Girls typically choose to enroll in the school when they are four or five months pregnant and their changing body "starts to show." Pregnant girls' other options in this district are to continue in their regular school or to dropout of school until they give birth. The program is designed for a one year stay, until the child is 4–6 months old, when girls are encouraged to return to their "home" schools. However, girls who have no child care provisions or who do especially well in the small, nurturant setting, remain until graduation. Girls must apply for continuation in the program and are chosen by staff on the basis of need and a positive response to the program in the past. Eighty-six percent of Bright Prospects' students complete high school, while only 60% of teenage mothers (by age nineteen) do so (Guttmacher Institute 1981). This graduation rate is part of what attracts visitors, reporters, and commendations from across the country.

The city's ethnic diversity is reflected in the school population of 54% Hispanic, 30% Anglo, 8% American Indian, and 7.5% Black. The Bright Prospects' staff describes its students as poor; despite low incomes, they live in their own houses and are members of extended families. The girls are perceived to be from homes where women maintain traditional roles and education for girls is not valued. One teacher estimated that 50% of the students live in families which are "in crisis," families in which alcoholism, physical, sexual, or psychological abuse, chronic unemployment, or drug abuse are present. Students were between the ages of twelve and twenty-one. Over fifty percent of the students in the year of the study were sixteen or seventeen years old; sixteen percent were fifteen years old and thirteen percent were eighteen.

Central to Bright Prospects' success are its three child care centers in the building; seventy-five infants through toddlers receive care while their mothers attend classes. Each student assists in a child care center for a class period each day. The nurseries are also used as "labs" for study of child development. Three staff nurses, supplemented by visiting health clinics from the state university medical school, provide regular health information and care for the babies and the mothers.

Its graduation rate, comprehensive program, eighteen year history, continued innovation (a teacher for homebound girls was recently created), and strong funding from the public school district (over ninety percent of its funds come from the school district) make it a model program. In addition, Bright Prospects' teachers continue to devleop curricular materials (e.g. in math and in pregnancy and motherhood) that are used across the country.

Bright Prospects School occupies a former middle school building situated at the intersection of a four-lane and six-lane road in the area of town sprouting the newest and finest shopping malls, office buildings, and hotels. The school is a dusty yellow stucco, surrounded by several large, handsome cottonwoods which shade the children's outside play areas. Temporary buildings flank two sides of the school. The building clearly denotes what it is: an urban school. However, when a visitor enters the school and encounters its long main corridor brightly carpeted in red and its female students with infants and toddlers in tow, it becomes clear that this is an unusual urban school.

The curricular focus at Bright Prospects School addresses the problems of teenage mothers, as identified in the broader discourse. The curriculum emphasizes helping its students overcome their problematic status through three interrelated avenues: as mothers, as secondary school students, and as individuals needing guidance. The school helps its students become good mothers, become successful students, and become people who can handle their personal and family problems. A school motto is "We believe a student can learn, be a good parent, and make good decisions." As once-deviant teenage mothers succeed in academics, make progress toward high school graduation, learn how to be good mothers, and are helped by counselors to make decisions for their futures, they transform themselves into people who no longer have problems, who are no longer emotionally disabled. As they are no longer women with problems, they also are no longer people who cause problems for society. Thus, they are socially redeemed, returned to an unproblematic status, returned to a 'state of grace.'

## Social Redemption as Mothers

Bright Prospects provides a nurturant atmosphere: The comprehensive nature of the program, the attention to details, the attempt to integrate emotional, physical, and cognitive learning, and the overall quality of staff 'tell' the students that they are people worthy of valuable time and resources. A tall blonde sixteen-year-old, Kay, commented about the school: "[The staff] makes you feel that you're special. They go the extra mile to make you feel like somebody." School district attendance requirements (which mandate a failing grade after eleven absences) are loosened at Bright Prospects because girls are frequently sick during pregnancy or, as mothers, must keep sick children at home. The school accommodates those facts of mothers' lives into its rules. In a similar way, the presence of on-site, free child care accommodates the reality that many students would be unable to attend school for lack of affordable child care. These examples illustrate how the school accommodates the several necessities of students who are pregnant or mothers, adaptations which facilitate their school attendance.

When girls enroll at Bright Prospects, they are placed in academic classes required for high school graduation and in one or more of three special parenting[4] classes. The first of the parenting classes covers personal health and the health of the fetus through delivery. Diet, exercise, anatomy, growth of the fetus, and labor and delivery are some of the topics covered in depth. The second parenting course on child development educates the young women about the growth and care of babies in their first year of life. This course involves standard classroom instruction alternating with classes devoted to infant care practice in the nursery. The third parenting course focuses on the care and raising of toddlers. About one-third of girls enroll at Bright Prospects when they are already mothers. They take only this last parenting course, regular academic requirements, and spend one hour each day caring for children in one of the nurseries.[5]

Students spoke highly about the program offerings and most consistently about the value of the first parenting course. This course teaches about the male and female bodies, so students learn the names of all parts of their bodies. One girl said, "When I go to a doctor, I can talk about this part or that part." She felt more competent to discuss health issues when she knew anatomical names. Students and faculty acknowledged that girls were well-prepared for labor and delivery. Nurses in the delivery room at the local hospitals reportedly commented that Bright Prospects' students were the best prepared and most knowledgeable young mothers. Susan, a sixteen-year-old student, testified to the thoroughness of the class: "When I went into labor, I knew *everything* that was going to happen to me." Ellen agreed, "You learn the name of every part of you and what's happening. You know *so much.*"

The school's curricular focus on knowledge and experience about mothering occurred in formal classroom situations, in the nurseries, and in spontaneous conversations among teachers and students. This curricular thrust 'said' that knowledge and competence in mothering were both interesting and important. For teenage mothers whose problematic status is due, in part, to the belief that they will be bad mothers, the Bright Prospects curriculum offers knowledge and experiences to become competent mothers. The curricular focus on mothering is one way in which Bright Prospects helps these problem teenagers redeem themselves.

### Social Redemption as Students

The nurturing atmosphere of the school carried over into the dominant style of pedagogy and classroom interactions between teachers and students. The pace of classes and personal attention accounted for the academic success of many girls. Students' opinions varied on the difficulty of the class work; some said it was comparable to that in their previous schools, but there was more time to complete it. Other girls thought the work was easier. More important for the students was the specialness of the Bright Prospects' teachers. Rosa said,

> The classes are hard, but it's more fun doing the work in this school. The teachers are different; they help you more. They sometimes crack a joke . . . At my other school, the teachers were real mean; if you said something, they'd just stare at you.

Julianna corroborated Rosa's account.

> The classes are taught the same [as in my other school], but they help you learn more. Here, the teachers talk about it more, make you understand it more, don't just give you an assignment.

She elaborated on how teachers gave the extra help at Bright Prospects.

> They see the expression on your face. (She makes a quizzical expression, one that says 'I'm confused.') And they come up to you and ask, 'Do you have a problem? Are you having a problem?'

Thus, students identified the attentiveness of teachers as a major factor in their academic success at Bright Prospects. Smaller class sizes undoubtedly also contributed to the attentiveness; a teacher-student ratio of 1:11 allows more personal attention. Both attendance and grade point averages rose while students were enrolled at Bright Prospects, though not dramatically so. A sample of thirty students showed attendance changes from 74%, the year prior to enrollment at Bright Prospects, to 79% at Bright Prospects, and grade point average increases from 1.77, the year prior to enrollment at Bright Prospects, to 2.16 (out of a possible 4).

Students interpreted their modest grade and attendance gains as being very significant. For many, this was the first time they had taken school tasks seriously. For others, the deviancy of pregnancy made success at school suddenly important and meaningful. Esther explained the impact of her higher grades, "They [higher grades] make you feel better. They make you feel like you've done something right." Ellen stated, "I feel proud. I had a baby and I finished school. I had to work harder. It gives you a good feeling."

Success in high school also carried implications for post-secondary schooling. As the new mothers became cognizant of the economics of providing for a child, many began to see a college education as desirable. Academic success at Bright Prospects made high school graduation (or a GED), the prerequisite for further education, a distinct possibility. School success for students at Bright Prospects, as for at-risk students in general (Wehlage et al. 1989), allowed them to consider brighter futures, futures which had formerly been considered unattainable.

Thus, success in academics and progress toward a high school diploma introduce prospects for the future that were otherwise unthinkable. School success is pivotal in the girls' social redemption, for only with graduation from high school can they realistically consider further schooling and living wage jobs. School success opens a door for the girls' contemplation of optimistic futures; and talk of graduation and post-secondary schooling redeems them from the hopelessness and economic dependency attributed to teenage mothers.

## Social Redemption as Individuals

Five counselors play an especially active role with Bright Prospects' two hundred students. The two men and three women focus upon the emotional supports necessary for the students to remain in school, to make life decisions, and to get to know themselves. In addition to seeing girls individually at least once a month, counselors conduct weekly sessions in each of the three parenting classes. One counselor said, "These sessions help the girls express and handle the emotions of being pregnant, of caring for an infant, or of living with in-laws or parents.'' In addition, one counselor offers an elective course, social psychology, another runs weekly discussion groups for girls undecided about keeping or relinquishing their babies for adoption, and another conducts an evening group for teenage fathers.

Students expressed a consistent, positive view of the counselors and the opportunities to discuss their problems. Nicole said,

> Talking with the counselors and in social psychology class makes you feel more confident in yourself and the people around you—how people are different. That's how it changed me. I wasn't as *down* as much. I feel more confident in myself to go and do things and not be embarrassed to go do it.

Lisa commented on her experiences talking to a counselor:

> You can tell him all your problems and he'll help you, so you don't have so much inside you; nothing builds up inside you.

Girls are urged to see their counselors when something is bothering them even if it occurs during a class. Just as physical health needs are a legitimate excuse to absent oneself from class, so are emotional health needs. When leaving the building at lunch hour, the assistant principal encountered a girl on the school steps who was teary-eyed and looked 'down.' The assistant principal's immediate comment was ''Are you O.K., hon?'' The girl gave a weak head nod and the assistant principal said, ''Go see your counselor. Go see your counselor.'' In this way, students were encouraged to use their counselor as the main confidant and helper. They did not leave it up to an individual girl to find a compatible adult to talk to, but urged again and again that the assigned counselor be used.

The kind of problems discussed with counselors is illustrated by a discussion in one of the counselor-led classes. The class had twelve students, eight of them Hispanic or American Indian; all the girls were juniors or seniors and already mothers. The counselor began the class and Stacie interrupted with a problem.

> I just don't know what to do. My boyfriend gets angry at me and calls me a slut, or a whore. I just don't know what to say. But it makes me so angry.

A classmate suggested, ''Slap him.''
Stacie replied, ''He'd hit me back.''
The counselor remarked, ''And then you would have the parents hitting each other in front of the child.''

Linda said, "Call him something back." The group was stumped, however, for they could think of no equally stinging epithet for males.

The counselor summarized the predicament by saying that there is no langugage of comparable derogation to men as 'whore' or 'slut' is to women. And then the teacher turned the class to another topic.

Although this class discussion was unsatisfactory in that it left the student without ideas of how to respond to verbal abuse, it illustrated the kinds of problems discussed among students and counselors. The classroom context appears to transform this very personal, emotional topic into a dispassionate discussion topic, which is allotted a certain amount of time and then abandoned as the class moves to another task (Sarason 1971). Students' comments suggest that talking about issues which are otherwise held secretly relieves some of their weightiness and helps girls think more clearly about alternative responses. As they gain confidence to make decisions, they begin to believe more in their capabilities, and enhanced self-esteem results.

One of the media characterizations of teenage mothers is that they are emotionally disabled. Through ongoing discussions of personal problems with counselors, students at Bright Prospects also redeemed themselves from this problematic status. They became confident decision-makers and more able to face the problems in their lives.

This section has described several curricular foci of Bright Prospects School which facilitate social redemption of pregnant teenagers as good mothers, good students, and emotionally sound people. Curricula intended to develop good mothers, successful students who graduate from high school, and emotionally mature young women also function to remove the problematic characteristics of teenage mothers and, thus, provide an avenue to social redemption. Evidence that the girls have returned to the 'state of grace' is provided in panel discussions. Across the academic year, girls volunteer to speak about their experiences as teenage mothers and as students at Bright Prospects as participants in panels which visit civic and church groups or junior high schools. These panel discussions provide an arena for girls to publicly confess their past sins and articulate how they have changed. With such public exposures of their former and transformed selves, the process of social redemption is completed.

## Success Stories: Responsible, Rational Mothers

The stories of problematic pregnant teenagers began with photographic exposures of their sexual bodies juxtaposed with young wistful faces on *Time* magazine's cover. The images of success, of socially redeemed young mothers, are less sensational, but, nevertheless, gripping. In one of many panel discussions for different audiences, six Bright Prospects' students sit behind a v-shaped table and look at a group of about twenty adults, mostly women. Two of the six panelists are Anglos, three are Hispanic or American Indian, and one is Black. Five have hair that hangs to their shoulders with bangs swept back to each side à la Farah Fawcett in the 1970s television show, "Charlie's Angels." They all wear pants and simple blouses or tee-shirts. Within the last six months, each could have posed for the alarm-inducing "Children Having Children" cover of *Time*.

The six are introduced as "representative" of most Bright Prospects' students. The girls range in age from sixteen to nineteen, five are single mothers, one is married. For thirty minutes they tell the audience of strangers (and a video camera) how they responded when they found they were pregnant, how they came to Bright Prospects, why they had previously dropped out of school, and how Bright Prospects helped them. Along the way, they also discuss the difficulties of being mothers, single mothers, and continuing their education.

The panel followed a formula according to which the young women first recounted their reckless pasts, getting pregnant, dropping out of school, and feeling hopeless. Then they narrated how they changed and how their futures are shaping up. Bright Prospects' students were very willing to talk about themselves, to make sense of their lives through such stories (Lesko 1988), and, thereby, to redeem themselves through the "new" selves they presented.

The panelists spoke of themselves as previously wild or reckless. Arlynn described herself when she got pregnant: "I was headed for dropping out; I was headed down. I hadn't been doing well in classes." Esther recounted a similar past, "Before [I got pregnant] I didn't go to school; I partied all the time . . . Now I respect myself more. I don't do things to embarrass myself." Dolores volunteered, "I was bad. I would go home, take a shower, pack a bag and leave for two weeks. My mom was getting really upset with me. We were fighting a lot." Each time a panelist spoke, other students' heads bobbed in recognition.

Then with the realization that she was pregnant, each girl discussed how she came to recant her previous behavior. Each student said that having a baby made her more mature. Having responsibilities for another and having that other totally dependent are circumstances that forced them to be consistent, dependable, to consider the consequences. What the girls meant by becoming "mature" was to leave behind behaviors dubbed immature. Debbie said, "I miss being crazy, being wild. I was a really wild kid." Suzanne added, "You can't do that anymore [sit around drinking and smoking pot]. If you do that, they'll grow up to do it, too. You have to set an example for your kid." Debbie noted, "It seems when you get pregnant, you mature just like that. We're not old," she added quickly. "You just mature." Arlynn said that Bright Prospects School intended "to help you take care of your baby and to take responsibility."

This theme of accepting responsibility and becoming mature centered around taking care of their babies. The oldest panelist, Cindy, admonished the audience to remember, "Young teenagers can take care of their babies." Once again, the other five panel members nodded in agreement. Cindy acknowledged that she often wanted to get out of her situation with a "crying baby, a hungry husband, dishes, ironing." She wondered aloud: "Why did I do this?" Then she concluded, "You have to give someone else your life; you have to put your husband and your child first."

In addition to becoming mature and responsible mothers, the panelists emphasized their regular use of birth control. They laughed among themselves when Dolores said, "I have my son on my lap. There is *no way* I will forget to take my birth control pill, with him there as a constant reminder." Most of the girls said they wanted more children but not until they were ready. "Maybe when I'm out of college and I don't have to depend on anyone, when I can take care of myself." Esther summarized, "I know not to do it again until I'm ready."

Every panelist described herself as now wanting to attend college. Esther said, "I think of college now, before I didn't want to. I want my baby to have whatever he wants." Dolores saw college as a prerequisite for a good job. And a good job meant self-sufficiency. Esther expressed her strong dislike of living with her mother, "I want to support me and my child, not have to live at home. I don't like that idea. I feel like me and my child are a burden to my mother."

The themes articulated in this public 'confession' of former sins and renunciation of those former attitudes and actions are identical to those in the discourse on teenage pregnancy in *Time* and in the Children's Defense Fund publications. Pregnant teenagers are portrayed as sexually irresponsible, bad mothers, and futureless. These successful Bright Prospects' students spoke of their pasts in which they had been irresponsible and directionless. But they juxtaposed their new, mature image as good mothers, responsible users of contraception, and planners of self-sufficient futures in which they hold good jobs and provide admirably for their children.

These representative Bright Prospects students willingly exposed themselves to strangers to tell their stories of former wildness being replaced with rational planning and child-centered lives. Their stories of difficulty and redemption are moving. Their willingness to confess their crimes, recount their deviance, and boldly and confidently declare, "Because of this school, I'm going to make it" was startling. Why would young women willingly volunteer for these public confessions?

These images — of mature responsible young women rising from the ashes of their past through the opportunity of a school with parenting classes and child care facilities — are comforting and uplifting. These girls tell us that they are like members of the audience. No longer deviant, no longer socially problematic, these girls' statements calm the fears raised by the discourse on the problem of teenage pregnancy. The confessions of these girls reveal that they are not "emotionally disabled," but young mothers with 'regular' problems of children and schoolwork. That the panelists seem ordinary is soothing. They communicate that they are not people who cause problems for others in society. They want to be independent, not even wanting to be a source of inconvenience for their parents. Thus, this panel proclaims that these teenage mothers are no longer women with unusual problems or people who will cause problems for others. In embracing good motherhood, responsibility, rational life-planning, and optimism for self-sufficient futures, these girls publicly complete their redemption. Their deviancy began in the public limelight; their sexual young bodies were necessarily publicly displayed. And their deviancy ended publicly with stories of maturity and school success.

These public panels function as rites of social redemption for the teenage mothers. They are listened to, empathized with, and applauded for their transformations. The audience represents 'society' who is interested in and approving of their stories' happy endings. But the panels also serve the school; an alternative school program is always in jeopardy of being eliminated as an 'extra' or 'frill' in a school district budget. The panels verify and personalize the real successes of Bright Prospects School and the importance of the program for the students it serves. Thus, these panels proclaim that both the girls and Bright Prospects are successes.

## SUMMARY AND CONCLUSIONS

This article has examined the overall curricular thrust of an alternative high school for school-aged mothers within the broader discourse of the problem of teenage pregnancy. Three themes dominate discussions of teenage pregnancy found in the media and in the topical reports of advocacy groups like the Children's Defense Fund or philanthropic organizations such as the Alan Guttmacher Institute: pregnant teenagers are sexually irresponsible, likely to be bad mothers, and futurelessness and dependent. The rhetoric of a crisis of teenage pregnancy is called into question by the actual decline in numbers of births to teenagers in the last eighteen years. To understand why the problem of teenage pregnancy grips the public imagination, the symbolic dimensions of this public problem must be considered. Births to lower-class, single teenagers alarm segments of the public who fear overpopulation, more poor people, a lower quality of 'human capital,' and more persons needing social services, such as special education and welfare. Since the problem is embodied in young, sexual, single women, both sexually active, single women and the young are categories of dangerous, or unstable, persons.

The curriculum at Bright Prospects School is structured by these same themes. The program strove to show girls that they could be "good parents, good students, and good decision-makers." Success stories of girls evidenced the same themes. In their voluntary self-exposures, the young women consistently stated that they used birth control, that they accepted the responsibility of being mothers, and domesticated their previously wild behavior. Finally, in firmly avowing their intent to finish high school and go to college, they show themselves on the road to self-sufficiency through setting goals and planning for their own and their child's economic futures.

This analysis argues that in the strong linkages between the public discourse about the problem of teenage pregnancy and the curricular thrust of Bright Prospects School, the school curriculum functions as a process of social redemption for its deviant, pregnant students. In focusing upon creating good mothers, good students, and good decision-makers, Bright Prospects helps the girls redeem themselves as they come to be girls who no longer have problems and girls who no longer cause problems for others. In this differentiated curriculum, girls succeed in becoming good mothers with good futures and the school succeeds by helping them. Given the alarm over teenage pregnancy, the praise for Bright Prospects' program is understandable.

However, if one is cognizant of the diminishing numbers of teenage mothers, of the symbolic loading of the discourse with economic, class, and gender issues, and of the less-alarming longitudinal studies of teenage mothers, then the curriculum of Bright Prospects School may be criticized for some serious shortcomings.

First, although it is an all-female school, women as a social category are absent from the curriculum except as mothers. That is, women as ghetto-ized workers, women as single parents, and women as victims of abuse in families are all omitted from the curriculum. The Children's Defense Fund admits,

> ... we've never had an America in which the average single woman with children could earn a decent wage at any age (1986, p. 3).

Nevertheless, there is no systematic curricular examination of the disparity between women's and men's wages, nor guidance in helping girls consider non-traditional occupations with salaries outside the pink collar ghetto. Even though the vast majority of Bright Prospects' students are single, there appears to be an assumption of a nuclear family setting in which women's wages are supplementary rather than the primary income. Middle class women teachers may be operating from a cultural bias which blinds them to the economic and marriage realities of their students. Similarly, the curriculum only responds to emotional, physical, and verbal abuse on an individualized basis. The general topic of women's position in families is also absent; anecdotal data suggest that the incidence of sexual and emotional abuse among the girls at Bright Prospects far exceeded the national average of one in three (Butler [1978] 1985). However, there was no attempt to raise issues of family abuse systematically in a group.

Adding these omissions to its accomplishments, Bright Prospects' differentiated curriculum replicates some curricular patterns in regular secondary schools. The school's curriculum is positive in that the girls learn to become competent mothers, but when that is the only way women as a group are represented in the curriculum, then the school fails to prepare them for the lives they will lead and perpetuates sexist stereotypes (Howe 1984; Spender 1983).

Thus, the curricular function of social redemption has both positive and negative dimensions. Bright Prospects' students exude self-confidence and optimism. The program succeeds in developing real competencies of immediate practicality which translate into enhanced self-esteem. At the same time, social redemption as good mothers, good students, and good decision-makers incorporates the girls into a social order that is oppressive for women, people of color, and lower social classes. A deviant status is a position from which to criticize the normal, the accepted order, although not sufficient to create a ''reverse discourse'' (Foucault 1980). A reverse discourse enables a subject of a mainstream discourse to speak in her own right (Weedon 1987). Girls at Bright Prospects were speaking in their own right, for example, when they asked about how to respond to verbal abuse or when a member of the panel discussion accentuated that teenage girls can provide good care for their children. Girls were articulating issues, and points of departure, and ''enunciating questions'' (Lewis and Simon 1986). Lewis and Simon suggest that female students do not need a curriculum that itself structures ''women as the question'' but rather a practice in which they could ''enunciate the question[s]'' (1986, p. 461). Teenagers enunciate the questions all the time, and Bright Prospects' students were no exceptions. Staff members need to begin listening to those questions in order to build a discourse around teenage motherhood, active sexuality, and women in families that is not limited to the patriarchal definition of being a good, i.e. non-problematic, woman: quiet, child-centered, consumed by domestic tasks, privatized, and isolated.

The differentiated curriculum of an alternative school for teenage mothers replicates the standard secondary school curriculum in its messages about women's primary social roles and characteristics, but differs from the standard fare in its immediate practicality, focus upon mothering, and its therapeutic dimension. However, it fails to allow a group of students defined as a public problem to enunciate questions about their problematic status within the broader social context of single mothers, sexuality, adolescence, and class which underlies the problem of teenage pregnancy.

What does this case study of the curriculum in a school for teenage mothers have to tell us about curriculum differentiation more generally? This case study illustrates, once again, that schools are normative and normalizing social institutions. Schools operate in tandem with other social units, such as governments, families, churches, to exert pressure on people to conform to the norms of behavior. Norm-following people are not problems for social institutions. The norms which typically operate move all students in the direction of white, middle-class (or lower middle-class) norms. The dimensions of those norms important in this case were general behaviors and attitudes such as: belief in rational life-planning, belief that school success leads to economic success, and the importance of becoming self-sufficient. But there are additional norms at Bright Prospects specifically related to female students: they are to become child-centered, to accept the responsibility and limitations of motherhood, to avoid having more children until they are "ready," and to strive for economic and psychological stability and self-sufficiency.

Socially problematic female students may be especially vulnerable to acceptance of normalizing behaviors and attitudes. These beliefs and attitudes may help them get through the secondary school, but are likely to be disabling myths beyond Bright Prospects School doors. They are disabling myths because they suggest that success is solely related to individual effort. If they try hard enough, they can succeed. While this is functional within a context of doing daily math assignments and studying for history exams, it is a deceit when the statistics regarding single mothers' lives are considered. Bright Prospects success stories only remain successes when they stay in the separate world of secondary schools or in the mythic world of individuals pulling themselves up by their bootstraps. When those individuals are single mothers, they have few bootstraps to grab.

Differentiated curricula may remain distressingly inadequate, and deceitful, when they remain blinded to students' prospective lives after high school graduation. Out of this blindness, they fail to teach students how to be survivors as they continue to struggle against sexism and classism. Rather, school success is predicated on accepting myths about individual upward mobility and taking control of one's life, which, by themselves, obscure real social impediments for successful single mothers' lives. Educators must begin to listen to the questions their students ask, look at students' present and future lives without the rose-colored lens of Horatio Algiers myths.

## ACKNOWLEDGMENT

This research was supported in part by a grant from the Office of Educational Research and Improvement (Grant No. OERI – G008690007) to the National Center on Effective Secondary Schools, School of Education, University of Wisconsin-Madison. The opinions, findings, and conclusions expressed in this publication are those of the author and do not necessarily reflect the views of the funding agency.

## NOTES

1. Bright Prospects School has been on the NBC nightly news, part of a television special, "A Generation at Risk," featured in a front page article in the *New York Times* and has received state awards. Marilyn Finch, principal, speaks frequently around the country and sits on national policy-making boards such as the Council on Economic Development.

2. All proper nouns are pseudonyms.

3. Race/ethnicity is, of course, also part of the teenage pregnancy discourse. It is likely that certain media presentations will emphasize race over class; it is likely that many readers and viewers will see enough black and hispanic images to see the problem as a racial and/or language-minority problem. The limitation of space prevents me from examining these additional elements of the discourse.

4. I share Peterson's (1984) objection to the term "parenting" (it obscures the fact that child care is work done primarily by women), but use it to be faithful to Bright Prospect's terminology.

5. Girls who are far behind in credits needed for high school graduation may choose to work toward a GED. Special education, classes for middle school students, and a jobs program (provides employment-seeking skills and knowledge and work experience) also are offered.

BETH L. GOLDSTEIN

Chapter 7

# Refugee Students' Perceptions of Curriculum Differentiation

Given the choice of two distinctive high school programs for limited English proficient students, how did Laotian Hmong refugee students decide which one to attend? In arriving at answers to this question I learned about high school curriculum differentiation for limited English proficient students from the perspective of the district's school staff and, more importantly, from that of the students. The narrative that follows considers the nature of the differentiation created for students, and their interpretation and use of it.

The account compares one school's transitional bilingual program with a second school's English-as-a-Second-Language supported mainstreaming program.[1] By looking at a district with both of these programs available to the same student population,[2] the study asks how, why, and with what consequences students differentiate the differentiation. Why did two high schools in the same district use different schooling strategies for the same group of students? How did the students interpret the two types of programs and what can student reactions tell us about the relationship between curriculum differentiation and social integration?

## CURRICULUM FOR LIMITED ENGLISH PROFICIENT STUDENTS

If we understand the curriculum to be knowledge as constructed and negotiated by participants within a school, then curriculum differentiation becomes not only the official, formalized differentiation that occurs through tracking and specialized educational programs but also that which occurs unofficially through interactive school processes (Page, 1987). This perspective allows us to consider several complex dimensions of differentiation as they become defined by school participants. This includes the academic dimension as it occurs formally and nonformally; it also encompasses the social knowledge of differentiation — what students learn about themselves in relation to others and strategies they develop to act on this knowledge.

For limited English proficient (LEP) immigrant students, these dimensions are colored by two distinctive factors. English language competency becomes a filter for the academic dimension. And cultural competency enters into the social dimension. What becomes school knowledge for LEP students depends first on their linguistic and cultural access to the formal curriculum, and then on the nature of their interactions with each other, with other classmates and with teachers. For the general student population, the socio-cultural dimension of the curriculum is usually not explicitly part of the formal curriculum, and basic English language competency is assumed; for LEP students, debates about education specifically revolve around whether and how to use formal differentiation on these two dimensions.

Hence, advocates of transitional bilingual programs hold that the formal differentiation of such programs (as characterized by dual languages of instruction, bicultural materials, and gradual transition to full English language instruction) enables LEP students to learn subject matter at individually appropriate grade and academic levels while they simultaneously learn the English language. They argue that this is a superior means to language and academic competencies which results in the desired social integration and participation. Other advocates contend that these programs actually decrease differentiation by making more of the grade level curriculum accessible to students through flexibility in language of instruction. In contrast, critics of bilingual education claim that the separate structure of bilingual programs, together with the status they give to languages other than English, increases social differentiation. From this perspective, bilingual education encourages separatist attitudes of and toward ethnic minority students. These critics advocate either mainstreaming with English-as-a-Second Language (ESL) support classes or direct immersion as alternatives that best promote linguistic and social assimilation. Also underlying these debates is disagreement about which strategies and programs meet federal and state requirements for equal educational opportunities and simultaneously satisfy local opinion on the appropriate balance between cultural pluralism and societal integration.

Both bilingual and mainstreaming programs make claims about their success in integrating immigrant students into the dominant culture. But their arguments assume that the differentiation that is significant for LEP students is that which occurs as a result of formal policy or structural arrangements in a school, particularly as they are expressed in bilingual and ESL classes: Yet we know that for mainstream students significant differentiation also occurs as a result of societal attitudes and inequalities that become enacted informally in the school context. We can no more assume that what is learned by LEP immigrant students is restricted to the formal curriculum than we can for other students. This paper compares the social consequences of curriculum differentiation for LEP students in one school's bilingual program to another school's mainstreaming program. To do so, this paper examines both the institutional construction of differentiation for refugee limited English proficient students and its subsequent, culturally-contextualized re-construction by students.

## THE ETHNOGRAPHIC CONTEXT

Lakewood School District[3] served a medium sized midwestern city. The city was predominantly white and middle-class; most of the relatively small minority population lived in a few residential pockets around the city. While the school district as a whole had a reputation for academic excellence, on a building by building basis, commitment of resources and quality of programs varied.

In its written policies for minority and LEP students, the district stated commitment to 1) assimilation of immigrant youth to local societal norms and 2) promotion of cultural pluralism. The district expected its schools simultaneously to provide their immigrant students with access to educational opportunities equivalent to other students' and to prepare them for their adult roles in a stratified society. Through the district's loose administrative structure, individual schools were left to resolve these policy contradictions as they met the demands of the distinctive community cultures they served. Each school's idiosyncratic internal order set the parameters of teaching and learning.

With the arrival of increasing numbers of migrant workers and then of large numbers of Southeast Asian refugees,[4] two high schools took specific steps toward defining courses of study for LEP students. The ESL staff at Ashmont seized upon the availability of federal funding earmarked for refugee resettlement programs to initiate a comprehensive bilingual program within that school. Its full-time staff included three

American teachers, two Vietnamese teachers, and one Hmong teacher's aide. The program that evolved came to serve as the magnet bilingual/ ESL high school program for the district. In contrast, Logan High School chose to establish a series of English-as-a-Second-Language classes to support simultaneous mainstreaming of LEP students. These classes were taught by the school's one ESL teacher with the assistance of two part-time aides.

When high school age Southeast Asian refugee students came to the district office as new enrollees, they were recommended to Ashmont's bilingual program. But, district rules stipulated that students could choose whether or not to enroll in that program. During the year of the research, all Hmong students attended either Ashmont or Logan. A simple review of student biodata records showed that some of the Hmong were exercising these options: some Hmong attending Logan lived within the catchment area for Ashmont and vice versa.

Teachers could not explain these attendance patterns. Those at Ashmont were astounded to learn that over twenty Hmong students attended Logan, about as many as at Ashmont; they had assumed the district ESL coordinator would have been more insistent that all Southeast Asian LEP students attend the bilingual program. Logan's ESL teacher, Mr. Rodriguez, hazarded a guess that the Hmong preferred to be with Americans instead of always being with other refugees.

Students initially suggested several reasons. Most said they had a preference either for the support provided by the bilingual staff at Ashmont or for the greater opportunities for contact with Americans dictated by the mainstreaming policy at Logan. A few who attended Ashmont, including the majority of the girls there, said they had heard that Ashmont had a better academic reputation so it might be a good place to pursue career aspirations. Nobody mentioned an advantage to attending a school close to their homes.[5] The students' responses seemed to confirm that they chose which school to attend by their preference for a bilingual or a mainstreaming policy; the first appeared to offer advantages of academic access and rigor, the second of greater social integration with Americans.


## THE HMONG OF LAKEWOOD

We understand that we are different people from you people. Other people they don't understand so they would treat us badly, but we don't care about that. The only thing we need now is to survive our life. (Hmong high school girl)

Lakewood's Hmong students brought to their relationship with American schools a lived history that contrasted significantly with that of their American-born classmates, teachers, and neighbors. The students were born in Laos, raised in Southeast Asian war zones and in refugee camps, separated from family and friends, and resettled as adolescents in a very foreign society. Their continuity with this past — personal and shared, lived, inherited, and reconstructed—was the basis on which they established a community in Lakewood and from which they negotiated school experiences. As essential background to discussion of Hmong actions concerning school differentiation,[6] the following paragraphs sketch the themes central to the context of their lives as Hmong in Lakewood.

Three general themes recurred in Hmong conversations about their past. They emphasized their political independence and economic self-reliance in Laos. They dwelt on living in homogeneous Hmong communities in balance with their spirit world. And they decried the threat to Hmong continued existence brought by the Indochinese War and its aftermath.

The Hmong are a patrilineal people with a strong tradition of extended kin groups as the central organizing principle of their society. Individual identity is derived from membership in a specific kin group. People think of themselves in terms of a collective group identity such that the fate of the group determines its individual members' status and well-being. The emphasis on group over individual results in behavioral norms that are distinctly different from middle-class American ones. Within the extended family, cooperation is stressed over competition. Collective action is preferred to doing things alone, with people ideally seeking the company and assistance of other family members. Income is contributed to collective use. The needs of family and community members take priority over individual ones. Individuals take seriously their communal responsibilities to maintain and reproduce the Hmong community because in their worldview, individual existence is dependent spiritually, physically and cognitively upon that community.

By Hmong standards, teenagers are adults duly responsible to the extended family for appropriate behavior, financial support and household maintenance. Ideally, girls meet these commitments within the domestic environs of the family activities while boys are more active in "public" spheres.

In Laos, the Hmong lived high in the mountains, maintaining a fairly independent, subsistence village economy based on swidden (slash and burn) agriculture. Prior to disruptions brought by the Indochinese War in the 1960s, only a few Hmong, mostly males, left the mountains to study or work for extended periods of time in the Lao lowland areas. Most of the men interviewed were employed by the Royal Laotian Army, and later by the U.S. CIA. During the war years and their aftermath, the Hmong population was decimated and scattered, with thousands fleeing Laos as refugees. Those who resettled in the U.S. became intent on re-establishing viable Hmong communities here as the only way of continuing to have Hmong identity.

Because schools were located far from their villages and could be relatively expensive, few Hmong had any formal education in Laos, and even fewer studied beyond the primary years. However, formal education was highly valued for its status and potentials for employment and income. The majority of those who did attend schools were boys because boys were more frequently allowed to travel outside of the village. Respect for teachers and schools continued in the U.S.; based on Laotian experience, Hmong adults believed that a secondary school education led to the desirable outcome of employment in the skilled, preferably white-collar, labor market.

> The parents want a better future for the children because they don't want their children's future to be like they are now. They want them to be better but they don't know how to help and that's very, very difficult. (Hmong leader)

Given their own limited experiences with formal education, parents relied on school personnel to guide their children through school. But while they desired occupational integration for their children, they did not desire cultural socialization for them.

Whereas the adults ''were Hmong,'' the teenagers were Hmong intrigued by what it meant to ''become American.'' While they agreed with their elders that school was the place for them to learn job skills, these students also articulated their expectation that high school was the place where they could explore what it meant to be American—to have American friends, speak English, look like American peers, and learn to move comfortably in American society.


## INSTITUTIONAL DIFFERENTIATION IN LAKEWOOD HIGH SCHOOLS

At the institutional level where my questions about formal curriculum differentiation began, societal values and forms of social organization were translated into school practices that variously informed Hmong students about themselves in American society. That is, students' particular experiences with schooling are related to the practices of their schools as social institutions. Schools establish bureaucratic orders and cultures that sort students, determine status relations among people in the schools, and restrict students' and teachers' options within the schooling process (Metz 1978; Rutter 1979; Bacharach 1981). These institutional contexts evolve in response to the specific dominant community served by a school.

As became clear, the particular institutional organization and ethos of Ashmont and Logan High Schools influenced the climate for teaching limited English proficient students, and differently defined these students' status and proper location within the school. The interaction of school and student cultures created different teacher perceptions of the Hmong. Whereas at academically-oriented Ashmont, mainstream teachers ascribed low status to Hmong students because their academic training was judged inferior to the school's norm, at Logan the institutional focus on social behavior accorded higher status to the Hmong for their studious and cooperative behavior. Yet within both these contexts, primary concerns for institutional reputations, teaching efficiency, and order mitigated against integration of the Hmong students.

### The Bilingual Program at Ashmont High School

Ashmont High School is the largest school in Lakewood. We have about 2100 students here. Approximately 80 percent of our students do go on to college or institutions of higher learning. We have the largest number of minorities in the district. We have the highest number of National Merit finalists. We have two presidential scholars this year. It's quite a unique school in that the make-up is different than most typical schools.

Our large number of black students make it very interesting. We do have a large number of Southeast Asian students that also make it very interesting. I think they have blended in very well with the rest of the school. We recently had a Fine Arts Week and had a group of students from Laos perform at one of the functions and the interaction was just fantastic. The Caucasian students asked them many questions and they, I think, learned a great deal about the Laotian culture. And that's the kind of interaction we witness here.

This statement by the principal of Ashmont in response to a request to describe Ashmont and its Southeast Asian students well characterized the nature of those students' relationship to the school. The type of interaction I observed between Caucasian and Southeast Asian students at Ashmont was indeed typified by the Fine Arts Week event alluded to by

the principal. Events during the week included classical and jazz instrumental performances, drama, poetry readings, art exhibits, and demon-
strations. The students in the bilingual program presented a cultural
show, modeling clothing from their home countries and performing folk
dances to taped music. At this cultural show, after being given the opportunity to ask questions about the cultures represented, the audience was
invited to join in a final dance. The questions asked made it clear that few
students in the audience realized that the refugee students even attended
Ashmont and that fewer yet had had any personal contact with them in the
school.

Whereas other Fine Arts Weeks programs had defined culture as
'high culture with a capital C,' the bilingual program's presentation identified it as ethnicity. The Southeast Asian students who were usually invisible in Ashmont had become temporarily visible to the school's dominant students in a display of exotic costumes and dances. The teachers
who organized the presentation did so as a way to have the students participate in a school-wide activity, something the refugees rarely did. But
the refugee models and performers had in fact been reluctant to participate because they feared just what had occurred. Their presentation
marked them as different from the majority of the student body without
promoting more than superficial peer exchanges.

Ashmont enrolled the children of Lakewood's professional and middle-class neighborhoods. The dominant culture of the school prized academic achievement foremost, using results from national academic com-
petitions and college admissions to measure its accomplishments. It had
the largest number of minorities in the district because of the Asian students enrolled in the bilingual education program, not due to high enrollment of any other single minority group.[7] Ostensibly, Ashmont housed a
comprehensive bilingual education program for the refugees because the
school upheld the district's equal educational opportunities policy. But
the program was viewed differently at Ashmont by those within it than by
those outside of it.

Within the bilingual program, the staff defined a climate that respected cultural differences and tried to make them explicit. In these
classes the students were taught that they should be proud of who they
were but that to learn to survive in the U.S. might require changing their
behavior and values. As a magnet program for LEP students throughout
the school district, the bilingual program had the tremendous advantage
of attracting to Ashmont students categorized as minority students
thereby helping the school meet its desegregation target. The bilingual
program was all-the-more acceptable to Ashmont's administrators and
most of its teachers because the program's organization brought these

students into the school but through its differentiated classes, separated LEP students from the majority of the school population, thereby removing any threat to the academic reputation of the institution. In other words, though the bilingual program created a context within which refugee students were expected to be able to learn, it also isolated them from their American peers and marked them as inferior to the dominant culture.

According to the teachers who taught its classes, the program offered an academically appropriate curriculum in a setting that promoted cultural pluralism among age-mates. As they conceived of it, the program was designed to provide a transition for the refugees into American society as it simultaneously promoted their cultural and self-respect. Brad Stewart, the program's coordinator, explained:

> If you look at the educational background of many of our students, it's minimal. In particular with some of the kids who have come from the highlands of Laos, the Hmong, but also other Vietnamese and Lao children. Some of them had no education before coming, no formal education. A number of them had one or two or three years. What we have been able to do here is create a program whereby we can take a high school-age student—sixteen, seventeen, eighteen, whatever—and put them into a high school setting and yet teach them at their level. . . . It [is] better to work with a student at his or her level and let them grow at that level, and they probably would learn English faster with their peers than they would with younger children. We think it's important that they be with American peers. This is where they're going to live. They need to learn to operate within that framework of high school-age students.

Given the perceived academic situation of the refugee students, the bilingual program was designed to offer five levels of English as a Second Language (ESL); bilingual social studies, math and science classes; four business and vocational education courses; and bilingual tutorial assistance. Students could complete virtually all their high school credit requirements within the bilingual program, which many of the students did. Ironically, the exclusive self-containment of the bilingual program precluded achieving Stewart's goal of placing the LEP students with their American peers. Little if any contact occurred with other students in the school except in physical education classes or in passing in halls and cafeteria.

Because the bilingual program was self-contained within Ashmont, a subculture developed among its staff and students.[8] This subculture brought flexibility into the curriculum and classroom structure, and made multi-culturalism an overt part of learning. Class size was smaller than average, eight to fifteen students as opposed to an average of twenty-five in mainstream classes. Classes frequently divided into small working groups through the use of teacher's aides. This allowed a variety of materials and languages to be used simultaneously, in response to students' varied educational backgrounds and languages. For example, a Hmong aide used Hmong and Lao to assist several Laotian students with a fifth grade American history text while the Vietnamese teacher worked with other students in English from an eighth grade text, frequently fielding Vietnamese language questions from the Vietnamese students.

The bilingual program teachers promoted a congenial but respectful classroom environment that was similar in climate to upper-track mainstream classes. Classes were managed in a disciplined, orderly fashion but order per se was not made a focus. Rather, teachers took their subject matter seriously, and expected their students to do likewise. As in upper-track classes, the teachers expected their ESL and Bilingual classes to be stimulating and academically focused, and their students to learn. But they also perceived their role as teacher as broader than instructor of subject-area material. The teachers spoke of themselves as culture brokers and counselors as well. They became knowledgeable about the home lives of their students and of their cultures. They explicitly and overtly included issues of cultural inter-reference in their curriculum. In ESL classes, teachers organized activities in such a way as to require students to work cross-ethnically; their purpose was to promote cross-cultural communication and to force the use of the English language. In ESL and history classes discussions, reading and writing about cultural mores, law, discrimination, and the history and experience of immigration were scheduled.

### Mainstreaming at Logan High School

My biggest disappointment in the ESL program and students has been their resistance to integration. Students should not remain separate. We want them to be Americans. School is the place for them to learn to mix with others, to learn communication skills. But Hmong students won't eat in the cafeteria with other students, don't get involved in school activities, they only want to attend classes and go home. . . .

Let me give you the example of Hispanic students. When they first came they only spoke Spanish, spent time among themselves. When younger siblings who'd gone through elementary school and middle school ESL programs came to high school, they had English communication skills and fit right in. They only switch to Spanish to talk secretly or curse. Now Spanish parents have no control over their children. The children are wild, just like American children. The children have become American.

Logan's principal made these comments when I asked permission from him to include Logan in my research on immigrant students. Logan High School served predominantly lower-middle and working-class neighborhoods. Its recognized strengths were its program for special education and its well-equipped vocational education facilities. As stated by the principal, the school prided itself on racial integration, and therefore emphasized rapid mainstreaming and assimilation of all immigrant students. In keeping with this, the LEP program was a service program to facilitate mainstreaming, offering only transitional ESL classes. For other classes, limited English proficient students were enrolled in low level courses on the assumption that the pace would be slow enough to compensate for their limited English skills.

The principal measured success in working with the LEP students by their social behavior in the school, the degree to which they mixed with other students and participated in school extra-curricular activities. Consistent with the dominant school ethos, although Logan had an elaborate system of tracking its academic curriculum, the school policy that evolved deplored special curriculum differentiation for LEP students because it contradicted racial integration policies. Curriculum differentiation that would establish separate classes for LEP students would delay their integration into American society. Rather, the school advocated rapid mainstreaming as the means to promote peer interactions that would achieve social assimilation. ESL classes were acceptable in conjunction with mainstreaming in that they might speed up linguistic skills for integration. Yet, as I learned, this absence of elaborate structural differentiation of the curriculum specifically for LEP students did not mean that the Hmong at Logan did not experience extensive curriculum differentiation. Differentiation occurred both *within* classrooms and in the flexibility allowed—and even urged on—Hmong students to use the ESL staff and rooms as their unofficial substitutes for attendance in other classes.

Formally, the LEP students' guidance counselor, Mr. Perkins, in consultation with Mr. Rodriguez, the ESL instructor, determined placement of Hmong students in classes. I asked Mr. Perkins to explain how he decided which classes to recommend to the Hmong students.

We've had good cooperation from the mainstream teachers who are willing to bend things in the classroom to accommodate these [Hmong] students. Our goal is to mainstream them as rapidly as possible. We want them to have the interaction with American students and to have the language opportunities that contact offers. So the cooperation of the mainstream teachers is important.

We do bend the rules some to allow them to drop classes even after the first
six weeks of the term. That way if they're failing they can get out of the
class. No point in penalizing them because they don't fit in with the others
who've been in school all along.

I'm afraid they won't ever do much better than dead-end janitorial work.
They haven't got the language skills. They'll probably have this kind of job
through their adult careers. Not a very happy prospect, is it? It's a vicious
cycle of school-work-family not helping with language learning but you
can't expect the school to solve it. It's too bad for them because they would
make loyal, diligent employees. But they are highly motivated. They're a
joy to work with compared with other low level students. They're cooperative and intent on learning but they sure don't learn well.

Mr. Perkins' evaluation of Hmong students was consistent with that of
other Logan staff members. Hmong students were appreciated for their
respectful attitude toward schooling and authority figures. But according
to Logan's staff, their foreignness precluded post-graduation occupational advancement. The best that Logan could offer them was the opportunity to acculturate and in the process to get a high school diploma.
Therefore, while enrolling Hmong students in the courses required for
graduation, the choice of specific classes was based on an estimation of
the student's likelihood of passing the classes.

Because of their limited knowledge of English and basic academic
skills, Mr. Perkins generally enrolled Hmong students in lower-track and
adaptive (transitional special education) classes. These were the classes
taught by "cooperative" teachers, those who were flexible in what work
they required of Hmong students, how they allowed them to complete
this work, and how they graded. First it is important to note that in assigning Hmong students to these classes, their counselors were using the
extant differentiated curriculum of the school, albeit one designed without explicit attention to English language proficiency, as a de facto form
of differentiation for LEP students.

At least as significant was the within-classroom differentiation that
ensued in the lower-track and transitional special education classes. In
these classes, student and teacher actions typically resulted in classroom
climates that revolved around negotiations of order and behavior instead
of around learning. The classroom management practices that provided
flexibility for Hmong students also frequently resulted in their within-
classroom segregation and assignment of tasks different from those assigned to their classmates.

In the interest of establishing behavioral order in often chaotic classrooms, teachers rewarded shy and submissive students for remaining

quiet. In the case of the Hmong, the teachers responded positively to their overt behavior as docile, teacher-cooperative students. They segregated Hmong students from their less tractable majority-culture peers, allowing Hmong to work together on class assignments while insisting that the other students work individually. These teachers exchanged passing grades for cooperative behavior without considering why Hmong behaved as they did or how Hmong students interpreted those grades. Typical of mainstream classrooms that enrolled both American and Hmong students is the following remedial French I class for students who had failed a previous French class or who were categorized as slow learners. Notice that the teacher incorrectly identifies the three Hmong in the class as Chinese.

> At first the class had thirty-five students, including the three Asians [all Hmong]. It was impossible. I couldn't control them. Almost all were slow learners and behavior problems. All my time was spent trying to maintain order. So I asked for the class to be split. Then some flunked out. Now I have about eleven students any given day though more are enrolled. Lots of skipping classes.
>
> The Chinese[9] didn't mix with the other students. At first the two girls always worked as a pair, the boy with an American boy who sat next to him. He was a good influence on the American because his seriousness calmed the other's rowdiness. But the American dropped the class. So now the two good Chinese work together and the third mostly is on her own. I know I should try to get them to mix with the other students more but . . .
> The Chinese students were flunking the class. They're so quiet and the others are so loud. I wanted them to continue so I offered to give them extra help during my free periods. One of the girls comes in a couple of times a week. She moved from flunking to being an A/B student. . . . The other girl is passing. She has a solid D. She memorizes the dialogues and does ok on quizzes but can't put it all together. But I hope she doesn't try to continue French next year. I don't think the other teacher would move as slowly as I do. In any case, they make a tremendous effort to learn French and do their best in here. [The ESL] teacher has created a good space for them where they can share with each other. I can tell they're working together there.

This French class illustrates the dilemmas faced by mainstream teachers and Hmong students in negotiating classroom environments. The class was noisy, students entered late and wandered around the room. When the teacher attempted drills from the front of the room, few students other than the Hmong participated, and they responded so quietly that they could not be heard above the chatter. Oral work quickly disintegrated into a shouting match in English between teacher and students over behavior. When the teacher attempted to establish order in the room by having students do paired oral work or individual written exercises, students spent a considerable amount of time talking with one another or sitting around waiting for teacher assistance or for the next activity to be assigned. In contrast, the Hmong did not participate in the general rowdiness or engage in social conversation when assigned oral drills. They completed their assignments, drilled one another outside of class, and sought extra help from the teacher.

Despite her professed commitment to integration through mainstreaming, the teacher preferred to have the Hmong work with other Hmong, separated from the Americans. While other students in the room were given individual sheetwork, Hmong students were assigned paired oral drills or groupwork. Unlike the other students, they were allowed to retake tests and correct their written assignments to raise their grades. For their combination of effort and classroom attentiveness, all three passed French I. Yet in the teacher's estimation none of them could pass the next level class because her low level course covered so much less material than the other French I classes did. And the French II teacher bent less in her expectations of students.

This type of within-classroom differentiation occurred in the adaptive classes as well. For example, many Hmong enrolled in a transitional special education business course. This class was team taught by two teachers, one a mainstream business education teacher, the other a general studies special education instructor. The two each described the arrangement as an ideal model of team teaching in which they contributed complementary expertise to the classroom. In my observations, they worked together by dividing the class. Miss Crenshaw, the business education teacher, dictated brief lectures from her teacher's manual as Mrs. Johnson, the special education teacher, wrote them out on the board. Then students were assigned the next set of workbook exercises. All Hmong students sat in two rows of desks on the right side of the room while the special education students sat in four rows on the other side. Miss Crenshaw checked the Hmong students' work and Mrs. Johnson checked the special education students' work. When asked about this arrangement, the teachers claimed to have been unaware of it and then explained it as a natural pattern to fall into since the special ed students were, after all, Mrs. Johnson's homeroom class. The Hmong students did not complain about being placed in a special education class—most were unaware that the course was differentially designated[10]—but they were resentful of the demographic arrangement within the classroom.

An additional form of unofficial differentiation developed under the auspices of Mr. Rodriguez. Many of the Hmong were encountering grade problems in their U.S. history classes, a course required for graduation.

Mr. Rodgriguez and Mr. Perkins consulted and decided that Rodriguez should teach an ESL U.S. history class off-the-record. The class could not be officially listed as a history course since Rodriguez was not certified to teach history. Students enrolled in other history classes but, with ready consent of their history teachers, attended his class. Hmong students eagerly took advantage of this opportunity to pass the required history course. Yet once again, they were physically removed from American peers.

If we accept that differentiation debates about LEP students explicitly include questions about social assimilation, then we must ask about the consequences of curricular decisions for LEP students in the formation of social relations and attitudes. As has been delineated above, even with Logan's mainstreaming policy, Hmong students were separated by teacher practices from interactions with other students. But as we know, teacher designated classroom interaction among students is only a small part of the peer socializing that occurs among high school students. However, for Hmong students, substantial social contact seldom took place with their American classmates. The Americans rarely initiated interactions with the Hmong. The additional absence of teacher-directed, American-Hmong student interaction left Hmong on their own to initiate contact with American peers.

In one science class a Hmong girl had been assigned an American girl as lab partner. Mai Yang, the Hmong girl, was very excited by the opportunity to finally have an American friend. She brought in photos of her family to show Gail and asked her to do the same. But the partner never brought in the pictures. During labs the American always joined two American friends to complete the assignment, leaving Mai Yang to work alone or join the two Hmong boys in the class. By mid-year their only contact was when Mai Yang would ask to borrow the American's lab notes overnight. Mai Yang interpreted this behavior as dislike for her and stopped trying to initiate conversations. Gail said they had nothing to talk about so she wanted to spend her time with other friends. One day in the science class when Mai Yang told me how disappointed she was with Gail and with her own unpopularity with Americans, I asked her about friends in other classes.

Beth: How about in your other classes—do you have American friends?

Mai Yang (quietly): No. Nobody talk with me.

Beth: Do you talk with them?

Mai Yang: No. I think they don't like me. If they like you then they talk. And be friends. But nobody talk me.

Beth: Maybe you should talk to them.

Mai Yang: Before I try but now too shy. They don't like me, don't want to be friend. (Shrugs)

Beth: It seemed awfully noisy in there today.

Mai Yang: Because he give us free time so they can talk.

Beth: But you were only reading.

Mai Yang: Nobody to talk. Maybe one time they talk to me but they talk too fast so I not understand anything. Now I read.

Beth: How about your math class—don't you talk with the girl behind you sometimes?

Mai Yang: You mean the tall one?

Beth: Yes.

Mai Yang: When we in 8th grade we have same sewing class and sometime the teacher tell her to help me. But now we don't ever talk.

Feelings of shyness, intimidation, and insecurity precluded Hmong students from initiating social interactions with American peers. Mai Yang longed for friendship with an American girl but she was unable to sustain exchanges that were of mutual interest. To protect herself from visible isolation, she "disappeared" into books during unstructured classtime. Similarly, Bee Yang, a Hmong boy, inadvertently alienated himself from the boys who sat around him in math while endearing himself to the teacher:

Bee Yang: The other day in my math class an American boy turned to me and said "Why don't you ever talk? Let's talk." I told him we were supposed to study not talk. He said I'm no fun and turned around. But I know classes are time to study. You shouldn't talk all the time.

The same cultural style that gained Hmong support from teachers put distance between them and their American peers. Although prejudice did occasionally enter into their relations, more commonly distance among students was a consequence of their use of different subjective values and standards to judge each other.

For the average American student, classroom instruction pertains to individuals and is not a topic of conversation or a basis upon which peer social relations are established (Everhart 1983). It has social utility as the butt of jokes and the site in which peer exchanges occur. Hmong students respected the formal curriculum as offering powerful knowledge. They could not understand how protecting classroom instruction prevented social relations with their American peers.

From the perspective of most American students, there was no tangible benefit to befriending Hmong. Hmong were strange to them in their appearance, language and demeanor; they represented a curiosity but not an attractive social opportunity. American teens, already leery about the Hmong because of their teacher-centered classroom behavior and differences in language and communicative style, were further put off by Hmong definitions of permitted social relationships. Whereas dating and cross-gender relations were leisure-time foci for so many American high school students, due to cultural as well as financial and time constraints, they were foreign to most Hmong. Given the communicated style of the Hmong, American peers made slight effort at more than casual exchanges. They interpreted Hmong behavior to mean that the Hmong were disapproving of or uninterested in the Americans or that they were incapable of participating on equivalent terms. As a result, most Hmong experienced social exclusion by the Americans in the schools.

After spending some time at Logan, I reflected back on the principal's comments on the status of Hmong students at Logan. He had accurately characterized the dominant perception of Hmong students' relation to Logan. They attended classes — and indeed, were prized by teachers for their classroom behavior—but otherwise were not part of the life of the school. Most assumed that the Hmong preferred as a group to keep their distance. Despite enrollment in the mainstream programs, they were ostracized in the school. Whereas at Ashmont they were formally differentiated on the basis of academic criteria, at Logan differentiation's basis was primarily behavioral and social.

The Hmong students' perspective on what transpired in their lower-track classes differed from their teachers' and majority-culture classmates' because they perceived it through their own cultural lenses. In contrast to the attitudes of their American peers, the Hmong respected the teachers because teachers were adults, had power and authority, *and* had desirable cultural knowledge and status. At the same time, they were aware that physical separation occurred in classrooms between themselves and the other students. Whereas teachers may have separated Hmong from other students for purposes of classroom management and the academic benefit of the Hmong, the Hmong understood that separation as reinforcing their social isolation. Yet Hmong had said they chose to attend Logan in the hope that they would have greater opportunity for sociable contacts with American peers there than they did in the isolating bilingual program. Since in practice, teacher, peer and their own actions resulted in social isolation from Americans, why did they choose to enroll at Logan when district staff had recommended they attend Ashmont? And why did only Hmong of the Southeast Asian refugee students choose to attend Logan?

## HMONG INTERPRETATIONS OF SCHOOL DIFFERENTIATION

Hmong beliefs, attitudes and aspirations described earlier helped me interpret the initially contradictory or patternless answers I got from students about how they decided which school to attend. Several students currently at Logan said they had begun high school at Ashmont on a counselor's suggestion that they attend the bilingual program. They switched schools because the only summer school ESL program was at Logan and they did not want to have to change back and forth from one school to the other. Those who attended the bilingual program said they liked being in classes with other refugees because they felt comfortable. Most who attended Logan claimed not to want to spend so much time with other Hmong. Some said they attended where other people in their family went to school. No pattern as to which students emphasized academic reasons for their choice and which social was apparent. This was particularly puzzling because the students at Logan who claimed to want to be with Americans were actually manipulating their activities in school so as to be with other Hmong. The answer began to emerge from a group discussion that started when I publicly asked one of the senior Hmong students about his reasons for attending Logan.

This boy said that he transferred to Logan from Ashmont after attending Logan's summer ESL program one year. The other boys began to tease him about being too lazy to do the homework required of him at Ashmont. He replied that his move had nothing to do with academic laziness but that he had too many fights with the Vietnamese boys at Ashmont and there were no Vietnamese at Logan. And once he had transferred, of course, his sister had to enroll at Logan also; it was not safe for her to attend school without his protection. All the other boys agreed, saying that they did not want to be forced to associate with other refugee groups. Several added that they felt better being in the same school with other family members. In other words, 1) though choice of school may have had a social basis, it often had less to do with desire for interactions with Americans than with desire for distance from other refugees and 2) proximity to other family members carried weight in students' school preferences.

Many of the boys chose Logan to relieve or avoid tension between themselves and particular other students who attended Ashmont — Hmong of other kin groups and/or Vietnamese or Cambodian classmates. They did not want enforced socializing with students identified as being their historical enemies or Hmong political rivals. Furthermore, the boys subtlely complained about having Vietnamese teachers in the bilingual program, accusing them of preferential treatment of the Vietnamese students. For the most part, the boys were grouped in the two schools according to immediate kin groups.

However, none of the girls had chosen to attend Logan for such reasons. The girls at Logan and most at Ashmont enrolled based on where their closest male relative(s) chose to enroll. Girls with male relatives in Lakewood's high schools attended the same school as those male relatives. The two Hmong girls who had no male relatives in the high schools and who could therefore act independently, chose to attend Ashmont where they thought they would get more staff support to prepare for and find a job.

What does this tell us about differentiation? The two types of institutional differentiation created by Ashmont and Logan were re-interpreted by the Hmong themselves. These types of curriculum differentiation may well have had distinctive academic and linguistic consequences but Hmong focused on the social dimensions. What initially drove boys, and consequently their female relatives, from Ashmont was forced interaction with other Southeast Asians. School differentiation practices contributed to sorting and labeling Hmong youth in such a way that they became a minority group "clique" within the schools. At Ashmont and Logan, school staff used overt ethnic characteristics as a structural classification in school (Bernstein 1977; MacDonald 1980) that constructed and maintained boundaries between different groups of students. Institutional structures reinforced categorization at Ashmont through the actual physical separation in the bilingual program of refugee students from others. At Logan, though the institutional prescription for integration should have discouraged such classification, within-classroom management techniques introduced it. In both schools, the refugee students began to learn that cultural distinctiveness could lead to marginality in American society. Through a combination of organizational, perceptual and attitudinal factors, Hmong students found themselves on the periphery of American academic and social spheres in the school. They remained separate and almost invisible. Clearly neither Ashmont nor Logan successfully promoted biculturalism, integration or cross-cultural respect. They taught about assimilation if by that we mean that Hmong students learned about being incorporated into American society as another underclass minority group.[11]

What Hmong learned from differentiation as they experienced it in both Ashmont and Logan was that they were excluded from majority culture acceptance. Both Ashmont and Logan High Schools had the unin-

tended effect of reinforcing Hmong ethnic solidarity through the direct
and indirect exclusion of Hmong students from majority-culture participation. The students learned to use the institution of the school in the best
way they could to reconcile sociocultural conflicts and personal needs for
identity and inclusion. Hmong high school students learned that schooling would not necessarily lead to their social acceptance into American
society, but they continued to believe that it held the key to economic success. They came to evaluate school's utility based on the likelihood of the
training available to them in school being important to their adult lives as
they expected to live those lives. In their re-evaluation of priorities at
home and in school, they arrived at an assessment of schooling similar to
their parents'.

Hmong students in essence established their own form of curriculum
differentiation in Logan. To the extent possible within institutional constraints, they manipulated their time and activities in school around prag-
matic considerations of graduation requirements and home responsibilities. To this end, they arranged their class schedules to be with people
who were supportive of them — LEP program teachers, select mainstream teachers, and other Hmong. They sought out and complied with
teachers who would reward teacher-centered behavior with passing
grades. To avoid unsupervised or disheartening contact with American
and other refugee peers, they created their own spaces within schools.
This was acceptable and even institutionalized in the bilingual program
at Ashmont. But the fact that they ate with other Hmong in the cafeteria
and used the ESL classroom as a haven at Logan violated that school's
institutional spirit of integration. In enacting their own curriculum to resist various expectations of Ashmont and Logan, Hmong resistance to
schooling was unobtrusive. Even in resisting the expectations of Ashmont and Logan, they reinforced their quietly peripheral, if not invisible,
relation to school life.


CONCLUSION


In the case of the high school bilingual and transitional programs studied,
students' subject area mastery and self-esteem were bolstered in the academically differentiated programs that presented knowledge and skills
in a linguistically accessible and cognitively challenging manner. However, both the bilingual and mainstreaming programs studied achieved
this through social differentiation that exacerbated ethnic segregation
and hierarchies. Thus, while formal differentiation may have contributed
to students' academic proficiencies, it undermined both their and the

schools' aspirations for social acceptance. The students did not initially have separatist inclinations but ironically their interpretation of school experiences as demonstrating a lack of receptivity on the part of the majority culture students and adults in the schools promoted such sentiments.

For the immigrant students in this study, curriculum differentiation occurred not only on formal levels but also, and with more import, within classrooms as participants negotiated the relationships among themselves and the curriculum. Immigrants' perspectives on the purpose of attending school and their response to experiences in school resulted in linguistic and social outcomes that contradict assumptions about bilingual and mainstreaming programs. Thus student interpretation of school structures and knowledge contributed to the definition and enactment of differentiation.

What immigrant students learn at school about their relationship to the larger society results from multi-faceted interpretations of that policy by administrators, teachers and the students themselves. A formal policy of assimilation or differentiation can be transformed through interactions within school. As for any student, school lessons are a consequence of the exchange, conflict, resistance, and accommodation that occur among the different people who act upon a school's internal culture and organization.

## NOTES

1. Five basic program models exist for teaching limited English proficient students in the United States. Three models include some component of bilingual instruction, with the distinction being the intent of such instruction—transition into the mainstream English language curriculum, long term maintenance of native language, or development of bilingualism without intention to eventually enroll in a single language curriculum (enrichment bilingual education). Two models emphasize immediate mainstreaming into the standard English language curriculum: a total immersion model and an English-as-a-Second-Language supported mainstreaming model (Ovando and Collier 1985).

2. The district also included three high schools without full-time ESL support staff, in which students were immersed in the mainstream curriculum for all subjects with occasional ESL tutoring provided on a "pull-out" basis. However, because none of the Hmong students enrolled in the district attended these schools, I have not included discussion of this option in this paper.

3. Pseudonyms are used for all places and people. Interpretive, qualitative research methods were used as the most appropriate means to examine the interactive processes with which I was concerned (Connell et al. 1982). The research

entailed observation, participation and interviews in two high schools and the one Laotian Hmong community they served throughout one year to explore how students, their families and teachers differently understood the school contexts and schooling's relationship to resettlement.

4. During the research period, 1983–84, approximately 1200 Southeast Asian refugees lived in Lakewood; about 100 of these were high school students. These population figures are approximations because the refugee community experienced continuous in- and out-migration as new refugees arrived from Asia and U.S. resident refugees relocated for purposes of family reunification, education, and/or jobs.

5. Upon reflection this made sense since secondary school attendance in Asia bore no expectations of a school being conveniently close to home.

6. For a fuller discussion of Hmong history and culture, see Barney 1961; Yang Dao 1975; Geddes 1976; and Goldstein 1985.

7. Logan had the highest black and Hispanic student enrollment in Lakewood.

8. See Goldstein (1988) for an elaborated discussion of this subculture and its consequences for students and teachers.

9. This teacher incorrectly and consistently identified the Hmong students as Chinese, a designation of "generic Asian ethnic" used by other teachers as well. Asian students stereotypically are expected not only to value education highly but also to be stellar students in academic achievement. The stereotype dangerously supports a lack of sensitivity to the variety of educational backgrounds, cognitive styles, and community values and motivations represented by Asian students, never mind individual differences in learning. Even this French teacher who regularly used her planning periods to tutor her Hmong students individually, knew little about them, not even understanding how their valuation of French was rooted in Hmong history in the French colonial system of Laos.

10. Other bilingual education students might have been aware of being in a special education class but Hmong students' limited experience with school did not enable them to recognize the class as such. To a casual observer the only obvious difference about the class was the presence of two teachers.

11. This paper does not address the differences in academic outcomes between the two schools. I argue elsewhere (Goldstein 1985) that Ashmont's bilingual program with its focus on academics rather than behavior provided a more effective environment for academic learning than did Logan. Also, at Ashmont bilingual instruction rendered more subject areas intelligible to Hmong still learning English.

MARGARET CAMARENA

Chapter 8

# Following the Right Track: A Comparison of Tracking Practices in Public and Catholic Schools

Why does the deterministic link between family background and school achievement persist, despite the egalitarian ideals of the public school system and the good intentions of school staff? This question has continued to perplex educators and intrigue social scientists over the years. Despite the efforts of school reformers, disparities in academic achievement between the more advantaged students and the disadvantaged (comprised primarily of children from poor and ethnic minority families) persist (Astin 1982). Indeed, the correlation between family background and academic achievement increases as students progress through school (White 1982). Recent research conducted in public and private schools suggests that the explanation for this disturbing connection lies in the differential practices employed by schools (Coleman, Hoffer & Kilgore 1982; Greeley 1982; Lee 1986).

One of the school practices which has been found to stratify students academically (i.e., produce groups of "achievers" and "under-achievers") and, eventually occupationally, is curricular differentiation: schools offer qualitatively different curricula depending upon students' interests and/or post-secondary plans. Recent studies of public secondary schools have found that the typical secondary school offers a variety of different curricular programs which differ in both content and function (Powell, Farrar & Cohen 1985; Oakes 1985). Substantial between-track differences in the instructional content and methods between college-preparatory and non-academic tracks, in teacher expectations for students, and in students' attitudes toward learning and themselves as learners have also been found (Oakes 1985).

For some time, educators have been concerned that the practice of tracking promotes underachievement among students placed in the lower tracks. The lower standards set for teacher and student performance in non-academic tracks than in the college-preparatory track (Oakes 1985) and the lack of upward mobility from non-academic tracks to the college preparatory track (Lee 1986) are evidence for concern. Rather than correcting students' skill deficiencies, and thus increasing their post-secondary opportunities, tracking as practiced in public schools essentially relegates certain groups of students, those in the non-academic and remedial tracks, to an academic career of sub-standard education and underachievement.

Although current research indicates tracking is a mechanism used in public schools to stratify students, an important question remains unanswered: is tracking *per se* divisive or is it the method of implementation that shapes the eventual academic outcomes?

## THEORETICAL FRAMEWORK

It is the contention of the author that the practice of tracking students for instruction need not restrict the academic mobility of less academically able students. The aim of this chapter is to illustrate how the instructional preparation which results from tracking is a consequence of a school's method of implementing tracking.

Recently sociologists have taken to comparing public and private schools as a means of studying the effects of different organizing conditions and institutional environments on the promotion of positive schooling outcomes (Salganik & Karweit 1982; Scott & Meyer 1983, 1984; Talbert 1988). Sociologists maintain that organizations which are subject to governmental regulation and centralized decision-making, such as public schools, have difficulties developing coherent programs that promote positive outcomes (Bankston 1982; Cohen, Deal, Meyer & Scott 1979; Rowan 1981; Scott & Meyer 1984). Mandates from local, state, and federal governmental agencies require public schools to embrace multiple goals, thus preventing staff from developing their own goals and reducing the likelihood that goal consensus will be achieved (Meyer & Rowan 1978). Furthermore, the legal norms which structure public school administration and practice, inhibit commitment to goals and programs beyond contractual obligations (Salganik & Karweit 1982; Talbert 1988).

Having to achieve multiple, sometimes conflicting, aims established by external agencies makes it difficult for staff to establish common standards for students. Rather than requiring all students to master the same curricular content or skill level, the instructional goals which are developed reflect differing standards for specific categories of students.

External regulation severely limits the professional prerogatives of school staff (Meyer & Scott 1983). Any changes made in instructional services and programs come to reflect criteria stipulated by governmental agencies rather than variations in the characteristics and needs of students (Meyer & Rowan 1978). Fragmented funding and authority for programs results in loose coupling (Weick 1976) and undermines the integration and supervision of services and programs (Scott & Meyer 1984). Greater centralization of decision-making restricts staff authority to set policy and leads to the introduction of standardized intervention and evaluation techniques (Meyer 1979, 1981; Slaughter & Johnson 1988). The introduction of standardized processes results in a devaluing of cooperative, supportive teacher-student relationships and attempts to supervise and coordinate programs (Bankston 1982; Meyer 1979, 1981; Slaughter & Johnson 1988; Stackhouse 1982). Under these administrative conditions, public schools find it difficult to synchronize their goals and policies in a manner that results in effective practice.

In contrast to the fragmented administration found in public schools, private schools are characterized by greater coherence of policies, programs, and practices (Salganik & Karweit 1982; Talbert 1988). A number of factors allow for the maintenance of greater integration in private schools: self-governance, the presence of a normative culture shaped by the school's history, philosophy, and traditions, and the freedom to establish institution-specific goals, policies, and practices. Having internally-developed goals and policies not only facilitates programmatic integration within private schools, but also enhances the development of commitment among staff to the school's goals (Salganik & Karweit 1982; Talbert 1988). Private schools have the flexibility to shift their practices to meet the needs of their students (Talbert 1988). These conditions make it more likely that private schools will develop educationally productive programs than public schools.

Recent research on Catholic schools indicates that they have a normative culture based on shared humanistic values that enhances the development of effective programs: promotes cooperation among staff and promotes the integration of decision-making processes (Cibulka, O'Brien & Zewe 1982). Catholic schools' philosophical commitment to

promoting the success of all students permeates their institutional practices (Kleinfeld 1979), and the curriculum resulting in the egalitarian
treatment of students (regardless of past academic performance) (Cibulka, O'Brien, & Zewe 1982).

Lacking the bureaucratic restrictions found in public schools, Catholic school principals have complete autonomy to set policy and to dele-
gate authority for instructional decision-making to faculty (Camarena
1987), a Catholic school tradition (Drahmann 1985). Lack of external regulation allows Catholic schools to be more flexible in their practices and
to be more tightly-coupled than public schools (Camarena 1987).[1]

Comparing schools in the public and private sectors provides the
conditions for a natural experiment to examine how tracking is enacted
under different organizing conditions. Since schools in the public and private sector differ in their organizing conditions, i.e., goals, degree of external regulation, and integration of policies and programs, the effect of
these variables on the implementation of school practices, such as tracking, can be studied by making public-Catholic school comparisons.

Given the egalitarian goals which guide their school policies and the
tighter coupling between policy and practice, Catholic schools should
employ instructional practices which provide more consistent academic
preparation to all students regardless of their incoming abilities. By examining tracking implemented under the more tightly-coupled administration of Catholic schools, it will be possible to determine whether tracking can, under certain conditions, lessen the achievement gap between
students in the high-track and those in low-track. In this chapter, the differences between the tracking practices employed by public and Catholic
schools will be examined, and the pedogogical and policy implications
will be discussed.


## THE STUDY

The study discussed in this chapter is an extension of an earlier study of
public and Catholic schools (Camarena 1987) that was conducted as part
of the Study of Stanford and the Schools (SSATS) research project. During a five-year period ending in the spring of 1986, Stanford University
conducted a series of collaborative studies of public high schools located
in a number of different school districts in northern California. This earlier school study (Camarena 1987) identifies differences in public and
Catholic school administrative and instructional practices.

## METHODS

In order to obtain the detailed information needed to accurately describe the tracking practices employed by schools, which included how they made initial assignments and subsequent reassignments and how they monitored and advised students, quantitative and qualitative data were collected from a number of different sources. School administrators, including principals, academic vice-principals, directors of studies, guidance/counseling directors and counselors, and heads of academic departments, were interviewed. Teachers in math, science, English and social studies departments were surveyed about academic practices and other school-related matters. School documents, such as course catalogs and informational handbooks for students and parents were also reviewed. The data presented in this chapter about school policies and practices were obtained from a content analysis of the interviews with school staff and of school documents. Teachers were surveyed about the effectiveness of school practices.

The purpose for collecting information from multiple sources was to describe more comprehensively and accurately school procedures than could have been provided by a single informant. This approach also made it possible to corroborate and clarify information provided by respondents. Administrators were able to provide information about the school's mission, policies, and to some extent, its practices. School counseling staff and department heads were able to describe actual school practices, and the teacher survey data made it possible to assess the extent to which established practices were routinely followed. Teachers were asked to assess the effectiveness of track placements and academic advising since they were the staff most directly affected by these practices.

Self-report data can be unreliable or incomplete at times. The use of multiple informants and the collection of both survey and interview data allow for the comparison and corroboration of responses and triangulation of the findings (Denzin 1970).

## THE SCHOOLS

The sample of schools in this study included three public schools and four Catholic schools. (Four Catholic schools were included in the sample so that the various types of Catholic schools would be represented in the sample, i.e., religious order, diocesan, parochial, single-sex, coed, large

and small schools.) The public and Catholic schools sampled were selected because they were typical of secondary schools in the public and
private sector. Private schools are commonly believed to enroll only high-
ability, affluent students. Contrary to this stereotype, the typical Catholic
school enrolls a fairly diverse population, socioeconomically, academically, and in some cases, ethnically (National Catholic Educational Association 1985).

## The Public Schools

East High was the largest of the public schools with some 1,700 students,
thirty-five percent of whom were ethnic minority students. In terms of socioeconomic status, East ranked slightly below average for the state's
public schools. It was located in a suburban area that was undergoing
rapid development and attracting more affluent families. Ocean High was
almost as large as East with an enrollment of about 1,600 students, but
had a much smaller proportion of minority students, only fourteen percent. It ranked in the middle of the state's distribution in terms of socioeconomic status, and was located in a middle-class suburban neighborhood. Oaks High was the smallest of the public schools with some 1,400
students, twenty-one percent of whom were minority students. It ranked
in the top quartile of the state's distribution in its socioeconomic status.
It was located in an older suburban neighborhood whose increasing prop-
erty values had attracted more middle and upper middle-class families.

## The Catholic Schools

The Catholic schools studied were located in urban and suburban areas
and had student populations that reflected the ethnic, economic, and religious diversity of the neighborhoods from which they drew their students. There was more variation in the composition of the student enrollment in the Catholic school sample than in the public school sample. The
entering abilities of Catholic school students varied considerably since
the schools did not have stringent academic admissions criteria. One
school admitted virtually all students who applied, and the other schools
admitted students who scored as low as the twenty-fifth percentile on the
STS High School Placement Test.

St. Mark was the largest of the Catholic schools studied, with some
1,400 students. It was originally established by the Holy Cross Brothers
as a school for boys, but had shifted to coeducation several years after its
opening. It had the smallest minority enrollment of the Catholic schools,
only twenty-two percent. This was probably due to its location in a predominantly Anglo, middle-class suburb and to its high tuition (relative to
other neighboring Catholic schools).

St. Basil was an urban, coed diocesan school which enrolled some 900 students. The ethnic and economic diversity of the student body had increased in recent years, which reflected the growing numbers of working-class, minority families in the neighborhoods surrounding the school. Thirty-one percent of the students were from minority backgrounds. Many of the students received financial aid from the school and worked after school to pay their tuition.

Two single-sex Catholic schools were included in the sample. St. Mary, a school established by the Sisters of the Sacred Heart, was located in a large urban area. St. Mary enrolled about 800 girls and thirty-four percent of these were minority students, a marked increase from its early years. Once its students primarily came from established, middle-class Catholic families, but now it enrolled many children from immigrant, working-class families.

The smallest of the Catholic schools, St. Jude, enrolled only 233 students, but had the largest proportion of minority students: sixty-two percent. As a small, suburban, parochial school, initially it had drawn students from its predominantly Anglo, middle-class neighborhood. In recent years, it had begun to attract students from working-class, minority families living in nearby urban areas. St. Jude was the least selective of the schools. Virtually all students who applied were accepted.

## PLACEMENT PRACTICES IN SCHOOLS

Tracking is the practice of grouping students into categories; e.g., college-preparatory or vocational, and assigning them to different sequences of courses. From an organizational perspective, tracking involves a sequence of interconnected decisions and actions by a number of staff at different organizational levels. The usual sequence of events which comprise the tracking process includes: (a) the initial assessment of students' abilities; (b) the initial assignment of students to tracks; (c) ongoing assessment of student progress; and (d) the reassignment of students based on performance. Although tracking may occur in any academic subject, this discussion of tracking will focus only on tracking in English and mathematics because these are the areas assessed in studies of school effects (Coleman, Hoffer & Kilgore 1982; Oakes 1985).

### Tracking in Public Schools: Placement Decisions and Mobility

In the following section, the tracking process in public schools will be described in terms of how initial placement decisions and reassignment decisions are made. The factors which hamper mobility between tracks in public schools (e.g., monitoring procedures, scheduling limitations, and lack of comparability in instructional content) will be examined.

## Tracking Decisions

In the public schools studied, tracking begins with a decision about initial course placement made by school personnel when students are scheduled for their ninth grade classes. Courses in mathematics and English are tracked into three levels: college preparatory, general education, and remedial education. The tracks extend from ninth grade through the twelfth grade. At all three public schools studied, the academic vice-principal is primarily responsible for making initial placement decisions, and at East High and Ocean High, department chairs and teachers are also involved. (Oaks High does not have department chairs.) Information regarding course selection is provided in a number of different ways. The academic vice-principal or department chairs from Ocean and East High visit "feeder schools" (junior high schools whose students will attend the high school) and meet with eighth grade classes to give students information about classes and to distribute printed materials about graduation and college entrance requirements. Oaks High staff invite prospective parents and students to attend an evening informational meeting to describe their school's curriculum and course requirements. Because of the large number of students who must be scheduled and the limited number of staff involved in scheduling, staff at these schools are not able to meet individually with parents and students to discuss course selection and track placement.

Public schools rely on standardized tests, teacher-developed tests, and eighth grade teacher recommendations. Staff at Oaks High also take grades earned in seventh and eighth grade into account. The most important criterion for initial track placement is the eighth grade teacher recommendation. The initial track placement can be altered by parent or student request. Even if a student is not identified as "college material" by an eighth grade teacher or by his/her performance on achievement tests, it is possible for him/her to be placed in the college-preparatory track by personal or parental request. If a parent or student requests a change of track against the recommendation of school personnel, parents are required to sign a form indicating that they absolve the school of responsibility for the consequences. Since schools' staff cannot legally prevent a student from enrolling in a course, staff will allow students to take courses even if they do not think students will do well in them. Students who are not identified as "college material" or "college bound" or who are not identified as needing remedial instruction, usually find themselves in the non-college-preparatory general education track by default.

During the spring scheduling process, public school students do not have the opportunity to meet individually with guidance staff to discuss track assignments, course selection, or post-secondary plans. Department chairs or teachers distribute informational materials and meet with homerooms each spring to pass along information. However, guidance counselors no longer have sufficient time to advise students. The academic vice-principal at East High describes the situation that has developed at the secondary level:

> We no longer have any "guaranteed services," where students sit down with a counselor and map out a four-year curriculum. Now we "batch process" kids. We go in and talk to students in classes and tell them about course requirements. We have no pro-active college counseling here. Students have little understanding about college.

Not only are staff unable to counsel students, but they are not able to monitor and assess students' progress on a regular basis. At East High and Ocean High, teachers and department chairs are primarily responsible for monitoring track placements and recommending track reassignments. At Oaks High, the academic vice-principal, and teachers to a limited extent, are responsible for monitoring track placement and recommending reassignments.

As a consequence of not having sufficient guidance staff to advise students, crucial decisions about course selection and track placement are left up to students and their parents. Despite the fact that public school staff are not confident that students are capable of making mature, well-informed academic decisions, staffing limitations have forced schools to shift responsibility for making these crucial choices to students and the responsibility for monitoring students' progress toward graduation to parents. The academic vice-principal at East High is skeptical that students and their parents can make appropriate decisions without some guidance:

> It's very nice to say a student should make his own choices. It's fine if you have faith in the ability of a fourteen year-old being able to make significant life choices . . . That's the job of the school, but we're not doing it. So we've left it up to parents. But I don't think a lot of our parents know any more than their kids. Many of them weren't successful in school themselves.

*Mobility Between Tracks*

As important as the initial placement is to a student's eventual academic preparation, mobility between tracks—the opportunity to move to a different track—is equally important. Any changes in track placement are usually made within the first several weeks of classes. Given the logistical problems of rescheduling large numbers of students and finding classes with room for additional students, school staff are reluctant to reassign students. Staff at Oaks High try to discourage students from requesting reassignment by charging a fee if they initiate a course change. The academic vice-principal at Oaks describes the logistical problems they face when trying to reassign students to a different track:

> I try to discourage reassignments. Sometimes its impossible to move kids out of a class. It's hard to reassign students who fail required courses, particularly at the upper grade levels. We can't fit a sophomore who failed English into a freshman English class, because the classes are already too large. And students can't go on to the next course because they must get a passing grade in the previous course. Then we recommend sophomores and juniors go to adult school or a community college or summer school to pick up some courses.

Several structural features of the public schools studied limit the flexibility in their tracking practices: the large numbers of students who must be scheduled, class size limitations, inadequate advising and assessment practices, and lack of comparability of instruction between tracks. At the three schools, enrollment ranges from 1,400 to 1,700 and none of the schools has more than a few staff responsible for scheduling and monitoring students. Consequently, staff cannot devote sufficient time to monitoring course selection and to reviewing track assignments each year. In fact, students' transcripts are not reviewed by school staff until the students' junior year. This lack of regular monitoring leads to serious problems for some students (Rosenbaum 1976):

> We've had parents come in here crying and threatening us with lawsuits because their kids won't graduate on time. They didn't meet our graduation requirements and they didn't know it until it was too late . . . Former students have come back complaining that they thought they were taking the right courses to get into college because they met our graduation requirements. [Academic vice-principal at East]
>
> We don't review students transcripts until their junior year when they have to take their proficiency tests. That's way too late. By that time, some kids

are so far behind that there is no chance they will graduate with their class. When they find out, a lot of them just give up and drop out. (Academic vice-principal at Ocean)

In addition to not monitoring course selection regularly, public school staff do not test students on a regular basis to assess learning gains or to judge the appropriateness of track placement. Although schools conduct standardized testing as part of the state's assessment program, school staff do not use these objective data to make decisions about track placements. The primary criteria for reassigning students to different tracks are teacher recommendations and grades earned. Even in the event that a reassignment is recommended by a teacher, it does not always occur, as indicated by the comments of the English department chair at East High:

It's hard to get a grasp on reassignments because our classes are so large and some students' problems don't surface until maybe a week or more into the semester. Then we recommend a schedule change if possible. Sometimes they are locked in and it's just impossible. Then they have to stay where they are and that can be a real problem for students. A student may not pass a course based on that inappropriate placement.

Incomparability of instruction between tracks and restrictions on class size further reduce the likelihood of track reassignment. Instructional content and materials differ substantially between tracks in public schools, which make it unlikely that students will succeed if they are reassigned to a more advanced track. This description of ninth grade math courses for the general track and the college preparatory track taken from East High's course catalog gives some indication of the disparity between tracks:

GENERAL MATH
Description: The course is designed to reinforce and improve arithmetic skills for consumers, provide job entry skills and give sufficient pre-algebra mathematics for those who desire to continue in the math sequence.

ALGEBRA I
Description: Algebra I is the first course in the college preparatory mathematics program and is a year-long class. The course is designed to provide an understanding of the real number system and its structure through introduction of the concept of the variable. The student should expect a fairly heavy homework load and . . . coping with the demands of Algebra will be useful to those who go on to college.

Reassignment in public schools is hampered not only because the academic preparation between tracks is not comparable, but also because it is difficult to find other classes to schedule students into. Academic classes are often too large to accommodate additional students given class size limitations. It is particularly difficult to reassign juniors and seniors who fail courses. Students are not required to retake failed courses. In fact, students often cannot be retained in courses in the English, math, and science sequences because the spaces must be reserved for the next cohort of students. This creates an academic "catch-22" for students: they cannot be retained in a lower-level course and yet they cannot continue on to the next course in the sequence without passing the prerequisite course.

Schools have attempted to resolve this academic "catch-22" by developing a host of electives in other departments that satisfy unit requirements for graduation. Students who fail courses in the standard English, math, or science sequences can substitute elective courses in vocational education, home economics, or business. For example, at East High, students can take "Consumer Math," "Industrial Arts Math," or "Business Math" if they still need more math units after completing "General Math," but cannot handle more advanced math courses. Although these courses satisfy graduation requirements, they do not satisfy college entrance requirements, nor do they provide students with rigorous academic training.

East, Ocean, and Oaks assess a student's eligibility to graduate by the number of units taken in math and English (and other subjects), rather than by the student's ability to master pre-college skills. Offering students a variety of courses that are classified as math and English courses but which have little academic content and allowing them to make their own unsupervised choices may only serve to keep students in an academic holding pattern: they do not improve their skills and they cannot move out of a lower-track because they do not receive appropriate remedial instruction.

Given the constraints under which staff at Ocean, East, and Oaks have to work, the lack of comparable standards and preparation between tracks, and the sparse monitoring of students' progress, it is not surprising that, with rare exceptions, students at their schools remain in the same track from ninth grade until twelfth grade.

## TRACKING IN CATHOLIC SCHOOLS

In the following section, the description of tracking practices in Catholic schools will illustrate how the different administrative conditions in Catholic schools affect tracking practices. Catholic school staff do not encounter limitations either in scheduling options or in the resources (e.g., staff time) they devote to tracking and to monitoring students' academic progress. Because their decisions are not restricted by governmental regulations, Catholic school staff can exercise more professional discretion when making decisions about tracking than public school staff.

### Tracking Decisions in Catholic Schools

The tracking practices employed by Catholic school staff differ from those of public school staff in a number of important ways. Upon being admitted to a given school, students and their parents are required to meet individually with either the academic vice-principal, the director of studies/admissions, or a counselor to discuss the results of the standardized admissions test, and students' academic strengths and deficiencies, course selection, and track placement. Staff at all four Catholic schools examine scores on standardized admissions tests, elementary school grades, and recommendations from eighth grade teachers when making initial track placements. St. Mary also takes into consideration elementary achievement test scores and recommendations from elementary school principals. St. Jude, which does not have minimum academic requirements for admission, also considers personal information (e.g., motivation, factors affecting past performance) obtained during the admissions interview to make placement decisions.

Catholic school administrators — academic vice-principals and directors of studies/admissions — assume responsibility for the initial placement of students, while department chairs and teachers play a more active role in reassigning students, recommending changes, and monitoring progress. Because St. Jude has such a small administrative staff, the principal is also involved in making admissions decisions and initial placements. In all Catholic schools, the counseling staff play an active role in both the initial assignment of students and all subsequent reassignments and assume primary responsibility for monitoring students' academic performance. Both counselors and teachers are responsible for monitoring course selection. To ensure that counselors and teachers have counseled students about course selection, their signatures are required on the course lists before the director of studies will schedule students.

Catholic school staff feel it is their professional responsibility to make decisions about track placement, and tend to be more directive in the tracking process than are public school staff. Although there have been occasions when parents questioned track placements, Catholic school staff usually convince parents that the school's decisions are appropriate, and consequently avoid making changes that would be disadvantageous for students. Not only do Catholic school staff not yield to parent pressure, but they also refuse students' requests to be moved to a less advanced track if staff think students can handle the work.

> We want students to succeed. We try to put them in a course they'll do well in. Some students need to be pushed. Some kids try to go to an easier level. They will try — it's human nature — but we won't let them. [English department chair at St. Jude]

With the increasing diversity of their student population, Catholic school staff have had to alter their curriculum and tracking practices to accommodate students needing remedial instruction. Rather than retaining students in remedial tracks for four years as the public schools examined do, Catholic schools have developed a two-year tracking plan. Students, whose admissions test scores are below grade level, are required to take study skills courses in addition to their regular sequence of math and English courses during their freshman and sophomore years.

> What we now have for incoming students who score low on the verbal part of the [admissions] test, they do not go into a foreign language in their freshman year. They go into a reading program and start their language in their sophomore year. Math does basically the same thing. Lower-scoring students do not go into algebra, they go into pre-algebra. They've revamped algebra to spread it over two years. [Director of Studies at St. Basil]

Students are homogeneously grouped in English courses only during the ninth and tenth grades. Students needing remedial work in English are required to take study skills courses in addition to their regular English classes to improve their reading and writing skills. St. Mary, because of its growing non-native-English-speaking population requires that students who need to improve their verbal skills take language development courses also. With the exception of honors classes, upper-division English classes are heterogeneous in their composition.[2]

Catholic schools have three different math sequences: a slower-paced sequence for students needing remedial help, a regular college-preparatory sequence, and an accelerated sequence for students who take algebra during eighth grade. At St. Mary, St. Basil, and St. Mark, all three track sequences require students to cover at least algebra and geometry. At St. Jude, students in the slowest-paced math sequence are required to at least complete algebra; students in the faster-paced track will at least complete geometry. Students are not allowed to substitute courses from other departments to fulfill their math requirements.

One of the most notable features of Catholic school tracking practices is the prominent role counselors play in the process. They are primarily responsible for monitoring students' course selection and completion of academic requirements, advising students about academic matters, monitoring students' academic progress, and scheduling and making track reassignments. The head counselor at St. Mark describes the role of counselors at her school:

> Our role is to work with parents, students, and teachers to help them achieve excellence . . . We talk with teachers about their courses and their thrust, and we comment on the appropriateness to students' college plans. We give feedback about how valid classes are, considering students' goals for the future. We also give informal feedback about how classes meet students' needs.

> We go into classes with worksheets and explain classes to students. Later they will meet with a counselor after they've worked out their first schedule with their parents . . . The third quarter of each year freshmen, sophomores, and juniors are called in to meet for at least twenty minutes with counselors. We also give them a questionnaire about their plans. We talk about what is down the road for them in relation to their classes so that it isn't an isolated discussion about "what I'm going to take next year."

As part of each school's monitoring process, students are required to meet with their academic advisors (counselors) twice a year to discuss academic matters. During these meetings counselors review students' performance, and discuss course selection and possible track reassignments. After the ninth grade, schools rely on students' grades and teacher recommendations to make track reassignments, and also standardized test scores at St. Jude and St. Basil.

> Students meet with counselors to select classes. During the scheduling process, teachers send lists of students who are misplaced and who they recommend for a change. The counselors talk about this with students. Teachers encourage students to move up [a track]. [Math department chair at St. Basil]

### Mobility in Catholic School Tracking Practices

School staff responsible for scheduling students report that between five and ten percent of their students are reassigned to a different track each year and the reassignment is usually to a more advanced level.[3] Catholic schools have the flexibility to shift students whenever a change in track is needed. Staff actively encourage students to try to move to more advanced tracks and will not allow students to move to a lower track if they can handle the work at a more advanced level. Catholic school staff play an active role in directing students into challenging courses:

> It (track placement) is brought up in discussion with the students: "This is where you are and this is where you should be next year." The counselors prod students to move up even though they are quite happy where they are. [English department chair at St. Mark]

Formal and informal monitoring practices enable Catholic school staff to play an active role in motivating students and encouraging them to overcome academic difficulties. As part of the school's monitoring practices, at the mid-point of each term, lists are circulated to all teachers with the names of students who are in jeopardy of failing. Teachers take an active interest in the progress of students even if they are not enrolled in their classes and are required to get involved in extracurricular activities or sports so they can get to know students better. The following incident described by a minority teacher at St. Jude, illustrates the special interest he takes in the progress of minority students at his school:

> After practice, I called Joe over and asked him whether he was having problems at home. I had seen his name on the list [sent out by the counseling department] with names of students who were failing at mid-term. He said he had been fooling around and hadn't been doing his classwork. I told him, if his grades didn't go up by the end of the term, I was going to come looking for him.

Catholic school staff use tracking as a mechanism for remediating academic deficiencies and promoting achievement among students with skill deficiencies rather than perpetuating academic stratification of students. One English teacher's description of her approach typifies the approach taken by the Catholic schools studied:

> Tracking should be an "upward-mobility" idea. It hasn't always worked out that way in public schools or smaller schools . . . I think sometimes kids get into a low track and then they find that it is the easiest way out, so there is no struggling up. I've had kids say to me, "I want to go in 'C' (level) again," because they knew that the other classes were more work. Then you see an attitude of getting by and getting out . . . I am sorry, but I'm not part of that "get by" generation. I won't let them just get by. [English department chair at St. Jude]

The comparability of instructional content between tracks combined with the careful, regular monitoring of students' progress insures that students have an opportunity to change tracks when warranted. Although there is some variation in academic standards between the four Catholic schools, all the schools have established standards for academic outcomes that all students are expected to master, regardless of track placement. These standards are evident in the course requirements established by the schools. The following description of the math options ninth grade students have at St. Basil illustrates the greater comparability of academic standards in Catholic schools than in public schools:

ALGEBRA A
This course reviews the fundamentals of arithmetic, fractions, decimals, percents and ratios, and introduces algebra topics at a slower pace. This course is to be followed by Algebra B in sophomore year (required in ninth grade if not taking Algebra 1).

ALGEBRA B
This course is a continuation of Algebra A. It will include the study of polynomials, factoring, solving equations and inequalities and quadratic functions. In completing this 2 year sequence, the student will have covered all the topics studied in Algebra 1 and will take geometry in the junior year.

ALGEBRA 1 (required freshman year)
This course studies the real numbers, equations, inequalities, word problems, polynomials, relations, function and rational expressions.


Unlike their public school counterparts, students in the four Catholic schools are not allowed to substitute non-academic elective courses for academic course requirements. Students are required to retake failed courses during summer school so that they will not fall behind their class, and will have sufficient academic units to graduate on time. Catholic schools consistently enforce academic requirements for all students regardless of their incoming abilities or post-secondary plans. Rather than modifying their instructional programs to provide less academically rigorous options for low-ability students — the approach adopted by public schools — Catholic school staff have designed an instructional program for low-ability students which provides extra academic support in the first two years in an attempt to narrow the achievement gap between these students and their better prepared peers. Such an approach is necessitated by the schools' practice of heterogeneously grouping students after the sophomore year.

Tracking in Catholic schools is a means for providing students with the extra time and instructional help they need to develop pre-college skills.

> The three-level track system works well for students. Students aren't locked into a track. They can move up and down at any time. We don't water down our courses. There isn't a lot of difference between tracks. Teachers usually use the same book; they just go faster and incorporate additional materials for the more advanced track. [English department chair at St. Mark]

> I believe remedial kids can learn anything. It just takes them longer. I think they should use the same book . . . It gets away from the stigma: "He's in that book." The method of teaching should be different. [English department chair at St. Jude]

The likelihood that students will attain their school's standards and will also have an opportunity to change tracks is increased by the close monitoring and advising that the students receive. Not only do the monitoring practices employed by Catholic school staff insure that students will attain the school's standards, but they also serve to motivate and challenge students to aspire to higher educational goals:

> The kids, whether they are in the low track or not, once they get into St. Mary decide they are college preparatory and want to take college prep classes. And they struggle to do that. [English department chair at St. Mary]

*Monitoring and Advising Practices in Public and Catholic Schools*

Simply examining how high schools schedule students into courses upon entrance does not provide a complete understanding of the complex interaction of school practices which affect learning outcomes and stratification. How schools go about advising students about course selection and academic problems, how staff monitor students' academic progress and completion of requirements, and how staff make decisions about track reassignment are also important factors affecting the stratification of students.

A survey of teachers indicates Catholic school teachers are more confident that their schools place students in classes appropriate to their abilities and monitor and advise them adequately than are public school teachers (Camarena 1987). Why do Catholic schools reportedly monitor and advise their students more effectively than public schools? An examination of assessment and advising practices indicates that Catholic schools make a greater institutional commitment to monitoring and promoting their students' progress than do public schools.

Despite their more limited financial resources, Catholic schools maintain a lower counselor-student ratio than public schools. The student-counselor ratio ranges from 60:1 to 300:1 in the Catholic schools studied and 500:1 to 1100:1 in the public schools studied. Because Catholic school counselors are responsible for a small number of students (relative to public schools), they are able to meet with students on a regular basis to discuss academic matters. At St. Mark and St. Basil, students meet with counselors on an annual basis, and at St. Mary and St. Jude, students meet with counselors twice a year. At St. Jude, the principal and vice-principal also advise students. In addition to regular meetings with counselors, homeroom teachers discuss course selection with students prior to their meeting with counselors, and provide informal advising to students as needed.

Frequent advising is combined with close monitoring of students' progress toward graduation. Counselors are primarily responsible for monitoring completion of graduation requirements. However, the directors of studies who develop the master schedule, department chairs, and teachers also are involved. The directors of studies check students' transcripts to ensure they have completed prerequisites before finalizing class lists. Department chairs and teachers are required to check students' study lists and sign them before students are scheduled into courses. Annual or biannual meetings with counselors also help insure that students are taking the required courses.

In the event that students experience academic difficulties, Catholic schools employ additional procedures for monitoring the performance of students in academic jeopardy. If a student is in jeopardy of failing at midterm, teachers are required to submit weekly reports to counselors. Students must meet with their counselors weekly until their academic problems are resolved. Because graduation requirements are so stringent in Catholic schools, it is imperative that staff closely monitor students' progress to insure that they complete their requirements on schedule.

By serving on academic committees and providing feedback to faculty about students' problems, counselors in Catholic schools form an important link in the school's ongoing cycle of curriculum planning and evaluation.

> We counselors can make pretty good judgments when scheduling students
> — what their needs are as far as curriculum is concerned. Right before we
> start scheduling we talk with department heads to get a sense of what their
> thrust is in their department, and it is at this time that we can make sugges-

tions about what we see happening in classes as far as teacher methodology, students' interests, and whether (a class) is appropriate given the college and career interests of our students. [Counselor at St. Mark]

Catholic schools' institutional commitment to promoting their students' academic success is reflected in their extensive academic support
services. The careful monitoring and advising prevents serious academic
problems from developing, and the coordination of programs helps to insure consistent academic preparation across tracks.[4] Because Catholic
school staff assume responsibility for making crucial academic decisions
for students and closely monitor their progress, students in all tracks
make timely progress toward graduation.

Due to high counselor-student ratios, public school staff are not able
to provide the same careful monitoring and frequent advising available to
students in Catholic schools. All the public schools studied have curtailed their advising services because of budget cuts, and Oaks has eliminated counseling services entirely because of its district's financial problems. At East and Ocean, counselors spend most of their time scheduling
—an almost never-ending process—or handling paperwork, and are unable to meet regularly with individual students. The head counselor at
East High describes the dilemma public school counselors find themselves in:

> I don't consider myself a counselor anymore. I don't know who I am any-
> more. We have two "counselors" for almost 2,000 students. It's mind-bog-
> gling. The best description of who I am is a "crisis person" . . . a scheduling
> "crisis person." I handle schedules and program changes and paperwork.

The academic vice-principals assume some of the advising burden. Given
the time constraints staff face, they only have time to provide counseling
in crisis situations. Counselors do not get involved in planning students'
four-year programs or evaluating instructional programs. Unless their
parents assist them, public school students make crucial academic decisions unsupervised.

Academic advising in public schools is limited to "batch processing"
of students. Department chairs and administrators periodically visit
classes to pass on information and to schedule students. Public schools
rely primarily on course catalogs and handbooks to provide information
to students about course selection, graduation requirements, and college
preparation. Staff, either an administrator or counselor, usually do not
review students' transcripts to check completion of graduation requirements until the students' junior year. Unfortunately, by the junior year

many students have completed so few of the required courses — either because they have failed courses or have not enrolled in the correct ones — that they cannot graduate on time.

The formal goal of tracking is that students successfully complete a sequence of courses which will remediate learning difficulties and provide them with skills that will enhance their post-secondary opportunities. Consequently, frequent monitoring of students' progress and course-taking patterns is important because it insures that students are taking an appropriate sequence of courses that will improve their skills and allow them to graduate on time. Advising plays an important role in resolving academic problems and motivating students to accept academic challenges. Without these components, tracking can lock students into patterns of underachievement. This appears to be the case in public schools. The academic vice-principal at Oaks criticizes the performance of his school in serving students:

> We don't provide the kind of flexibility of curriculum and materials or atmosphere in this school that demands excellence and shows that there is something to be gained from learning. I would say 50 percent of the kids here finish high school with a low ability of learning ... If the purpose of high school is to enhance students' life changes, then we're not getting the job done.

Because public school students' academic decisions are not supervised by staff, they often do not take a sensible sequence of courses which improves their skills and increases their post-secondary options (Delaney & Garet 1986). Given insufficient supervision of track placement and course selection in public schools and lack of advising, mistakes that students make in selecting appropriate courses may go undetected for years. Students in the lower-tracks are particularly prone to making mistakes in course selection (Delaney & Garet 1986). School staff report that many students in their schools drop out during their junior year because they have fallen so far behind in completing their academic requirements that they will not graduate on time.

Why do Catholic school teachers have more confidence in their school's ability to effectively track, monitor, and advise students? Because Catholic schools make a greater institutional commitment to supporting these services. Despite more limited funds, Catholic schools allocate substantial institutional resources, particularly those rare human resources of staff time and attention, to insure adequate monitoring and advising occurs. Catholic school staff also assume responsibility for developing an appropriate program of studies for students and for making

crucial academic choices for them which prevents mistakes in course selection from being made. In contrast, public schools have curtailed the
resources they allocate to monitoring and advising students to the point
that students are essentially responsible for planning their own program
of studies. Making crucial choices without consultation with counselors
results in public school students making mistakes which may not be detected until it is too late to remedy them.


## CONCLUSION

This comparison of tracking practices in public and Catholic schools indicates that different methods of tracking can be enacted with corresponding differences in the consistency of the academic preparation provided to students and their subsequent opportunities for "upward
mobility." In other words, the answer to the question posed at the beginning of this chapter is that tracking per se is not divisive. Although it cannot be assumed, given the use of a small non-randomly selected sample,
that conditions in the schools studied are indicative of all public and private schools, the findings are significant in that they illustrate how, under
certain conditions, tracking need not hamper the academic success of
lower-ability students. Tracking may have a beneficial effect in schools
with a commitment to promoting similar academic standards for all students and with the institutional capability to enact policies and practices
which will enable them to attain this goal. In schools like the Catholic
schools studied, whose policies and allocation of resources reflect an institutional commitment to the egalitarian treatment of all students, and in
which school staff have the authority and flexibility to develop practices
and services which match the needs of their students, tracking can result
in comparable academic preparation across tracks and promote academic
success for lower-ability students. The stratification of students into
"achievers" and "underachievers," which is usually attributed to the homogeneous grouping of students, is actually a result of the cumulative effect of a number of school practices. These include: inflexible scheduling
practices, inadequate monitoring of students' performance, inadequate
advising and monitoring of course selection, homogeneous grouping for
four years, non-comparability of academic standards and demands, and
non-comparability of instructional material taught between tracks.

This study has serious implications for the effective education of
schools with diverse populations. Both social scientists and practitioners
should be cautious in interpreting the findings as support for the use of
tracking as an effective means of dealing with academically heterogeneous student populations. Although practitioners will be tempted, they

should not conclude from this study that tracking can effectively promote achievement for all students (including those with poor past performance) in any and all schools. There is now a substantial body of research which indicates that tracking in public schools does not produce the desired effect of remediating the academic problems of traditionally underachieving groups of students. The crucial question confronting both researchers and practitioners is: why does a strategy which was initially adopted to help meet students' needs actually hinder their progress?

The findings of this and previous studies (Bankston 1982; Cohen, Deal, Meyer & Scott 1979; Meyer & Rowan 1978; Meyer & Scott 1983; Rowan 1981; Scott & Meyer 1984) indicate that the public school system is plagued by conditions which hamper the effectiveness of its programs and the promotion of success for all students. Organizing conditions in the public school system hamper the development of consistent standards for all students and comparable academic preparation across tracks. Due to increasing governmental regulation and centralization of decision-making, public school staff have been stripped of the authority to establish institution-specific goals over which they feel ownership or to develop programs which match the needs of their students. They have had to curtail services crucial to the provision of effective instruction, e.g., soundly-based teacher evaluations and careful monitoring of students' placement and progress, thus reducing the likelihood that students' academic problems will be detected and effectively dealt with. Lacking the authority and structural flexibility to modify programs and to shift staff and students, public schools implement rigid, routinized programs which in many cases do not meet students' needs. Under such conditions, tracking becomes an instructional practice which locks low-ability students into patterns of underachievement.

An additional factor makes it unlikely that an instructional practice such as tracking will result in similar achievement outcomes for all students in public schools. Public and Catholic schools are distinguished by the underlying assumptions which shape their practices and the goals they set for students. Public school staff assume that differential student outcomes are the result of innate differences in students' ability rather than the result of exposure to qualitatively different instructional programs (i.e., poor or inappropriate instruction). This leads to public schools' divestment of responsibility for insuring that students master a common set of skills, and lack of commitment to developing programs that will reduce the achievement gap between advantaged and disadvantaged students. In contrast, Catholic school practice is based on the philosophical principle that all individuals have talents, although they may differ, and that they are equally deserving of nurturing (Kleinfeld 1979). The practices in the Catholic schools studied reflected a stronger institutional commitment to the successful academic development of all their students (regardless of incoming abilities) than was characteristic of the public schools. Catholic schools not only imposed a common set of standards for all their students, but they also committed more of their resources to helping lower-ability students attain them. Practitioners' assumptions about students' potential and the role they play in their development undoubtedly play an important role in determining the goals and practices a school commits itself to.

The important lesson to be learned from this study is that the practice of tracking is not solely responsible for the stratification of students in secondary schools, and more importantly, merely modifying tracking techniques will not reduce the achievement gap between the more advantaged students in the high tracks and their disadvantaged peers in the low tracks. The problem of academic stratification will not be resolved simply by eliminating the use of tracking. Policy-makers and practitioners concerned with providing more egalitarian treatment of public school students must closely examine the underlying assumptions about students' capabilities and the ability of schooling to affect student aptitudes which guide school practice, and the effect of organizing conditions on the development of school goals and the implementation of school policies and programs.

## NOTES

1. Catholic school staff carefully supervise instruction (i.e., monitor the instructional content of courses and the pace of instruction, evaluate teachers frequently), coordinate programs and services, and carefully monitor students (Camarena 1987).

2. The shift to heterogeneous grouping is done for pedagogical reasons: to provide students with the opportunity to interact with peers of differing abilities and to maintain a challenging academic climate.

Schools' size does not determine how the Catholic schools studied group students for instruction. Catholic schools' tracking practices are the same regardless of their size, i.e., larger ones do not develop the rigid, routinized practices found in public schools.

3. Staff are referring to the movement between tracks which occurs during the first two years when students are homogeneously grouped for instruction.

4. The academic standards across tracks are described in Camarena (1987). The work standards and academic preparation vary substantially between tracks in public schools, but are consistent between tracks in Catholic schools.

CAROLYN ANDERSON AND REBECCA BARR

Chapter 9

# Modifying Values and Behaviors About Tracking: A Case Study

The conventional wisdom about organizational change has always argued that change occurs in rational, predictable, and linear ways, that its direction can be fully controlled when managed with clearly defined steps. This assumption is based on the bureaucratic image of schools and the belief that educational organizations operate as coordinated structures, in which goals and activities are linked in rational and logical ways.[1] An alternative viewpoint suggests that organizations and the people in them do not always act according to predictable patterns. Multiple and often conflicting organizational goals may compete for prominence.[2]

Schools have been placed in the category of "organized anarchies" (Cohen, March, and Olsen 1972) or "loosely coupled systems" (Weick 1976), in which goals may develop as a consequence to, not a determiner of, events in the life of the organization. Cohen, March, and Olsen, for instance, noted that an organized anarchy "discovers preferences through action more than it acts on the basis of preferences." Bureaucratic models of organizations assume that decisions are made in an environment of certainty. In reality, especially in the introduction of innovations, decision makers may be less sure about what they need, and may not have dealt with the problem before. In such an environment of uncertainty, an organic system of management, with continual adjustment and redefinition of tasks and communication channels, may be more appropriate (Zaltman, Duncan, and Holbek 1973).

It is also possible that school innovations can take into account both the rational and nonrational characteristics of organizations. House (1981) suggested that the most successful change projects include three elements: a technical or rational approach, a political perspective which recognizes power relations as they affect change of behavior, and a cultural emphasis on shared norms and values. A model of change which relies on broad-based involvement and communication and uses the process of negotiation and collaboration rather than standardized mandates would appear most likely to tie together these three elements (Erickson 1988).

Grouping for instruction is illustrative of all conditions in schools which are resistant to change, which rarely change in a rational or linear way, and for which decisions must take into account group beliefs, values and contextual factors — all characteristics which mitigate against any quick and easy solutions. First, changes in instructional grouping strategies, especially in the curriculum differentiation and tracking which characterize grouping at the secondary level, require major adjustments. Scheduling of students; curriculum guides and materials; teacher expectations, habits, and planning style; and teaching strategies available in a teacher's repertoire all must undergo change in order to modify the way in which grouping of students for instruction occurs. Grouping patterns in schools occur within well-coordinated systems; changing one aspect without considering the consequences to another part of the system may create failure in the first. Second, teachers tend to hold strong beliefs, if for different reasons, that ability-grouping is beneficial for both students and teachers. They may believe that it benefits students at both ends of the ability spectrum by providing "appropriate" instruction, or that it is necessary for teacher management of time and energy. Change under such conditions requires a multilevel, incremental, and interactive strategy.

In this chapter, details from a case study are offered to show that while change in complex systems can be facilitated by a planned and rational approach, the process becomes iterative, circuitous, and time consuming whenever the issues are value-laden. The case study describes the process by which one school district attempted to modify its approach to tracking and curriculum differentiation. To accomplish this purpose, key leaders had to renegotiate values with staff, design interactive strategies to elicit their commitment, and accept new approaches to the original plan. The original plan assumed a rational three step approach: study the research, identify the issues, write guidelines based on research. Such an approach, however, failed to take into account both the complexity of the grouping question and the implicit values strongly held by staff about how and why schools group students for instruction. Central to the chapter are selected critical events involving beliefs or values which affected the change process. These events acted both as roadblocks and as stimuli to redirect the change effort.

The chapter is introduced with a district profile, a discussion of methodology, and an overview of the chronology of the project. In this context critical events are then discussed and conclusions drawn.

## DISTRICT PROFILE

Some brief facts about the demography and organization of the district provide a picture of the context in which the study took place. Also described here is the nature of tracking and curriculum differentiation as they existed when the study began.

The school district in this study was a rural-suburban district of over 4000 students from kindergarten to grade twelve. The schools were as ethnically, religiously, economically, and racially diverse as the surrounding communities, which included a small rural and mostly white farming town, an older predominantly white small town with newer multiethnic subdivisions, an established and stable suburban community with a diverse population, and a new planned suburban community with rapidly changing ethnic and economic composition. The student body was about 35% black, although schools varied in racial composition from about 15% to 90% minority. At the time the study began (August 1985) there were five elementary schools (K–6), two junior high schools (7–9) and one high school (10–12).

Traditionally the responsibility for placement of students in tracks at the secondary level rested with counselors and individual departments, based on guidelines which used standardized test cut-off points, prior course and grade prerequisites, and a generalized category called "teacher recommendation." Principals (unlike their elementary counterparts) had little personal involvement in placement, save to resolve conflicts involving parent disagreement with placement decisions. The advent of K – 12 Curriculum Committees in 1984 (composed of one administrator and about six teachers representing all levels and appointed by the curriculum office with input from staff) provided a new and welcome vehicle for establishing placement criteria. For example, one principal claimed at the beginning of the project neither to have nor to want responsibility for deciding how many levels (tracks) to provide in a given subject area, citing that as "the curriculum committee's responsibility."

Curriculum differentiation in the district was typical of most secondary schools. Math, Science, and English departments were explicitly tracked, with three to five levels in each subject. The study provided evidence of Jeannie Oakes' (1985) observation that in secondary school tracking, explicit and visible procedures for tracking tend to underrepresent the true extent of tracking because they exclude an entire system of informal differentiation which also occurs. This informal system contributes to the nonrational characteristic of instructional grouping because it distorts the full picture of how grouping occurs and because it is based on unarticulated or overtly denied values.

Informal tracking, or what might better be called "implicit" tracking, occurred predominantly in two ways: First, teachers and counselors often held a tacit understanding that certain courses and/or sections of a course were most appropriate for certain students. Placement in these courses occurred in much the same way as in those with explicit tracking and placement guidelines. For example, speech or art, while ostensibly heterogeneous, were understood as a place for students who lacked strong academic skills, or for transfer students with insufficient records to allow placement in explicitly tracked courses.

Second, a domino effect often created informal tracking when several classes in students' schedules were part of a tracked sequence. Other classes, even if explicitly heterogeneous by placement criteria, by default became tracked. If, for example, a single section of honors seventh grade math was scheduled for fourth hour, there could be no honors students enrolled in other heterogeneous classes (such as physical education or typing) during that hour. This master schedule tracking phenomenon was observed to occur most often in this district when close to half the courses for all students were explicitly tracked, and where tracked classes tended to be singletons in the schedule.

A related factor which served to cloud even apparently explicit tracking was the lack of formalization in placement criteria, especially teacher recommendations. Levels of courses ostensibly distinguished on the basis of student knowledge and academic background often differed more on the basis of prior student performance. Placement tended to be based on "applied ability" (student effort) rather than on "potential ability" based on a student's existing knowledge base. If teachers themselves used their own subjective criteria in making recommendations, the actual placement criteria became further blurred across multiple sections of a single course in one building.

## METHODOLOGY

The case study described began not as a research study but as an attempt to solve a school district problem. The authors of this chapter worked collaboratively to propose and implement alternative solutions to address the problem, one working as an outside university-based consultant and the other as an in-district curriculum administrator. Both worked primarily with the Program Council, the group charged with reevaluating the existing procedures for grouping students. Near the end of the first year of the project, they decided to become observers/researchers of the change process and began to collect data more systematically. Nevertheless, the process of study was always secondary to the need to accomplish the goals of the project. In addition the researchers were never, as they observed the project, objective outsiders and in fact played roles which directly influenced the change process which they were at the same time trying to observe and document.

When the project was first conceptualized as a research study, the two collaborators began a retrospective collection of data, including primarily documents such as meeting agendas and minutes; information about the district which was given to the consultant such as test data, school philosophy, information about the group with whom she would be working, written descriptions from principals about the use of grouping in their schools, documents describing the tracked sequence of courses within departments, a district brochure, summary of research studies used in the initial district work to identify the problem, and a letter from the teachers' association expressing fear about the impact of grouping changes on class size. In addition, summaries that various members of Program Council made about their reactions to ideas presented by the consultant, written correspondence between the two authors, and a retrospective summary of critical events (chronologically organized) were all collected as data. All drafts of the grouping guidelines were saved, and attempts were made to write more descriptive minutes to capture the flavor of the discussions which helped to generate them. Since this project involved a K–12 school district, it should be noted that data used for this chapter involve only what was relevant to the secondary schools.

## CHRONOLOGY

The following summary offers an overview of events which occurred from the spring of 1985 through the spring of 1988, as the project evolved from central office concern to school board policy and administrative guidelines. This brief sketch provides the outline from which selected critical events are then highlighted and explicated in detail.

During the 1984–85 school year two central office curriculum administrators (including the one author) reviewed data on course enrollments, curriculum materials, and student grades. They informed the superintendent that tracking and curriculum differentiation may have been causing negative consequences for student performance and for the equal allocation of resources. In August 1985, the superintendent then directed the Program Council, a district committee responsible for considering district curricular issues, to address the issue of instructional grouping and to prepare a proposal to improve the current procedures. His original plan for a one year study was gradually shifted to a three year timeline.

The curriculum administrators (who were also the chair and assistant chair of the committee) approached the question initially in the fall of 1985 as a literature search and organized a series of discussions which centered on readings about the issue of instructional grouping. However, as the research was explored it became clear that the issue was neither clearly defined nor clearly formulated as to appropriate solutions. Furthermore, the Council felt frustrated about how to translate what they were learning into actual practice, given the realities of school life.

By the end of November 1985, the curriculum administrators agreed that a consultant would be useful in proposing the next step and in organizing the Council's thoughts. A consultant with an interest and background in instructional grouping was found. She held one all-day workshop with the Program Council early in 1986, two follow-up meetings with the curriculum administrators, and numerous phone conversations with the primary administrative contact. The Council's work on this project was discussed informally in the buildings, where copies of the minutes were posted and where information about the project was spread through the grapevine. There was some early expression of concern about the implications for building autonomy and teaching conditions. These concerns were addressed by Council members informally and by the curriculum office administrators more formally through meetings with groups of teachers, letters, and phone calls.

The first draft of the guidelines was written in April 1986 by the curriculum administrators. The Council received the draft with hostility and much criticism because it included ideas which had not been discussed in their meetings and because it articulated values on which apparently no consensus existed. This event caused the administrators to redirect the process with a full day in May 1986 spent clarifying the Council's shared values and planning a way to re-draft the guidelines with more committee input.

Brief written information about Council-generated values and beliefs was disseminated to the staff in June 1986. Plans were made over the summer to train administrators, who would then inservice teachers, on the grouping issue. The training was designed to share the major research findings and to generate conversation with the whole staff about the shared values developed by the Council. These discussions took place in August and September 1986.

Beginning in the spring of 1986, the Council began informally to solicit volunteers who would pilot some alternative grouping strategies. These projects served to generate interest, to model possible alternatives, and to test on a small scale what might work for the district. A total of five secondary pilot projects operated during the 1986–87 school year (in addition to several elementary projects).

Between the values clarification exercise (May 1986) and the following spring, several versions of the guidelines were drafted by a subcommittee, with modifications coming from full Council discussions of the draft. Between March and May 1987, teachers were asked to meet and discuss the most recent draft of the guidelines, with written feedback submitted to the Council before the last day of school. This feedback was summarized and discussed by the Council during the 1987–88 school year, and resulted in a final draft of the guidelines which was used to generate a board policy as well.

Both the revised guidelines (available on request) and board policy (Appendix A) were approved in June 1988. Implementation during the 1988–89 school year occurred primarily in the context of restructuring one junior high school into a middle school. Other structured plans for implementation were delayed because of district reorganization issues, including the closing of a junior high school, a shift of ninth graders to the high school, and major staff changes. However additional work by individual teachers was supported by the district, including the following: a) a regular high school science teacher and a special education teacher team teaching the critical skills and concepts of the regular science curriculum to a special education class and b) inservice for staff members on cooperative learning (given by the fifth grade teacher who had piloted the technique with a heterogeneous class).

## VALUES AND BELIEF SYSTEMS

Since a major focus of this chapter is the impact of values and beliefs on the change process, the next section includes a summary of the views held by key groups in the organization, from the most involved in direct-

Table 1 — Belief Systems at Different Organizational Levels

| Subgroup | Initial View(s) of Tracking | Reactions to Grouping Study | Dealing with Reactions |
|---|---|---|---|
| Central Office Administrators | tracking concerns<br>• quality<br>• equity<br>• cost | desire for consensus | atmosphere for dialogue |
| Program Council | teachers pro & con<br>building administrators: pro<br>central administrators: con | intense disagreements | values clarification<br>subcommittee involvement |
| Secondary Administrators | tracking beneficial<br>decision belongs to curriculum<br>committee | fear of change<br>fear of parent/teacher reaction | inservice training<br>alternatives offered |
| Teachers | tracking beneficial<br>(minority of staff disagreed) | fear class size increase<br>fear change without training<br>hope for minority students | dialogue opportunities<br>voluntary participation<br>feedback requests |
| Parents | depended on their student's<br>placement | fear of losing honors program<br>hope for more equity | answer questions informally |

ing the change process and most informed (central office administrators) to the least involved and least informed (parents).

During the 1984–85 school year, the two curriculum administrators discussed with the superintendent problems associated with tracking. In the process of evaluating curriculum and observing instruction, they questioned the quality of lower-track programs in ensuring student progress and success. The bottom track used a less comprehensive curriculum, created behavior problems for teachers, was associated with less time on task, locked students into lower expectations for achievement, resulted in lower student self-esteem and success (proportionally more D's and F's). Multiple levels of a course were costly both in master scheduling difficulty and in creating artificially low class sizes because there were more levels than the grade level in a given school warranted. Furthermore, it was believed that the lack of a clear policy and guidelines encouraged the operation of implicit tracking and prevented consistency in how principals and curriculum committees managed grouping.

The Program Council, the group responsible for developing grouping policy and procedures, included four teachers and five administrators from different grade levels and different ethnic groups. They were chosen by central office administration (with staff input) on the basis of their ability to conceptualize curriculum issues on a district level and to operate effectively in a group. In addition to the grouping study, this group set guidelines for other curricular issues in the district. The members formed, although not intentionally, a microcosm of the attitudes extant in the district as a whole. Their discussions and decision points will be discussed in depth later in the chapter.

Secondary administrators, including those on the Council, tended to favor tracking and/or to believe that the decision belonged at the curriculum committee level. Echoed in all of their reactions was considerable caution, fear of change, and fear of reactions from parents and teachers. Most secondary teachers, like their administrators, believed that tracking was beneficial. Exceptions largely occurred among minority teachers who noted the unequal access to knowledge which accompanied tracking. There was also considerable fear that if tracking were eliminated, class size would increase or that change would come without adequate training for teachers. For example, a letter in January 1986 from the teachers' association executive board raised these concerns: "It is hoped that any change in class grouping would not be used as a reason to increase class size or to reduce the number of staff members. The individual attention provided by the professional staff to the students in heterogeneous grouping would require much more time and effort than in a homogeneous grouping situation."

Although parent reaction was not assessed formally or directly, it was reflected by administrators and teachers in informal conversations with parents. Parents whose students were in honors programs were fearful that these prestigious programs would be dropped or restricted to fewer students. Other parents hoped that there would be an improvement in course offerings for the average and below-average student.

## CRITICAL EVENTS

The management of this project was a delicate matter and one which involved steps backwards and sidewise as well as forward. In this section we highlight several of the events which blocked the process, provided evidence of problems to come, or illustrated possible solutions. The events, presented in roughly chronological order, illustrate the value-laden nature of the case study project and the importance of dealing with beliefs in effecting change.

### Program Council Discussions of Grouping Literature

The first critical event proved to be the research based discussions in Program Council meetings. The initial articles chosen for discussion were taken from the Project Rise materials of the Milwaukee Public Schools. They were chosen because they provided a clear explanation of the case against curriculum differentiation. However, because they represented a clear bias without specific studies to provide supporting data, they were rejected by those on the Council who believed tracking was a positive condition for learning. On the other hand, most minority teachers and curriculum administrators on Program Council strongly agreed with the values presented in these articles. Also expressed was the concern that the curriculum administrators would control the flow of information so that only material with this bias would be presented for discussion. Attempts were then made to generate articles which dealt with the positive as well as the negative side of grouping and with alternative strategies for grouping. Three to five articles were read and discussed at each meeting, for a total of about twenty during the semester. (See Appendix B for a list.)

The effect of reading and discussing so many articles in common was that certain ideas, which contradicted the initial view that tracking was good for all students, continued to surface and could not be dismissed. They allowed the Council to discuss questions about the differential impact of grouping and tracking: for whom was it effective, under what conditions was it damaging, what grouping strategies can be useful. Building administrators had to deal with the conflict between the research results and their perception of teacher resistance to change. In particular, the research identified as a fallacy the broadly accepted teacher premise that low achieving students always benefit from instruction in homogeneous groups.

By the end of the fall semester, two viewpoints emerged on the Council: some members argued that the disadvantages of homogeneous grouping to low achieving students is inherent in homogeneous grouping itself. Others began to talk about how the disadvantages are linked to the way instruction is delivered and to the content of the curriculum for these groups. The former viewpoint was best represented by minority teachers and curriculum administrators, who pointed to the inherent inequity of ability grouping because of its resegregation potential. The second viewpoint was best summarized by a building administrator on the Council, who wrote in a January 22, 1986 letter to one curriculum administrator:

> "I also believe many of the evils pointed out in the literature are the result of behaviors which we can control and manipulate if we are aware of their adverse effects on learners. Are the problems associated with low-level classes solely due to the presence of only low-level students in the class, or are they exaggerated by administrative practices of late-afternoon scheduling or inordinately large class sizes? Are teachers aware of what research says about their behavior in interacting with low-level students? What about the self-concept of low-level students? These and the other problems associated with low-level classes need to be discussed with administrators and teachers and suggestions for correcting these problems given. It would seem that in-service education at the adminsitrative and teacher-level are needed."

## Consultant Input

The need for a consultant as outside expert was recognized at the end of first semester by the curriculum administrators and her subsequent involvement proved to be the second critical event. The search began for someone with a background in the social organization of schools and instructional grouping, who could help to build consensus on the Council, propose options to the current system, and suggest how change could be made while assuring ownership at all levels of the organization. The consultant chosen had a strong research interest and experience in all of these areas. Her willingness to work with the district was based on an interest in collaboration in which her researcher's skills could be applied to an existing organizational problem, defined by the district but with application to her own research focus.

The consultant held several prior discussions and exchanged information with one of the curriculum administrators (and later her co-researcher), as discussed in the methodology section. During three meetings and additional phone conversations, the consultant performed some critical functions in defining the problem and suggesting approaches to developing guidelines. In particular, she provided a theoretical perspective for understanding schools, grouping, and change; interpreted district data in a new way for the Program Council; suggested that guidelines be developed to allow flexibility and local control in creating instructional groups; suggested that volunteer teachers and administrators be solicited to pilot some alternative practices; and identified some alternative strategies to meet the needs of all students in different grouping approaches.

The theoretical framework used by the research consultant who advised the curriculum office and Program Council involved a view of work in schools characterized by a division of labor among levels of school organization, each with its own productive activities and outcomes.[3] Each level has a different role to play in the development and implementation of grouping policy. For example, district level administrators are responsible for such activities as procuring and maintaining buildings, securing personnel, obtaining the resources that teachers need for instruction, and the like. With respect to grouping policy, they are charged with insuring that all students be given the educational opportunities they need to fulfill their highest potential. School level activities include the assignment of students to teachers, the development of the school time schedule, the distribution of instructional materials, and the assessment and coordination of learning. At the classroom level, teachers must organize students for instruction and teach them.

While each level undertakes different activities, the levels are interrelated in complex ways. The activities of one level directly influence those of adjacent levels, and policies are effective to the extent that they support and facilitate the work at other levels. With respect to grouping, since conditions vary from school to school within districts, policies at the district level must permit variation in decision making at the school level that is responsive to the conditions of each school. In other words, they must enable the formation of class groups that can be effectively managed and instructed by teachers. Similarly, decisions made at the school level must not restrict the practices of teachers so that they are unable to develop instruction that is responsive to the needs of students. At the same time, the policies at district and school levels must safeguard the rights of individual students. This organizational perspective was considered in developing grouping guidelines which specified basic conditions which had to be met, such as placement based on objective and multiple criteria, without specifying the exact formulas for grouping.

The consultant commented on the research studies that the Program Council had been reading, noting that most researchers considered the effectiveness of ability grouping in terms of achievement outcomes. She argued that the existing evidence does not support the practice of grouping students into classes on the basis of ability nor that of regrouping them within grades; however, some evidence does suggest the effectiveness of cross-grade grouping and honors track placement (Slavin 1987). At the same time, recent reviewers also emphasize the social and emotional costs of tracking, particularly for low achieving students.[4]

The consultant stressed the inconsistency in findings among studies. For almost any grouping or tracking arrangement, the research literature shows that some teachers are able to help their classes to learn effectively, while others are not. What this means is that there is no direct relation between a grouping method and learning outcomes. A social arrangement, in and of itself, does not lead directly to achievement and attitudinal outcomes. Rather, it is the activities and knowledge that students experience as part of instruction that bear directly on what they learn and how they feel about their learning. The curricular content introduced during instruction and the time devoted to instruction influence what and how much students learn (Oakes 1985; Fisher et al. 1978). This emphasis on instruction was later reflected in the guidelines through specification of the instructional characteristics which must be available to all students in any grouping arrangement (i.e., instruction in higher order thinking, enrichment activities, a common set of essential skills to be mastered, the coordination of special services, and the control of class size based on grouping strategy).

The consultant suggested a relationship between the nature of the content being learned and the need for ability grouping. Particularly those content domains which can be divided into hierarchically related areas of learning, with earlier learning serving as the basis for later more advanced work, may require some degree of homogeneity in past learning among students. For example, instruction in some areas of mathematics involves sequentially ordered concepts. Accordingly, if students lack basic knowledge, it is difficult for them to profit from more advanced instruction. In comparison, other subject matter areas may not demand instruction as closely matched to the abilities of group members; that is, if instruction is sufficiently broad gauged and meaningful, most students can benefit from it at some level. For example, many short stories read by students can be understood and appreciated by them on a number of different levels. Ability grouping would seem to be needed for curricular areas involving the achievement of specific objectives that are sequentially organized, but less necessary for tasks that can be approached in different ways. Alternatively, if more diverse ability groupings are used in a subject area, methods of teaching and the organization of content needs to be changed so that students can benefit from instruction in different ways.

The consultant examined the achievement scores of students composing different tracks in junior high and high school English, mathematics, and science. The analysis revealed that tracks were highly overlapping in achievement; on this basis, she suggested that one or two of the tracks could be eliminated. Yet, the elimination of some tracks would require teachers to rethink the content of courses and its organization. Because of the social, curricular, and instructional ramifications involved in modifying grouping arrangements, the consultant suggested the use of pilot projects for teachers and administrators to try out new forms of grouping and instruction. Then, if the projects were effective, they might be implemented on a broader basis. Thus, in addition to developing grouping guidelines, the Program Council was encouraged to support the development of pilot studies which would identify the nature of curricular modification and staff development that would be needed to implement new grouping arrangements.

Dialogue with the consultant provided the basis for the first draft of guidelines for grouping. As discussed in the following section, however, a rational basis for policy development is insufficient.

*Values Clarification*

The extremely negative reaction of the Council to the first draft resulted in a significant refocusing effort. The primary curriculum administrator involved in the project and the consultant then discussed by phone a new strategy in which the rational approach was abandoned and a plan was designed to gain consensus within the Program Council about shared beliefs. To this end, the draft of guidelines was discarded and replaced with a values clarification exercise which was identified as the third critical event. At a day-long meeting in May, Program Council members succeeded in agreeing about a set of assumptions or values with regard to grouping and a plan to share these values with the staff.

The day-long work session included two parts. The first discussion centered around a review of three alternatives which could serve as the basis for proceeding to develop procedures for grouping. These three options had previously been discussed in principle, but the group had not articulated clearly its choice.

1. Leave as is

This is the way things are now. Teachers are making judgments on the basis of their understanding and preparation, and in terms of the desires of the building principals. Building principal's input is based on felt needs and some reference to the curriculum. The Curriculum Office's input is based upon the curriculum and needs of individual schools.

People are not doing things under any commonly understood guidelines, short of the actual curriculum.

e.g. At 7th and 8th grade math, dialogue between department, counselor, and principal determines interpretation of "Teacher Recommendation" for placement

2. Top down, common mandates

In this situation we would develop mandates and guidelines concerning grouping and expect that building principals and teachers would follow them. There would be no differences among buildings.

e.g. 5 levels of math at both Hubbard Trail and Deer Creek for 7th and 8th grade, with established CTBS cutoffs and specific criteria for teacher input

3. Flexible guidelines

In this instance, we would develop guidelines for teachers to use, with the approval of the building principal, in grouping children for instruction. The use of these guidelines would depend upon the uniqueness and diversity of the building population.

e.g. Based on a profile of the group, number of levels could vary between schools, based on the diversity of the population

The second possibility was rejected for the elementary level where flexibility and differences among buildings were seen as valuable. At the secondary level it was agreed that buildings should be the same, but that grade levels and subject levels could be allowed to vary when differences were warranted. Another option, to leave things as they are, with no common understandings and with unique rationales for every grouping decision, was also rejected, although it was recognized that many current grouping patterns were very positive and should be maintained. The premise which received the most support was the idea that procedures should be developed which act as screens to specify what a given grouping system must and must not do. It was also noted that elementary and secondary schools have different needs; for example, at the secondary level curriculum committees make the majority of decisions that affect grouping, while at the elementary level principals and teachers tend to be more involved.

The major focus of the work session centered on the discussion of beliefs. The basis for this exercise was the consultant's view that much of the decision-making in instructional grouping is based on values held, and that options for the guidelines would be easier to develop if Program Council could agree on its beliefs in critical areas. Eight pairs of beliefs were constructed by the curriculum administrators, based on prior Program Council discussion of the research themes, and presented to the rest of the Council for individual response. Some of these themes had been implicit in the initial guidelines draft, but again, were never articulated as positions to be affirmed or rejected. Members were asked to circle the one statement in each pair with which they most agreed:

A  1. Purpose of basic level is to instruct at ability level.
   2. Purpose of basic level is to prepare for higher level.

B  1. Basic levels need remediation in basic skills.
   2. Basic levels need higher order skills, in addition to remediation.

C  1. Low achievers and high achievers do not need to interact during the day.
   2. Low achievers and high achievers benefit from interacting during the day.

D  1. It is not a problem if minority kids are de facto segregated during the day.
   2. Minority kids should be integrated with other students in academic classes.

E  1. High achievers need acceleration more than enrichment.
   2. High achievers need enrichment more than acceleration.

F  1. The only reasonable way to group is by ability.
   2. There are many characteristics besides ability which are useful for grouping.

G  1. All subjects need the same type and number of groups.
   2. Subjects need different numbers and types of groups.

H  1. Many lower achieving kids cannot learn high order skills and concepts, regardless of the structure provided.
   2. Many lower achieving kids can learn anything, given enough time, motivation, and quality instruction.

When individual responses were tallied, it was evident that consensus already existed for all beliefs except A, whether the purpose of basic courses was to instruct at students' ability levels (e.g., meet innate unchanging needs) or to prepare students to enter a regular level program by modifying their entering characteristics. Additional discussion led to a consensus for the later, after members agreed that curriculum should be structured to sequence skills among levels so that movement is possible. Other minor modifications were made to the language of the exercise, so that meaning was clarified for use in later documents.

This day proved to be the glue which allowed Program Council to proceed with a common understanding and shared convictions that what they were trying to produce (guidelines for grouping) was both valuable and achievable. Subsequent dialogue and disagreement over specific language in drafts of the guidelines was much less strident and frequently referred to the language of these common beliefs. Their value is clearly seen in the fact that they were reclaimed over and over by the Council: incorporated in information disseminated to staff, used to train administrators, and ultimately included in the language of the board policy approved in June 1988. (See Appendix A.)

*Staff Input*

As a result of the consensus which had emerged in Program Council from all of the reading, discussing, and negotiating, it was decided that the staff would need some similar amount of time and inservice to consider the same value questions. The consultant strongly urged this approach, suggesting that if teachers and other administrators came to the same consensus about values relative to grouping, this consensus would be a foundation for accepting a later set of guidelines.

Two formal opportunities for feedback were provided and were the fourth critical event in the change process. The first opportunity occurred in the fall of 1986 when administrators and teachers were inserviced on both the values the Program Council had accepted, and on the research they had reviewed which led to these values. Teachers were encouraged to look for alternative grouping strategies to pilot (two examples are provided below), and to provide feedback to the Program Council members and their principal. Schools varied in the quality of this inservice, based largely in the interest principals had in the issue of grouping. Where effective inservice was given and teachers encouraged to explore grouping alternatives, good feedback emerged and was communicated to the Program Council. From these pockets of interest grew several pilot projects which the Program Council endorsed and which the curriculum office administrators supported with time and money.

In the spring of 1987 (the second formal opportunity for feedback), teachers received a copy of the guidelines drafted during the prior year and were asked to respond formally. Responses were in writing from each department within a school, and from some individuals who wanted to add a personal critique. They were asked to respond to four questions, after reviewing the proposed guidelines:

1. The guidelines are designed to provide conditions rather than inflexible rules. To what extent does the written document reflect the flexibility that we intended?
2. Thinking about your level and subject curriculum, *what* would you have to change in order to meet the guidelines? How you group students within your class? How the curriculum committee determines criteria for placement? The materials you use? The way you allocate your time? The way you deliver instruction? Etc.
3. What information do you need in order to meet these guidelines adequately, other than information already provided in the document?
4. Can you suggest some additional examples, specific strategies, or specific criteria which could be added to this document?

In general the staff endorsed the proposed guidelines as theoretically commendable, but they reported considerable skepticism about both the feasibility of implementation and the effect on students. Constraining factors were personal ("I would have a lot of adjusting to do in order to insure each student is benefitting from my daily presentation.") and organizational or curricular ("Grouping for part of a week is great in theory, but this notion will be the first to be dismissed when scheduling problems arise.").

Teachers seemed to associate heterogeneous grouping with larger class size. There was approval of the recommended class size limit of fifteen for basic classes, but also a fear that heterogeneous classes would grow in size as a result. The mainstreaming of special education students was mentioned as a factor which should influence class size.

Another problem (highlighted earlier by the consultant) was that the current curriculum, largely skill based and sequential, best matches homogeneous grouping. In addition, a topic-based curriculum finds less support in available textbooks. One department asked skeptically, "Will any [textbooks] truly meet the specifications in this section?" Curriculum revisions would be needed to imbed more thinking skills and problem solving skills for all students. The maximum of three levels would require some reductions in departments which currently have four or five levels. A major curriculum change would be to make the lower-track more challenging so that movement to the regular track would be easier. One teacher stated that "The differences between 9th grade algebra and pre-algebra are so great that no reasonable amount of effort will overcome them."

Teachers reported a tendency to teach only to the middle group, and a fear of managing vast student differences in one classroom. ("I have imagined myself with some kids at a 5th grade level and some at an 8th grade level in the same class.") Traditional lecture formats would not be possible with heterogeneous grouping. Multiple lectures or alternatives to lecturing would be needed. Time would have to be reallocated. Teaching multiple levels in one room was anticipated to require considerably more planning and preparation on the part of teachers, and increased use of grouping within the class. New instructional strategies (including more reliance on right brained activities) for reaching a mixed group of students would be needed. The guideline that special services be better coordinated with regular education, especially by providing in-class support, was applauded.

Teachers expressed a desire for more inservice on topics such as classroom management, grouping in heterogeneous classes, teaching for thinking and understanding, evaluating student progress on higher order skills, and use of criterion-referenced tests to place students. One department summarized the need this way: "Educating teachers is paramount. Old habits die hard."

Some concern was expressed that requiring heterogeneous grouping for part of each student's day would adversely affect the education of high achievers. Behind this fear is the implied assumption that heterogeneously grouped classes are less rigorous and less challenging. One department reported, "In practice this is bound to be unfair to the honors level student. It doesn't seem so on paper, but in reality this is what will happen." Also reported was the fear that heterogeneous grouping was difficult and frustrating for all students. Students may not learn as much, it was argued, when there are too many levels in one room. Slow learners need the opportunity for a slower pace. Although elimination of stigmas associated with the low-track was seen as the positive side of the plan, only the social studies department, which used heterogeneous grouping already, tended to prefer it.

*Pilot Projects*

In its efforts to communicate with and encourage some alternative thinking and practices regarding grouping, the Program Council and curriculum administrators supported several pilot projects. These formed the fifth set of critical events which facilitated the change effort. Several were initiated by Program Council members or by teachers who had talked extensively with Program Council members. A few were begun by teachers who were intrigued by the first inservice (fall of 1986). Some projects were very successful and others proved less workable. All, however, were useful in pointing to impediments inherent in making change. Two projects are described below which illustrate these successes and impediments.

During the 1986–87 year, a pilot program operated in which the basic science level in ninth grade was eliminated and these students were scheduled into the regular science course. A review of test scores by the teacher (a member of the Program Council) who was interested in conducting this pilot had indicated that except for six very low-scoring students (most of whom were mainstreamed from special education), the students scheduled for the basic course did not differ in reading and language scores from the regular level students. Although they did differ in math scores and in prior performance (grades) in science class, the ninth grade science teacher thought they would be able to handle the regular program with some adjustments to instruction, via multiple learning styles strategies.

Midyear review of grade distribution and discussions with the teacher indicated that the increased heterogeneity did work well when instruction was modified to meet the needs of less abstract thinkers. The original basic level students were not distinguishable from their regular level peers in unit test scores and semester grades. Classes in which a distribution of lower achieving and special education students did not exceed 25% were the most successful. Interventions by curriculum office administrators with the principal and counselors were necessary, however, to assure that the proportion of special education students and transfers was regulated so as to maintain the composition of classes close to the 25% level.

Another program which did not involve a change in instruction or curriculum, but rather an attempt to work within the existing structure to accelerate students, was less successful. In the fall of 1986, a pre-algebra teacher identified twenty out of seventy students as capable of more challenging work. Because of the vast curricular content differences between pre-algebra and algebra, he selected only the five most able and most motivated students for extra help. These students were given intensive outside tutoring (2–3 hours per week for two months), and at the semester, three were still in the tutoring program, passed a proficiency test, and were moved into algebra. One immediately dropped out; he could not adapt to the social differences between the two classes. Two remained, but by the fourth quarter, one was described as "seriously struggling." The teacher summarized his project in this way:

> One student out of five students who tried out of over twenty students capable out of seventy students in pre-algebra has been able to successfully move up — and only thanks to many hours by the student and the staff — That's quite a track record. Without curricular changes in the middle and lower tracks upward movement simply will not occur.

Eliminating levels and/or changing the curriculum to accommodate change seem more realistic approaches than trying to move students flexibly through an existing curriculum.

Out of this pilot came a proposed model junior high math curriculum to employ course leveling by skill/topic rather than by grade level. Five topics would be offered in both semesters so that students who can progress need to jump only one semester and not one year ahead. In addition, students with the same skill level regardless of grade would be scheduled in the same course. For example, high achieving seventh graders would take pre-algebra along with ninth graders who are only now ready for this skill. (The existing curriculum included separate courses for pre-algebra at each grade level.)

## CONCLUSIONS

In this chapter we have tried to portray curriculum differentiation as a condition in schools which is value laden and resistant to quick and tidy rational change. We have focused primarily on how the issue of grouping and tracking came to the surface in one district and received a major focus of attention for three years. We have discussed the influence of critical events which affected the way in which the topic was explored by the key leadership group.

This portrayal of a specific, focused effort to change practice in the area of grouping and tracking suggests several conclusions. In our analysis of the data and in these conclusions, we have avoided imposing the categories of a specific discipline. Rather, we have tried to let the categories emerge from the data. Having described the data as clearly as possible, we looked at the events in their own terms:

*Change requires passionate and corporate leadership.* The commitment of key administrative leadership, the empowerment of a leadership group within the district, and the strategic use of a consultant created the conditions for change. Despite the presence of strong leadership, the process at its best is not subtle authoritarianism, but an interactive and iterative process of involvement at many levels of the organization.

*Change is organic and evolutionary.* The change of attitudes is slow, and the leadership's beliefs will always be ahead of the rest of the district staff. Pilot projects make the change visible and concrete to more members of the organization, create the climate for flexibility and experimentation, and legitimize mistakes.

*Solutions are contextual.* Solutions are best received when they emerge from the people in the context and are not packaged programs imposed from without. Finding appropriate solutions is complex because of their contextualized nature.

*Clarifying and consensing on beliefs is a prior condition for change.* The Program Council reached a point beyond which they could not proceed without consensing on a common set of values. The broader group of staff had clearly not reached the same level of consensus when surveyed, although the pilot projects and inservice helped to focus on areas of possible change and probable roadblocks. The ability of the district to set forth its beliefs in board policy sets the stage for specific implementation of new practices in grouping students for instruction.

*Change requires major curriculum and structural modifications.* Feedback from teachers and the results of the pilot projects suggest that grouping patterns cannot fully be changed unless structural and curricular changes occur. Teachers must teach differently and the organization of curriculum must be modified. It is not sufficient to move a few students more flexibly through the existing system. It is not sufficient to change the classification/placement criteria. Levels must be dropped, curriculum reorganized, and teachers retrained.

## NOTES

1. There is a long history of work based on this rational assumption, including Max Weber (1947), Talcott Parsons (1956), and more recently Bennis, Benne and Chin (1969), Callahan (1969), and Scott (1981).

2. Good summaries of this perspective appear in the work of: Patterson, Purkey, and Parker (1986); and Baldridge and Deal (1983).

3. Primary sources for a more detailed description of this perspective include Barr and Dreeben, with N. Wiratchai (1983) and Dreeben and Barr (1987).

4. See, for example, Oakes (1985).

## APPENDIX A: BOARD POLICY

5:19 Grouping for Instruction

A.  The Crete-Monee School District 201 – U Statement of Educational Philosophy (BEPM 5.1) provides the basis for decisions about grouping students for instruction: "All children can learn, and should be given opportunities to fulfill their highest potential."

B. To provide guidelines for instructional grouping, the Program Council surveyed the attitudes of the professional staff and examined current research to derive the following eight principles:

1. The goal of instruction for low achievers is to increase their mastery of skills, so they may achieve at higher levels.
2. Students functioning at basic levels need higher order skills as well as remediation.
3. Many low achieving students can learn higher order skills and concepts, with enough motivation, time, and quality instruction.
4. Low achievers and high achievers benefit from interacting during the day.
5. Minority children should be integrated with other students in academic classes.
6. High achievers need enrichment more than acceleration.
7. Many characteristics, in addition to academic ability, may be considered when grouping students.
8. Different subjects and grade levels may need various numbers and types of groups.

C. To promote the potentially positive effects of grouping for instruction, and to minimize the negative aspects, the Program Council will establish standardized criteria for grouping practices in Crete-Monee School District 201-U.

D. All recommendations by curriculum committees, administrators, and teachers for grouping will be submitted to the district Curriculum Office for approval. These recommendations must conform to the current board policy and grouping guidelines as established by Program Council.

Approved: June 20, 1988

## APPENDIX B: PROGRAM COUNCIL READING LIST

Bossert, Steven T. and Bruce G. Barnett, *Grouping for Instruction: A Catalogue of Arrangements*. San Francisco: Far West Laboratory for Educational Research and Development, January 1981.

Esposito, Dominick, "Homogeneous and Heterogeneous Ability Grouping: Principal Findings and Implications for Evaluating and Designing More Effective Educational Environments." *Review of Educational Research* 43 (2): pp. 163–179.

Good, Thomas L. "How Teachers' Expectations Affect Results." *American Education* 18 (December 1982): pp. 25–32.

Goodlad, John, "Access to Knowledge." Chap. in *A Place Called School*. New York: McGraw-Hill, 1981.

Jaeger, R. M. and J. C. Busch, "A Meta-Analytic Longitudinal Evaluation of the Effects of Ability Grouping on Student Achievement." Paper presented at the Annual Meeting of the American Educational Research Association, Chicago, April 1985.

Jongsma, Eugene, "Research Views: Grouping for Instruction." *The Reading Teacher* (May 1985): pp. 918–920.

Kulik, Chen-Lin C. and James A. Kulik, "Research Synthesis on Ability Grouping." *Educational Leadership* (May 1982): pp. 619–621.

Marsh, Herbert W., "Self-Concept, Social Comparison, and Ability Grouping: A Reply to Kulik and Kulik." *American Educational Research Journal* 21 (Winter 1984): pp. 799–806.

Milwaukee Public Schools, "Educational Interventions: Grouping and Differentiation," *The Milwaukee Teacher Expectation Project*. Milwaukee, WI: The Milwaukee Public Schools, no date.

Milwaukee Public Schools, "Examination of School Deficit Theory," *The Milwaukee Teacher Expectation Project*. Milwaukee, WI: The Milwaukee Public Schools, no date.

Murnane, Richard J., "Interpreting the Evidence on School Effectiveness." Working paper No. 830. New Haven, CT: Yale University, Institution for Social and Policy Studies, 1980: pp. 6–8.

Olsen, Kenneth, Untitled discussion paper on grouping students by ability, Wheaton, IL: School District #200, February 1984.

Purkey, Stuart C., Robert A. Ruder, and Fred M. Newmann, "U.S. High School Improvement Program: A Profile from the High School and Beyond Supplemental Survey." Madison: Wisconsin Center for Education Research, September n.d. 1985 (Revised).

Stallings, Jane, Unreferenced pages selected from an ERIC document regarding assignment of classes to teachers and assignment of students to classrooms.

Summers, A. A. and B. L. Wolfe, "Do Schools Make a Difference?" *American Economic Review* 67 (September 1977): pp. 646–647.

Summers, A. A. and B. L. Wolfe, "Which School Resources Help Learning? Efficiency an Equity in Philadelphia Public Schools." *Federal Reserve Bank of Philadelphia Business Review* (February 1975): pp. 17–18.

Veldman, D. J. and J. P. Sanford, "The Influence of Class Ability on Student Achievement and Classroom Behavior." *American Educational Research Journal* 21 (1984): pp. 629–644.

Wilson, Barry J. and Donald W. Schmitts, "What's New in Ability Grouping?" *Phi Delta Kappan* 59 (April 1988): pp. 535–536.

NANCY M. SANDERS[1]

Chapter 10

# *Organizational Meanings of Curriculum Differentiation Practices*

Within the frame of reference provided by the educational research literature, curriculum differentiation practices of tracking and grouping are conceptualized and studied as educational treatments. Most of the research in this area has been conducted within the traditional rational/evaluative paradigm, assessing academic and social effects of various differentiation strategies on students (similar to the search for effective teaching methods or optimal class size). The underlying model is inherently one of organizational rationality, in which practices are assumed to be designed in response to *student* characteristics to maximize achievement and post-secondary attainments.

Naturalistic and interpretive research studies have challenged the normative assumptions in the traditional research and reveal significant social and academic stratification effects of curriculum differentiation (cf. Rosenbaum 1976; Lightfoot 1983; Cusick 1983; Oakes 1985; Tye 1985; Sanders and Stone 1987) and widely varying practices and perceptions of practices. The traditional research paradigm has limited power to explain these findings or to explain the persistence of practices given the lack of evidence demonstrating educational benefits of curriculum differentiation.

In this chapter, I propose that curriculum differentiation practices resolve organizational problems in schools as well as providing educational treatments. The thesis is that separate from planned or accidental effects on <u>students</u>, activities associated with curriculum differentiation provide means of organizational control and important sources of institutional legitimacy for *schools*. Drawing on understandings from organizational sociology, curriculum differentiation practices can be interpreted in terms of their importance to schools as well as to students. Shifting the frame of reference from educational to organizational meanings provides a different set of contextual referents for understanding and interpreting curriculum differentiation activities.

The first section of the chapter describes a debate among teachers about their department's curriculum differentiation practices. The discussion illustrates the importance of local context for understanding the meanings these activities have for these teachers. Subsequent sections of the paper use organizational constructs such as bounded rationality and institutional legitimacy to interpret the teachers' discussion and related research on curriculum differentiation. The final section suggests that organizational interpretations of curriculum differentiation help to explain contradictions in the research literature.

The discussion and data are from comparative case studies of twenty-five high schools, which were conducted for a curriculum policy study in California (Sanders and Stone 1987).[2] The schools were selected to capture the demographic and achievement variations in California high schools. The schools studied range in size from fewer than 100 to nearly 4000 students. They represent all community types, various ethnic and socioeconomic compositions, and varied patterns of achievement distributions. Field workers, working in pairs, spent several days at each school interviewing administrators, counselors, and teachers in three academic departments (English, math, and science). The case reports consist of a set of short answer and open-ended responses to questions about the schools, curricular policies, and curricular practices.

The curriculum differentiation practices in these schools, in addition to being justified as educational treatments, were found to provide means for administrators and teachers to resolve organizational problems and to maintain public support for schools. Organizational problems for which tracking is a solution include limited educational technology for handling low-achieving or poorly motivated students, scheduling and logistics (e.g., fluctuations in enrollments), competition for rewards and status among those in schools, and the need for public support of schools (Sanders 1989).

## MANAGING ORGANIZATIONAL ISSUES THROUGH CURRICULUM DIFFERENTIATION — A LOCAL DEBATE

In the English department of one of the study schools, interviews and records of teachers' discussions about proposed changes in curricular structure indicate how these teachers perceive and negotiate a set of organizational problems. The English curriculum in this mid-sized suburban school consisted of a core sequence of required courses integrating basic skills and higher-order learning. A separate sequence was offered to gifted students, culminating in Advanced Placement courses.

The teachers perceived that this structure had worked effectively before a court-order desegregated the district. The school, which had been predominantly higher socioeconomic status, high achieving, and white, now included about one-third lower socioeconomic status, low achieving, Black students. Teachers felt that the students who were being bussed into the school were inadequately prepared for the existing core courses.

In response to the change in student characteristics, teachers initiated what were called Special Help sections with the basic content and goals of the regular ninth grade core course, but oriented toward students reading slightly below grade level. For ninth grade students reading below sixth grade level, there was a special Remedial Reading Laboratory intended to prepare students for the core course sequence. The focus in both lower tracks was on entering the regular level of the core courses after one or two years. A teacher estimated that 40% of the incoming freshman class read below ninth grade level, and after a year in the Special Help sections about half of those students entered the regular sections as sophomores.

Because most of the teachers had been in the department for a number of years, they shared some beliefs about the curricular structure, its purposes, and effects. They had debated the "perennial dilemma" about whether to continue heterogeneous grouping in regular classes or to establish distinct college-preparatory and lower-tracks, even before desegregation. They agreed on the necessity of separating the very lowest and the very highest achieving students into categories of remedial readers and gifted but maintained the importance of heterogeneous grouping for the majority of students.

The problem provoking this discussion was that higher socioeconomic status, primarily white parents increasingly insisted that their children be placed in the AP or gifted track. The teachers attributed this problem to parental perceptions that regular core courses were not as rigorous as they had been. Teachers felt that the consequent growth of the Gifted and Advanced Placement courses drew the better students out of the regular classes, contributing to the loss of confidence in the academic quality of the regular program. They were concerned about the corresponding decline in the level of work in the gifted track, since non-gifted students were now included.

One teacher proposed offering alternative pacing as a solution. High achieving ninth grade students would be given the opportunity to test out of English I (the first course in the core sequence) and skip to English II, rather than be placed in gifted classes (as was becoming the trend). The proposal also included organizing the regular core courses more tightly around the minimum competency requirements, rather than relegating competency skills and students needing such skills to a lower-track.

The expected result was that more students could directly enter the regular courses, integrating the regular track in the ninth grade. "Bored" (i.e., higher achieving) students would be encouraged to test out of the initial course, taking English II as freshmen and English III as sophomores, but not to take the gifted/AP sequence. Junior and senior year electives would be offered after English III and would be clearly identified as college-preparatory courses, designed solely to meet the needs of college bound students. The same students who tested out of the basic course would be expected to self-select into the college-preparatory electives as juniors and seniors.

We would, in effect, set up two alternative tracks through the core curriculum. One track would serve the college-able student who is nevertheless not gifted, who would enter at English II in the ninth grade. The other would serve the non-academic student who is nevertheless not handicapped or severely limited, who would enter at English I. We would set up these tracks without changing our curriculum except for one adaptation: we would so arrange the curriculum of English I, II, and III so that middle and lower range students can experience more success. We would, paradoxically, increase the academic rigor of our college-prep program by lowering the demands in the English I, II, III sequence. We can do this because the college-prep student would start the sequence at English II and after English III, would start (as a junior) two years of rigorous courses designed to prepare her/him for college.

To the parent of a college-able student who asks about the apparent dilution of the regular program, we could point to a clearly delineated college-preparatory program. To the parent of the average or low ability student, we could point out that this program restores more academic talent to the regular program (by, for example, bringing more students back to the program from the AP sequence). Whatever advantage that is gained by heterogeneous grouping would therefore not be lost, the only difference being that the heterogeneity is achieved by mixing academically talented students who are a grade level below their less capable classmates. The lower half of the class would have had a year's preparation in English I and a year's growth to compensate for the differences in ability.

This teacher believed that the alternative, "old fashioned tracking into academic and non-academic tracks, will not work." The department had tried it twice and each time eliminated it because the lower-track classes "became disciplinary nightmares and because we lacked a coherent idea about the lower-track program." She felt that those problems "were obviated, in part, during the electives/arena scheduling era" which was past and would not likely return.

Opponents of the plan had raised several objections. They questioned whether teachers in the eighth grade should be expected to teach the content of English I (so that higher achieving students could test out). One teacher asked whether a test could adequately capture the expected coverage in the course. She also felt that college-preparatory and gifted students have very special needs which cannot always be satisfied in heterogeneous classes. "They need, for example, to spend more time with research problems, with close reading, with critical thinking, with advanced and complicated forms of writing, with vocabulary." In her opinion, this type of coursework in heterogeneously grouped classes risked losing the lower achieving students.

Alternative proposals focused on how current practices were managed and described to the public. A teacher advocated investigating how many students in the AP sequence were not actually "gifted" (defined as above the 90th percentile on achievement tests) and whether students who did not maintain at least a B average were allowed to remain. To counter the erosion of confidence in the regular core curriculum, another teacher suggested that the teachers should strongly reaffirm "that the regular English sequence is a rich, challenging college-prep sequence for students reading at or above grade level and that the AP sequence is for gifted students as determined by test scores, not parent request." Finally, a teacher suggested placing more students who "cannot survive in regular English" in the Special Help sections. Her perception was that very little actual change would result, but that confidence in the curriculum would be restored.

## ORGANIZATIONAL FACTORS AND
## CURRICULUM DIFFERENTIATION

The immediate problem for discussion in this department was the increasing pressure from higher socioeconomic status, white parents to enroll their students in gifted classes — a sort of white flight within the school. The discussion helps to illustrate how organizational factors affect teachers' decisions about curriculum differentiation. The factors which can be identified as *organizational* are those associated with the problems of managing collective activities (such as logistics and working relationships), problems of technology (or work processes) to achieve the organization's goals, and problems of legitimacy or maintenance of public support for the organization. These factors as represented in the teachers' discussion are:

1. the *managerial and logistical* effects of separating students for different forms of instruction (e.g., racial segregation, behavior problems, unclear curricular focus in low tracks);

2. intrusion by parents into organizational activities, another *managerial* problem;

3. beliefs of individual teachers about students, curriculum, and teaching which affect *work activities and relationships;*

4. the changed achievement characteristics of students, which affect *technology* or the type of work to be performed;

5. the political effects of heterogeneous grouping eroding *local parental support* for the school; and

6. the broader set of institutional requirements (that high schools must provide college-preparatory and advanced placement courses and that students must meet minimum competency standards) affecting *public support* from local and state-level constituencies.

As illustrated in this discussion, teachers' decisions about curriculum differentiation are not simply about maximizing learning opportunities. But this discussion of curriculum planning is not irrational or without regard for student outcomes. The teachers are concerned about achievement and about the stratification effects of curriculum differentiation.[3] They negotiate various organizational constraints and factors facing them in deciding how to structure activities.

Reframing activities in organizational terms provides a different set of understandings and interpretations of curriculum differentiation. Instead of seeing tracking and grouping as rational, technical solutions to *educational* problems, we can also understand them from a larger, organizational perspective. The tasks of school are not only to provide activities oriented toward educational goals for students but also to keep order, maintain the physical plant, fulfill legal and financial requirements, manage delivery of curriculum by scheduling teachers and classrooms, and so on. The day-to-day organizational problems in schools that affect curriculum (and for which differentiation offers partial solutions) include the logistics of class scheduling, decisions about what is to be taught, and work arrangements assigning students and teachers to courses. While appearing to solve some of these problems, differentiation activities cause others, such as when the process of scheduling students and teachers into differentiated courses results in segregation and behavior problems.

### Curriculum Differentiation as a Technical Solution to Limits of Current Teaching Methods

Curriculum differentiation provides a solution to what are seen as problems of technology or the work of schools. Technology is not only computers and media. In organizational terms, teaching and curriculum are the technology of schools in the same sense that medical knowledge and treatments are the technology of medicine. They are the work or transformation processes of the field.

Goodlad (1984) and others have described the technology of teaching in high schools to be extremely consistent and limited, consisting mostly of lecture and drill. High school teachers use traditional whole class lecture methods and rely on curriculum differentiation as a way to vary content, pace, and expectations across classes or across groups within the same class (instead of changing their teaching approach, for example, by individualizing instruction).[4] Curriculum differentiation enables teachers to specialize and narrow the focus of instruction, similar to specialization in any profession. It defines their activities in ways that alleviate the problem of differences in the clients (or products)—in this case, the students.

Curriculum differentiation is a form of internal, structural differentiation that not only provides different educational treatments, it also organizes students, teachers, and courses into differentiated units. Structural differentiation is a common organizational feature, like departmentalization in schools and differentiated product lines or service units in firms. Structural differentiation is one solution to problems of technology; another is changing the technology itself (e.g., team teaching, cooperative learning).

Only one English teacher questioned the technological capacity to teach heterogeneously grouped classes (with the extreme ranges of achievement removed to gifted or remedial classes). This teacher thought that some students would be lost using the methods appropriate for the college-preparatory orientation of the classes; that is, that the same technology might not work for all the students. However, the primary issue in the department was not the technological capacities of teachers but rather restoring public confidence in the technology. They considered the effects of changing the achievement boundaries in each track but did not consider different technical approaches to the problem.

## Maintaining Stable Work Conditions Through Structures

In addition to achievement differences among students, another problem facing teachers in determining what and how to teach is environmental instability. The environments surrounding schools are highly unstable. Enrollment, attendance, funding, staffing, accountability measures, and expectations change continuously. Confronted with unpredictable environments, people in organizations turn to structural arrangements to obtain some certainty and control over their tasks. Given a narrow teaching technology and continually changing environments, teachers rely on curricular structures to provide stability in planning and conducting instruction.

The English teachers, faced with changes in student characteristics, sought to maintain stability of their work by keeping the core course structure but adding special sections for low achieving students. They attempted to stabilize the gifted track sequence through bureaucratic control over student selection (which was also proposed to control parental intrusion).

Cusick (1983) and Powell, Farrar and Cohen (1985), using the metaphor of *The Shopping Mall High School,* describe elective curricular structures in high schools as a means of keeping order and keeping students in school. They link elective structures to a marketplace model in which individual teachers create specialized courses to attract and retain students who can choose to be elsewhere. As described by the teachers here, elective tracking at one time might have provided a solution to problems of selection and segregation faced by the department, but this option is no longer seen as a viable alternative.

## Institutional Beliefs and Requirements for School Legitimacy

Public expectations about formal organizations (as opposed to, for example, informal collectivities or kinship groups), reflect conceptions captured in classical economic rationality as it is applied to an idealized type of organization, the manufacturing firm in a free market environment.[5] In this ideal type of organization, internal structures are expected to reflect the technological attributes of work and the pursuit of profits. For example, the assembly line production of automobiles or hamburgers reflects the available technology in each industry and organizational goals of efficiency and profit maximization. (As indicated above, curricular structure reflects the technologies of teaching and curriculum.)

Public beliefs about rationality extend to all types of organizations, from government bureaucracies to private industry. These beliefs emerge most clearly from criticism of organizations when they *fail* to fulfill our expectations about their functioning and goals (e.g., failure to deliver the mail on time or to produce cars that run). Rhetorical arguments about how schools should be organized to maximize achievement (measuring organizational production in terms of test scores) and the need for competition (a free market environment through choice) reflect the classical economic ideals of organizational rationality applied to schools.

However, organizations not only need profits, they need social and political support or legitimacy to survive, and legitimacy is crucial for non-profit and public organizations such as schools. As argued by Scott, "empirical research has convincingly demonstrated that many organizations cannot usefully be viewed as technical systems and that no organization is merely a technical system" (Scott 1983: 13). Maintaining legitimacy — the support and resources obtained by conforming to important social beliefs and values — is of fundamental concern in schools.

Beliefs about organizations like schools in modern societies are widely shared or *institutionalized*. Institutional beliefs and formal rules and regulations specify what organizations must do to maintain their legitimacy and support. Institutional beliefs about high schools include what schools and classrooms look like, what students and teachers do, how curriculum is organized, and more abstract conceptions of meritocratic and egalitarian educational treatment. Institutional rules and regulations include college entrance, accreditation, and accountability requirements.

A normative ideal that schools differentiate curriculum to provide training for specific student destinations is central to public beliefs about students and about comprehensive high schools. Conant (1959) popularized this ideal in *The American High School Today*, which espoused differentiating the curriculum within comprehensive high schools to provide for students taking college-preparatory, vocational, and general programs. Kliebard (1987) describes the historical importance of college entrance requirements, the social efficiency movement, and the rise of vocationalism for understanding current public expectations about curriculum differentiation in high schools.

Organizations like schools that are strongly dominated by institutional beliefs and rules—public bureaucracies and firms in regulated markets—have been termed "institutionalized organizations"[6] in the sociological research. The structures of such organizations reflect public expectations rather than purely rational planning in pursuit of organizational goals (i.e. achievement). Institutionalized organizations are frequently criticized for apparent inefficiency and irrationality — for *not* conforming to the free market model of rational organization (e.g., being loosely coupled). Meyer and Rowan explain that in organizations which depend on public support, incorporating institutional rules and social beliefs such as the three track system is necessary for organizational legitimacy and survival.

The effect of institutional beliefs and rules is to require schools to conform (or at least *appear to conform*) to expectations in order to maintain legitimacy and public support. These public displays of activities may be significantly different from actual behavior. School respondents sometimes openly describe the discrepancies between formal policies and day-to-day practices. The English department's teachers seemed very aware of the need to conform to public expectations, and, if necessary, to promote an image of increasing rigor while not making any significant changes in the curricular structure.

Informally, individuals use personal skills, beliefs, and sources of power to affect the structure of their work as, for example, when seniority enables teachers to garner more desirable classes and students. Powell, Farrar, and Cohen (1985) and Sizer (1984) describe the informal treaties and bargains which teachers negotiate to improve their work conditions and to increase job satisfaction. Because many of the rewards of teaching are intrinsic, teachers engage in informal activities to enhance the rewards which do not come formally from salaries or professional status.

Informal tracking activities described by Finley (1984) indicate the effect on the curricular structure when teachers prefer to teach high-achieving students. Teachers in one school promoted their courses in ways which screened out lower-achieving, lower aspiring students. Thus, they created informal ability groups within a formal system of elective courses. Counselors contributed to the systematic informal structuring of the curriculum by steering students into different courses according to ability distinctions: lower-achieving students were guided into the less demanding courses such as Current Fiction and higher-achieving students were guided into more demanding courses such as Shakespeare. The counselors' position was that they were concerned about students' success, and, knowing teachers' expectations in different courses, guided students into classes in which the students had the greatest likelihood of success (Finley 1984: 236).

Outwardly schools match their formal descriptions of activities to socially legitimized beliefs about schools (e.g., describing choice of tracks which offer college-preparatory and vocational curricula) to maintain legitimacy and support. Internally, strategies may deviate from the "official" portrayal, as in the example by Finley, when students are segregated by achievement or aspirations into courses with different content. The formal description provides legitimacy by adherence to social beliefs about comprehensive high schools. Descriptions of activities in naturalistic studies often capture the discrepancy between formal descriptions and informal activities of teachers and counselors.

The comments by the English teachers about the curriculum stress the importance of public or formal descriptions providing legitimacy. The teachers specifically address the way in which the curriculum is explained to parents, illustrating the importance of rationalized formal descriptions. They reaffirm rigor through evidence of test score criteria for track assignment without changing the curriculum, a formal change that does not affect activities. Informally, the teachers disagree in their views of students and courses — and probably in their actual teaching and course content as well.

### Bridging and Buffering Strategies to Protect Legitimacy

When schools do not or cannot fulfill public expectations and institutional requirements or when standard organizational arrangements come under public scrutiny (such as the perceived erosion of the core courses), organizational strategies are used to draw on external sources of support or to conceal problems. Particularly under variable, unpredictable conditions, with unreliable, limited technology, or with unclear or conflicting goals, people in organizations use what are called bridging and buffering strategies to increase stability and protect legitimacy.

Bridging strategies link parts of the organization to external sources of support and stability. For example, schools use ritual category names such as "College-Preparatory" for courses and tracks which may actually be quite different within and across schools (Hanson 1985). Formally, curriculum differentiation links schools to external sources of legitimacy by using institutionalized names and categories, such as the college-preparatory courses (for higher achieving students) and vocational or basic courses (for lower achievers). Schools avoid formally labeling such differentiations as "high achievement" and "low achievement" because to do so violates egalitarian norms.

Institutional categories of courses and students provide schools with stable organizing principles during uncertainty; for example, the college and university entrance requirements provide structure for the organization of the track called college-preparatory. This external source of structure can be maintained while other features of schools change, such as the student characteristics or public attitudes about content. Thus, traditional categories of curriculum differentiation provide two kinds of organizational benefits to schools: they provide symbolic evidence of adherence to social beliefs and rules and they provide stable organizing principles.

All of the schools studied by Sanders and Stone (1987) provided the appropriate institutional categories of courses even though each system was different. The English teachers described here were careful to adhere to institutional rules as a bridging strategy, protecting their curriculum differentiation practices while their course structure was significantly different from many of the other schools studied.

Buffering strategies include decoupling and concealing activities and structures. Cicourel and Kitsuse's (1963) classic study of counselors indicates how student placement in tracks is buffered from public inspection and challenge through decoupling and concealment. They found that professionalization of counseling conceals the placement process and allows it to be affected by the subjective judgments of individual counselors. The criteria used for placement are not explicitly linked to the placements or to evaluations of performance. Rosenbaum also noted that counselors exhibit a "recurrent pattern of vagueness and evasiveness" about tracks and tracking (Rosenbaum 1976: 117). Concealing and decoupling the placement processes protects schools from challenge and public scrutiny about curriculum differentiation practices.

Harvey (1984) describes how concealing information about tracking contributes to socioeconomic stratification. "Pupils differ in their knowledge of how present performance is linked with school organization characteristics such as curriculum grouping and subject choice" (1984: 62). He found their knowledge to be related to social class and expectations.

> Essentially the process centres on the capacity of the pupil to determine his location in the network of career pathways of the high school, to anticipate irreversible status passages before they occur and to have an awareness of the contingencies which influence movement to a desirable pathway beyond any choice point. This requires an open awareness context of the significance of school organisation factors such as curriculum placement and subject choice and the development of a personal identity which centres on the attainment of school success. (Harvey 1984: 64)

Harvey's findings illustrate the assumptions of rationality that are inherent in beliefs about student choice and curricular structures and how schools buffer themselves from exposure of their limited adherence to this ideal. The English teachers' proposal to formally portray courses as rigorous and to use bureaucratic rules to control enrollment in the gifted sections are also buffering strategies, protecting the teachers and the school from the parents' criticism and political influence.

## Social Beliefs and Organizational Realities

By exposing informal curricular structures (as different from normative expectations or formal descriptions), ethnographic studies challenge pervasive expectations and assumptions about schools as rational organizations and curriculum differentiation as a rationally planned, educative treatment. Teachers structure the curriculum to garner desirable students, as well as to promote achievement. Counselors provide ambiguous information, as well as assist students in making informed course choices. Students choose courses for a wide variety of reasons, only some of which are rational and well informed about post-secondary destinations.

Buffering and bridging activities conceal the actual activities necessary to function on a day-to-day basis from public inspection but provide an image of rationality. Describing curriculum differentiation practices and what goes on in schools is complicated by buffering and bridging activities used to avoid exposing the contradictions between formal, public appearances and informal, private behavior. When researchers fail to acknowledge the distinction between formal and informal behavior or fail to understand the organizational benefits which schools derive from bridging and buffering strategies, they do not adequately capture school phenomena such as curriculum differentiation.

> The history of schools has been misinterpreted as the emergence of organizations that coordinate the technical work of education — and schools have been frequently criticized for their failure to manage this work efficiently. From our point of view, this criticism is misplaced: educational organizations arose to bring the process of education under a socially standardized set of institutional categories, not necessarily to rationalize the "production processes" involved in carrying out this work. (Meyer, Scott, and Deal 1983: 46)

The types of activities described here — using ritual categories, decoupling activities from formal descriptions, and concealing activities from public inspection — are judged to be deceptive and disfunctional from a rational/analytic paradigm. Recast within the broader framework of understandings about organizations, these same activities take on different meanings. They raise questions about the unstable conditions and contradictory expectations of schools in our society that lead to widespread use of protective organizational strategies.

## FORMAL AND INFORMAL DESCRIPTIONS OF PRACTICES

Conflicting descriptions of curriculum differentiation practices in the schools studied in Sanders and Stone (1987) mirror those found in other naturalistic research. We discovered in pilot interviews that tracking is a pejorative term in California schools. Most of the administrators and teachers interviewed objected to labeling curriculum differentiation strategies as "tracking." Instead, they often attributed academic and social stratification to "self-tracking" by students. Their explanations indicated a perception that tracking is an illegal or inequitable practice. Although publicly accepted in the 1950s and 1960s, subsequent legal challenges apparently resulted in schools buffering their curriculum differentiation practices from public view by denying tracking and decentralizing structures to the department level.

Therefore, the formal, publicly "correct" response about tracking is that schools do not "track" students. In five of the schools, there are formal policies *against* tracking. In the other high schools, administrators described curricula that were differentiated although they did not usually call the practices tracking. In the schools with formal policies against tracking and in some others, we found explicit attempts to mitigate stratification effects of curriculum differentiations through heterogeneous grouping or elective systems.

Curriculum documents and maps, course catalogues, enrollments, and teachers' descriptions of courses and sequences provided indicators to develop descriptions of the operational curriculum differentiations in each school (as contrasted with participant reports of informal activities). All of the schools operationally differentiated courses in the three academic departments studied (English, math, and science), regardless of their formal description of tracking practices. Each of the schools provided the two institutionally required categories of students and courses in California, college-preparatory (including advanced placement) and remedial (for minimum competencies). At the same time, within the consistent adherence to broad institutional parameters, the total number of differentiations, kinds of courses, structural relationships among courses, student assignment criteria, and proportion of students in each track varied across schools and within schools across departments. Respondents in each school described theirs as "unique" in explaining local differences in courses and sequences of courses which make up the tracking systems.

> Each school had its own system for differentiating the curriculum, and many labels were used for the same organizational phenomenon. Some schools assigned alphabetic or numeric codes to the courses within a track,

others distinguished tracks on the basis of students' intended postgraduate destination, and a few schools characterized the track by the content of the track itself. (Sanders and Stone 1987: 30)

Each school used relative achievement as the primary criterion for assignment to operational tracks. Students' achievement status vis-à-vis the distribution of achievement in a school determined their course and track placements. Seventeen of the schools offer the highest achieving students courses that are variously labeled Honors, Advanced Placement, Gifted or Gifted and Talented, or, less informatively, courses designated only by number or letter. The courses offered at the next-highest achievement level — Academic, College bound, and so forth — fulfill selective college entrance requirements, such as those of the University of California and elite private colleges. The courses for middle-achievement level students (e.g., Non-academic, College Interest, Community College) fulfill graduation requirements and also enable students to attend junior and community colleges. Finally, the courses for the lowest-achieving students (e.g., Remedial, Remedial Transition, Developmental, Basic) are usually oriented toward the minimum competency tests.

In this group of twenty-five schools, the congruence between the schools' formal and operational versions of tracking was low. The number and kind of formally described and operational tracks were the same in only four of the schools. There was a significant difference between descriptions of the formal tracking practices and the activities reflected in internal documents and descriptions.[9] The discrepancies between formal and operational practices underscores the need for treatment specification in research on effects. Use of formal descriptions of tracks in research may have little or no connection to the actual experiences of students.

### Characterizing Different Approaches to Curriculum Differentiation

There appear to be three basic approaches to curriculum differentiation in these schools, which I have characterized as highways, byways, and freeways, fitting the California context (Sanders 1989). The highways are linear systems and most closely fit the popular and research conceptions of tracking. Students set out on different course sequences or tracks and move in distinctly different directions—toward elite universities, regular colleges, junior or community colleges, vocational training, or to unknown or unnamed destinations.

Once placed on a track or highway according to their achievement characteristics, students can motor along successfully to the announced destination or exit from the track. They can also switch to a different track, but only to one that is "lower," that is, one with a less prestigious destination. Students usually cannot move to a "higher" track because to do so requires re-entering at the initial starting gate, and there are logistical difficulties and sanctions against doing so.

The byways are elective systems as captured in the shopping mall metaphor of Powell, Farrar, and Cohen (1985). Students select a path through the array of (seemingly) independent courses offered. They meander here and there through the countryside, changing direction quite abruptly at each junction to a new course. Some junctions have signs, others do not. Some students who know their desired destinations (or who have parents who know) use the elusive road signs to plan their courses. They also obtain directions individually from various sources (siblings, parents, counselors, teachers). Other students, called the "unspecial" by Powell, Farrar, and Cohen (1985), who have no special attributes to signal their destinations (such as extremely high achievement or severe learning disabilities) simply wander through the countryside enjoying the journey with their peers, seemingly oblivious to the importance of their course decisions for their futures.

The freeways are interrelated systems, with cloverleaf interchanges, clearly marked on-ramps and exits, signs saying "WRONG WAY," and bold markings on road maps. They represent a technologically more complex type of curricular structure. Although students who start in the fast lane and who do not attempt to exit or change lanes will make the most progress and reach the farthest destinations, interrelated systems do allow for changes of speed and occasional rerouting (getting off, circling around, and getting back on) within the limits of the time available. These systems are designed to propel students who enter slowly and without clear goals along paths which keep their future options open. All students are headed the same direction; the emphasis is on high status or college-preparatory content rather than on differentiated content and destinations. The English department's core course sequence with Special Help sections is a freeway model, intended to move low achieving students into the main flow of traffic in core courses. The structure and technology are more complex than linear and elective systems with side tracks of remedial courses feeding into the core and with heterogeneous grouping in most classes.

Few schools in the study were found to follow one approach exclusively. Most used combinations, with emphasis on one strategy or another. Approaches also varied within schools by department, with math most often using the linear approach while English and science more often offered courses as electives after assigning students to achievement levels.[10] Schools with highway (linear) or byway (elective) systems were found to be significantly different in size from schools with freeway (interrelated) systems. Linear and elective systems are found in large (over 2000 students) or very small (under 400 students) schools. The interrelated approach is found only in schools between 400 and 2000 students, indicating that size is a limiting factor for tracking approach.

Schools using different approaches also vary significantly in terms of student characteristics of achievement and socioeconomic status (which are highly correlated). Schools using interrelated systems have, on average, higher levels of achievement and socioeconomic status than those using elective or linear approaches.

According to participants' explanations of local practices, interrelated systems are more difficult to plan and carry out. Apparently, coordination, communication, and scheduling problems of very large or very small schools preclude the use of complex strategies. Teachers in schools with very low socioeconomic status students and low achievement levels report struggling with overwhelming problems and few resources to provide an elaborate or complex curriculum. This is exemplified by the English department's difficulty in adapting a complex curricular structure to the technological problems resulting from having a large proportion of low-achieving students who appear to need remedial instruction.

Finally, environmental stability is important in organizing the curriculum. The schools with interrelated or freeway systems tended to have more stable environments in terms of enrollments, personnel, local politics, and funding. Organizational instability such as funding cuts or enrollment changes affects staffing and curricular planning. When positions are cut, teachers frequently end up teaching outside their main preparation area. Teachers with the appropriate credentials in each area choose or are assigned to teach higher-achieving students and more advanced level courses. Lower level courses are planned around standard content and materials to make it possible for itinerant teachers to handle them. When students are highly transient, courses are segmented into repetitive units and placement is routinized to handle the volume of incoming students.

Conditions of organizational stability, higher overall achievement, and manageable size appear to provide the context in which teachers can focus on curriculum and develop more complex, interrelated course structures. When problems of achievement and stability are not overwhelming, teachers can develop strategies intended to reduce the stratification effects of differentiation. Courses can be coupled across achievement levels to promote access and mobility. However, even teachers in the more stable, high-achieving schools studied complained that institutional requirements and their communities did not support their efforts to create and maintain complex curricular structures.

Although these three operational tracking strategies have been contrasted in terms of their overall structure, there is no evidence about how they differentially affect *students* in terms of achievement and equity. The data from these schools cast doubt on the meaningfulness of assessing the effects of tracking as a unitary phenomenon across schools. A more appropriate approach for the research might be about the effects of different strategies on students.

## ORGANIZATIONAL PERSPECTIVES ON PROBLEMS IN THE RESEARCH ON TRACKING

Using the organizational constructs described here and reframing curriculum differentiation as an organizational feature illuminates three fundamental problems in the tracking research. These problems are:

— First, conceptions of tracking differ between definitions used in traditional research and descriptions of practices from naturalistic studies (e.g., Lightfoot 1983, Oakes 1985, Tye 1985, Sanders and Stone 1987);

—Second, descriptions of practices sometimes differ between researchers and respondents and even among respondents in the same settings (e.g., Rosenbaum 1976, Cusick 1983, Oakes 1985, Tye 1985, Sanders and Stone 1987, Sanders 1989); and

—Third, practices vary so greatly across settings in terms of numbers and kinds of tracks, criteria for selection, and content that aggregating data and drawing conclusions about the practice of tracking are highly problematic (Oakes 1985, Gamoran and Berends 1987, Hanson 1985, Sanders and Stone 1987, Sanders 1989).

Oakes explains that "tracking is a complex phenomenon in schools and, while an integral part of the organizational structure at most schools, it is obscured by a variety of factors" (Oakes 1981b). In an analysis of the data from the same schools studied by Oakes, Tye (1985) attributes contradictions in descriptions of practices in schools to the "multiple realities" within schools. However, neither Oakes nor Tye explain why tracking is obscured or why multiple realities about tracking occur. In a recent review of the literature, Gamoran and Berends (1987) emphasize the methodological differences in tracking studies. They attribute the difficulty of synthesizing research findings in the literature to the different approaches taken in survey and ethnographic studies.

> Dissimilar findings result from differences in the basic issues addressed as well as from the usual differences between survey and ethnographic methods of data collection and analysis. (Gamoran and Berends 1987: 415)

The preceding descriptions of the teachers' discussion, organizational understandings, and comparative practices suggest alternative explanations for the problems in the literature. In the first instance, the contradictions between research definitions and descriptions of practice reflect researchers' failure to acknowledge the difference between normative beliefs about tracking (reflected in Conant's three track system) and organizational realities in schools. Second, the contradictory descriptions of tracking within schools derive from the distinction between formal and informal activities in organizations and are compounded by buffering and bridging strategies used to conceal controversial activities like tracking. Third, the variation in tracking practices across schools appears to be related to organizational factors such as school size, student composition, and environmental stability.

### Conflicting Definitions in the Research: The Conflict Between Normative and Descriptive Conceptions of Tracking

Survey research frequently utilizes large data bases such as High School and Beyond (e.g., Peng 1981) to investigate tracking effects. Tracking is defined to be the provision of different curriculum programs organized around students' post-secondary destinations. The categories used in survey research (college-preparatory, general and vocational tracks) represent the social belief or normative perspective on tracking rather than descriptions of activities.

The conception of tracking popularized by Conant (1959) is explicitly rational (or rationalized) in terms of post-secondary destinations and this conception has dominated traditional research on high school curriculum differentiation practices. However, naturalistic research describes a mixture of achievement and post-secondary destination groupings in the high schools studied (Rosenbaum 1976, Cusick 1983, Oakes 1985, Sanders and Stone 1987, Sanders 1989). As described earlier, ability or achievement differences undergird differentiation practices in high schools, allocating students across the normative and rationalized structure of post-secondary destination programs.

Research definitions, although inaccurate descriptions of practice, reflect the importance and pervasiveness of the normative conception.

Oakes (1981a, p. 1) defines tracking to be "the process of identifying and grouping together school children who appear to have similar learning aptitudes or academic accomplishments for the purpose of providing them a differentiated course of instruction." Such definitions reinforce the image that tracking is a rationally planned, technically based, primarily *educative* strategy while naturalistic studies challenge this hegemony.

### Contradictory Descriptions of Tracking within Schools: Strategies for Maintaining Institutional Legitimacy

In addition to the differences between normative conceptions of tracking and descriptions of practices, formal and informal descriptions of practices by those in schools have been found to conflict. Rosenbaum's (1976) study of one socially homogeneous working-class high school found that the curriculum policy provided three curricular distinctions: college, business, and general tracks (the normative ideal of the comprehensive high school). However, according to his analysis of school records, there were actually five differentiated curricula: upper-and-lower college, business, and upper-and-lower-general tracks.

Cusick (1983) found that tracking was formally prohibited in three schools, but informally practiced so that better students took one set of classes while the poorer students took another set. He decided that the courses were divided into levels of ability rather than three distinct tracks. Similarly, many principals in our study of California high schools (Sanders and Stone 1987) said that their schools did not track students. However, in all of the schools studied, curriculum differentiation policies and practices resulted in academic stratifications (although these varied considerably across schools).

Organizational explanations for discrepant accounts of tracking include decoupling formal and informal descriptions of structure and activities, bridging practices to institutional beliefs using ritual categories, and buffering practice from public exposure. Each of these contributes to confusion about tracking while protecting schools from the political problems that might result from public attention to actual activities.

### Variation in Practices Across Schools

In addition to the variations in structures and approaches described above, Oakes (1985) found not three destinations but different numbers and kinds of tracks across thirteen high schools. One school had six distinct tracks, three oriented toward college preparation, one oriented toward preparation for entry-level positions in business and marketing, and two general programs that, in the words of a guidance counselor, 'do not necessarily prepare students for college.' (Oakes 1985: 47)

Another school offered either an academic or vocational curriculum, with students in the academic curriculum separated into ability tracks. Five schools had separate vocational and academic programs, with ability tracking within the academic program. The remaining eight used ability or achievement level tracking exclusively. (Rosenbaum (1976) described five ability based operational tracks in one high school.)

In general, organizational structures develop in response to technological factors, logistical and managerial problems, political contexts, and so on. The variation in curriculum differentiation practices conflicts with researchers' attempts to assess the effects of tracking and grouping practices on students aggregated across schools. A more appropriate research approach might investigate the range of practices, the associated organizational factors, and the effects of various approaches on students.


## SUMMARY

While curriculum differentiation is usually interpreted as a rationally planned, educational treatment, schools face organizational problems for which it becomes a potential solution. As reframed here, curriculum differentiation serves organizational needs in schools separate from a rationalized conception as an educational treatment. Therefore, we can understand and interpret curriculum differentiation practices not only in terms of their impact on students but also for the benefits they provide to teachers, to administrators, and to schools for managing and controlling activities and securing and maintaining public support.

The teachers' discussion described here brings the organizational factors affecting curriculum differentiation to life: technological problems (the different achievement levels of students and limited teaching methods); unstable working conditions (changes in students); political intrusion of parents into activities; and conflicts between institutional beliefs and requirements (e.g., desegregation and the college entrance and minimum competency requirements). In response to these factors, teachers decouple formal and informal structures, describe formal structures which maintain legitimacy but do not match activities, and develop informal structures which satisfy internal needs for control of work conditions and match individual teacher beliefs about students. The discussion illustrates how teachers use curriculum differentiation to resolve organizational problems, such as how to structure stable working conditions in a school buffeted by changes. For these teachers, curriculum differentiation is not only an educational treatment, designed to increase achievement and post-secondary attainments, but also a means of ordering their work, responding to political pressure, and maintaining legitimacy.

The research literature on tracking reflects the rational-evaluative perspective, confusing normative ideals with actual practice. Schools use buffering and bridging strategies to protect public support, and researchers have not acknowledged the reasons for conflicting and confusing descriptions of practices. Further, the research literature ignores significant differences across tracking systems in efforts to aggregate tracking effects. More appropriate questions for the research might be: Why do schools track? Why do curriculum differentiation structures vary across schools? And what are the effects of *different approaches* to the problems for which curriculum differentiation is a solution?

## NOTES

1. I wish to acknowledge helpful comments on earlier drafts of this paper provided by the editors, Reba Page and Linda Valli, and by my UCD colleagues Michael Murphy and Lance Wright. I also thank Dean Phil DiStephano and the faculty at the University of Colorado at Boulder for conversations and hospitality during my initial thinking about these issues.

2. The study, commissioned by the California State Department of Education, provided information to policy makers considering state level changes in secondary curricula, especially statewide graduation requirements.

A policy report about the findings (Sanders and Stone, 1987) primarily responds to the question, what courses do students take in high school—and why? The analysis focuses on curriculum differentiation strategies and the differential effects of curriculum structure on students. Students who enter high school at relatively higher achievement levels have access to and tend to take more academic courses (and more sequentially planned courses with higher expectations), increasing the likelihood that their achievement will increase. Relatively lower achieving students have access to and take fewer academic courses (and fewer sequentially planned courses with lower expectations), suggesting that the achievement gap between low and high achieving students can be predicted to increase throughout high school. These findings are consistent with Goodlad (1984) and Oakes (1985) about track differences.

3. Sorensen and Hallinan (1984) also found that teachers do not organize groups on the basis of race, but that race is an organizational factor in classrooms.

The main conclusion of our analysis is that there appears to be no direct individual level effect of race on ability-group assignments, but that race influences the formation of ability groups . . . Race, in sum, affects the way teachers organize instructional groupings and the criteria they use. We have not found evidence that race overtly became a criterion for the assignment to ability groups. (Sorensen and Hallinan 1984: 102)

4. See Metz (1986) about the effects of teaching technology on activities in magnet schools.

5. References to schools as organizations often refer to the "factory model" of schooling, a pejorative connotation. This focuses on a narrow production analogy rather than understanding structural and environmental factors important in research on formal organizations.

6. Meyer, Scott, and Deal (1980), Meyer and Rowan (1983), Meyer and Scott (1983).

7. Differentiations in three academic departments (English, math, and science), not including Special Education, Compensatory Education, or other targeted programs.

8. Federal policies, such as P.L.94–142, have not been included in this discussion. These requirements tend to be handled in special programs outside the academic departments studied here.

9. The mean number of formally described tracks across the schools was 3.2 (minimum two, maximum five) while the mean number of informal, operational differentiations was four (minimum three, maximum five).

10. These approaches vary within schools by department, that is, each subject reflects differences in beliefs and traditions about content and sequence and differences in institutional requirements. Graduation and college requirements in English are greater than in math or science, resulting in typically longer sequences planned in English. Higher education requirements also strongly affect the structure, for example, in math and science departments which offer the traditional Algebra-Geometry-Algebra 2 and Biology-Chemistry-Physics sequences. Math is more consistently tightly coupled with regard to course prerequisites and content than English or science.

REBA PAGE AND LINDA VALLI

Chapter 11

# Curriculum Differentiation: A Conclusion

As editors, we have spent more than a few hours with each of the chapters in this volume. Quite apart from our strictly editorial responsibilities, however, they have engaged us, compelling us into long conversations about curriculum practices, teachers' and students' lives, metaphors of schooling, and the relationship between curricular and social differentiation. Our cross-coast dialogues extended as well into broad discussions with each of the contributors. At this closing, because of the richness of our experiences with this volume, we assert our editorial prerogatives one last time to engage readers in an afterword about some of the directions in which we see the volume and its individual chapters pointing. We assume readers will not let it be the final word.

## CURRICULUM DIFFERENTIATION: A TOPIC DESERVING SUSTAINED DEBATE

As we indicated in the introduction, we began thinking about this collection in light of the tracking debate that the various national reports on the American high school inadvertently regenerated. Those reports took the short step from considering secondary institutions to noticing their proliferating curriculum, and from there to noticing curriculum's differential allocation among groups of students and (with less frequency) kinds of schools. We applaud the renewal of a debate which was muted in the seventies by back-to-basics, minimum competencies, and a retreat from the notion that schools and school knowledge make a difference. However, as we also noted in the introduction, we worry about the debate's premature closure. Like those of the past, present discussions of curriculum differentiation are dominated by simplistic, doctrinaire, either/or claims that the practice should (or should not) be continued. Critics and proponents alike are adamant in their positions, with opposed camps glossing over the persistently contradictory research corpus and conflicting perspectives.

This book contributes to the debate by demonstrating the importance of sustaining rather than settling it. It posits curriculum differentiation as a provisional, recursive, interactive process of negotiation, rather than a unilateral, final, tidy solution. Theorists may find propositions for debate eminently sensible since, as the studies in this volume suggest, the usual formulaic characterizations of tracking are inadequate. However, superintendents, teachers, or policy officials may find sustained debate a dubious suggestion since, after all, they cannot simply sit around and philosophize but must act. Nevertheless, these studies address and recast this important point. They document that talk about tracking—explicit and implicit, in lessons, in faculty lounges, and in district, state, and national documents, not to mention research reports—is, in a fundamental sense, constitutive of curriculum differentiation. And, they indicate that where diverse perspectives and negotiation are unacknowledged, unintended consequences result. To paraphrase Maxine Greene (1985), the most serious consequence of forestalled debate is that curriculum and schooling cease to be public institutions: they fail to center the distinctive, public speech and hearing of individuals through which all may come in touch with a rich, common humanity and, thereby, each with his or her own uniqueness.

Differentiation's debate is also important because the practice is extensively implemented in American secondary schools but with ambiguous processes and uncertain effect. For example, the studies in this volume support the national reports' documentation that the practice has not disappeared from schools, even though tracking was formally abolished in many districts in the 1960s. Indeed, because the studies delineate differentiation's multifaceted forms, they suggest that the practice is even more pervasive than surveys, typically of ability grouping or tracking, indicate. Less frequently counted manifestations include differently structured grouping in the private and public sectors; tracking by choice; teen pregnancy programs (and many other "special" programs); skills-based, traditionally liberal, and "relevant" subject matter; differentiated instruction with "parallel" topics; locally-responsive curricula from the persumably common, standardized, American high school. By making visible differentiation's many guises, the collection documents schools' deep attachment to differentiation and challenges the alluringly simple choice: either differentiated or common curricula. For example, would critics of tracking argue as vigorously for the repeal of the differentiated curricula we name special, gifted, and bilingual education?

At the same time that sustained debate clarifies schools' attachment to differentiation, it may also unveil institutions' equally deep but often overlooked concern for social integration. As the studies in this collection suggest, U.S. schools must not discriminate, even as they are compelled to differentiate. Accordingly, in curriculum differentiation schools confront a paradox, in which they attempt to provide *both* for equal educational opportunity for all as well as for the individual education of each.

Yet this double aspect of curriculum differentiation is lost in the conventional characterization which poses the practice dualistically: schools' purposes in curriculum differentiation are *either* personal and individualized *or* social and communitarian. In this view, differentiation is unambiguous, comparisons of various grouping patterns will yield robust results, and policy options should be straightforward. However, such a view is contradicted by the anomalous research corpus. Nor can a dualistic formulation account for the persistent contradictions in the research.

By contrast, this volume delineates paradox as at the heart of curriculum differentiation. Moreover, it suggests that curriculum differentiation's ambiguities translate a fundamentally ambivalent American culture, articulated around equally cherished but contradictory precepts of individualism and community (Bellah et al. 1985; Kammen 1977; Merelman 1984; Varenne 1977). Thus, US schools (like US culture) cannot choose either an individualized or a common curriculum (or polity) because selection of one option would contravene the seriousness with which the other is regarded. Conceptualizing curricular and social differentiation as intertwined, endemically tense processes makes understandable the confusions that surround the topic: we expect that its practice will be variable and muddled-appearing, its debate vehement and enduring, and its effects mixed and even contradictory.

Hanson demonstrates in Chapter 4 just how the double imperative drives one district's confused, confusing oscillations. Two of the district's high schools offer able students college-preparatory classes. However, as Hanson details, the high-track content is not identically "high-status," but is different at each school. Indeed, closer inspection reveals surprising inversions: the middle-class, suburban students are presented the routinized lessons often associated with lower-track placement or impoverished schools and, equally surprising, the urban students receive a liberal-like, discussion-based curriculum. Yet, in a still further twist, although the suburban curriculum does not engage students meaningfully, it does provide for their success on the Scholastic Achievement Test and thereby facilitates their entry into college.

Garnering such multilayered data, the studies in this volume challenge the adequacy of a theoretical formulation of curriculum differentiation as a neutral, solely scholastic technique of matching children's skills, tasks, and achievement test scores. They also throw in question the notion that the school order corresponds mechanically to a social order that is clearly either open or irredeemably inequitable. Instead, they show that curriculum differentiation is indeed always contextualized rather than neutral, but that context's influence is not so readily predictable as traditional or revisionist social theory would suggest. For example, like Hanson but with a wider lens, Hemmings and Metz (chapter 5) specify the interactive, oblique impact of national and community norms as well as of students' perspectives and abilities on teachers' designations of appropriate classroom knowledge. In their schools, not everyone sees college-preparatory coursework as high-status, desirable, or pedagogically appropriate, despite the pronouncements of the experts. Moreover, complying with "high" curricular standards for all had serious unintended consequences: students at imperiled Grant High School did indeed proceed through a syllabus that included algebra, but the cost of such study was that inadequately prepared students failed to improve fundamental math skills and may have been alienated from school knowledge they might well perceive as arcane.

Thus, in contrast to decontextualized or deterministic theories, the studies in this volume offer a reconceptualization. Curriculum differentiation is a sociocultural and political as well as an academic process; it involves tacit as well as conscious choices; creativity as well as pattern marks teachers' and students' definitions of each other's roles and of school knowledge in particular, intricately connected, classroom, school, and community contexts. In short, curriculum differentiation is a resource. School participants *use* it in ways that are sensible (albeit not inevitably nor necessarily justly) given their situations. Its use frustrates algorithmic description because people in diverse school-communities can and do draw on the multifaceted resources of the pluralistic culture to create a wide variety of amalgamations of individualism and community.

The studies in this volume detail rather than average out or control for local variations in tracking's meaning so that we can begin to account for both positive and negative enactments. By specifying the processes and contexts of meaning's construction, they explicate tracking as what we make it, not what it, in some mechanical or necessary fashion, makes us. For instance, Valli's description of Central Catholic (chapter 3) shows us the circumstances in which a school constructs curriculum differentiation positively: academically and socially disadvantaged students "try" because they perceive the seven differentiated levels of curriculum and teachers' strictness as keeping track of them, rather than as keeping them in track. By contrast, the construction of curriculum differentiation that Page describes in one of Maplehurst's public high schools (chapter 2) is fundamentally ambiguous: teachers direct lessons in which they expect lower-track students to "try" but also to fail, to care about school knowledge but also to disdain it, to engage but also to passively comply. As a result, students, like their teachers, both engage and disengage in an uncertain performance.

Such studies — closely described and carefully conceptualized analyses of school participants' meanings and actions — have implications for practitioners and policy-makers as well as theorists. We hasten to add, however, that the implications are not statistical. These studies consider only a small number of schools and cannot be tallied to generalize that tracking "works" (or does not "work"). Instead, each chapter provides a detailed cultural analysis of a particular case. With one case in hand, readers can meaningfully compare differentiation's complexities and contradictions in other settings, whether those of other case studies or those in which readers live. In other words, the studies provide no directives, only clarified models. Appropriate action is the determination of school personnel who reflect on their particular situations, using such data and concepts from research as are intellectually, analogically apt.

What these studies provide, then, are careful probes of how, not whether, curriculum differentiation "works." Because they examine the "black box" of real schools and classrooms which statistical surveys and controlled experiments typically reduce or ignore, they recast seemingly self-evident correlations, say between track placement and ethnicity. As Goldstein shows us (chapter 7), Hmong students choose programs for reasons unfathomed by teachers or policy-makers. Similarly, Sanders (chapter 10) suggests that organizations track for their own survival, quite apart from considerations of pedagogy. Furthermore, these studies argue that only by knowing the very specific ways in which tracking "works" can its practice or policy be effectively modified. For example, changing Ashmont's bilingual program to a mainstreamed program would not attract more Hmong students. Nor would abolishing tracking remove the organizational imperatives to differentiate. Indeed, as Anderson and Barr document in chapter 9, tracking policies fulfill multiple political agendas. Crete-Monee teachers, some of whom remained adamant about the advantages of tracking, may not have been simply stick-in-the-mud pedagogues: from the teachers' perspectives, the district office's motives to de-track were suspect, with the innovation seen principally as a means to increase class size rather than to promote equity. One can well imagine the strange ways in which dictates to de-track might come to life in such teachers' classes.

## CURRICULUM DIFFERENTIATION: SOME PERENNIAL ISSUES

Taken as a whole, these studies also point to recurrent issues that bear considered reflection. The bases for grouping students are consistently problematic: pregnancy, academic ability, behavior, social class, future destination? Also problematic are both the explicit and unconscious modes of curricular and instructional events and their unintended, frequently negative effects. For example, teachers of academically unsuccessful students are often counseled to provide "relevant" lessons or lessons "at the student's level." But such lessons may work to fulfill prophecies of who students are by maintaining rather than enhancing the knowledge students bring to school. Equally perplexing is the relationship between curricular and social differentiation: is the relationship transformative, transmissive, or translational? That is, is curriculum differentiation so powerful that it can promote equal educational opportunity and transform the social order? Or, is the curricular order so weak that it simply replicates, or transmits, the social order? Or, using the third metaphor, does curriculum differentiation have some limited autonomy, so that it can mediate, or translate, between the more stable text of society and those idiosyncratic versions that individuals construct in their face-to-face interactions?

Furthermore, because the studies in this collection look inside schools, they identify not only perennial issues but new ones whose importance convention may lead us to overlook. For example, three of the studies (Goldstein's, Lesko's, and Page's) consider gender's interaction with curriculum differentiation. Yet practitioners, policy-makers, and theorists have paid scant attention to the topic, perhaps because girls are underrepresented in lower-track classes, because race and social class are deemed more predominant structuring principles, or because schools are generally considered less structured by gender than other social institutions.

Overall, the volume also documents the crucial importance of the meanings and actions of school participants, even as they are rather routinely silenced. Its chapters capture the words with which people talk about curriculum differentiation. As we noted above, participants' words serve not to verify the accuracy of researchers' interpretations, nor are they included simply because they vivify abstract concepts or bare-bone statistics. Rather, they are the stuff out of which differentiation is constructed. As people speak and listen, they understand how and what differentiation means and is. Yet, as the volume describes, teachers rarely debate tracking among themselves or with students and policy-makers rarely consult either of the groups for whom tracking is most significant. In the face of such silence, this volume contributes concretely to sustained debate by making noteworthy some of the elements of what can be called the vocabulary and grammar of the language of education.

Some of the language of education that these chapters record consists of powerful, theory-like metaphors with which to view schooling. Lesko's article (chapter 6), for example, plays with the evocative metaphor of schooling as like redemption. As Lesko points out, the word connotes a broad, if loose, constellation of ideas which center on a notion of exchange. Seen through such a lens, curriculum and schooling are not autonomous practices of the ivory tower but are contextualized. For instance, the metaphor connects processes at Bright Prospects School to economic processes: as in a pawn shop, the women in the school redeem past pleasures in present pledges for future rewards. It also connects schooling with religion, another social institution, as when participants speak of the pregnant women's "salvation" through the high school equivalency program. The connections spill over further into psychiatry (perhaps the modern era's religion) when the teachers present students a "therapeutic" curriculum. Thus, the metaphor of redemption is a key to the meaning system, or ethos, that makes Bright Prospects a particular kind of school and its practices meaningful for participants. It signals the relationships among internal school domains as well as the school's relationship to external domains.

For readers, metaphors such as redemption furnish a means to compare and accumulate interpretive studies as well as to analyze individual cases. For example, Lesko's metaphor resonates with Brother Michael's discussion of the good leader/good follower at Central Catholic. It contrasts with the stark legalisms of public school tracking procedures in Camarena's survey (chapter 8). It suggests the trade-offs that teachers in Hemmings and Metz's schools make in the face of classroom, school-community, and national imperatives.

Moreover, although Lesko herself does not frame Bright Prospects as part of the recent debate about character education, the redemption metaphor provides the possibility for such a culturally analytic "exchange."

For example, for us it evoked Leacock's (1969) intriguing study of urban elementary schools, in which teachers differentiated curriculum for less-able students principally by overlaying academic information with moralisms. Spelling sentences, story interpretations, and writing assignments were filled with sermonettes which implored students to straighten up and fly right: "Correct. The *correct* way to behave is to raise one's hand." Leacock speculated that academically unsuccessful students' rejection of remedial lessons had less to do with their skill-level or intellectual interest than with their resistance to the teachers' epigrams which, ironically, teachers took for granted as a way of reaching kids with personalized or "relevant" curriculum. Because Bright Prospects students receive an equally moralistic curriculum but embrace rather than resist it, we wonder, with Lesko, about the vulnerability of teen mothers to school's messages. The comparison also leads us to wonder about the commonsensical rationale, or theory, on which differentiated curricula rest. That is, remedial curricula are often designed to take students' personal situations into account as a means of motivating students, yet such designs also justify lessons that can be personally invasive or demeaning.

The chapters, considered together, also record less-singular terms in the language of education. Although common, they become noticeable by virtue of the remarkable regularity with which they recur across settings. As markers of differentiation's specific parameters, their comparison allows us to plumb the layers of signification of the commonplace.

For example, "ability" and "effort" punctuate school participants' talk about curriculum differentiation. When teachers speak of "ability," they often refer to inherent, given talent. By contrast, teachers use "effort" to refer to students' willingness to "try," a volitional, attitudinal phenomenon. Together, the two terms set up a pedagogically salient structure of opposition between the intellectual and the social, or the academic and the behavioral. However, as the chapters in the book indicate, the structure is multi- rather than unidimensional, so that "ability" and "effort" connote different meanings in different contexts. Thus, as Goldstein notes, Ashmont teachers confound "ability" and achievement: the "ability" to read is reading's performance, not a capacity or potential to learn to read. Moreover, for some Ashmont teachers, low "ability" takes on added weight to signal students' fundamental unteachability. By contrast, as Valli describes, Central Catholic teachers expect that "effort" is the crucial determinant of school success. Since all students, regardless of "ability," can "try," all can succeed. Valli's analysis also shows that making an "effort" is not limited to students but is required of the school as well, hence the provision of a differentiated curriculum according to students' levels of "ability." In such a program, students who read at a fourth or fifth grade level are not expected to tackle *Julius Caesar.* Nor, however, are they treated like fourth or fifth graders, to whom, for example, *Julius Caesar* might be read aloud. Instead, less able students read high interest/low ability texts rather than the classics, but they discuss the same ideas as the upper-track classes — ideas of importance and interest to adolescents moving toward responsible positions as adults. "Effort" is also multivocal however, as the comparison with Page's chapter indicates: teachers expect lower-track students to "try" but, in Maplehurst, "trying" is largely a slogan for compliance and social control.

Other terms, as common as "ability" and "effort," also recur with varying connotations and denotations. For example, many school participants in these studies justify curriculum differentiation as a means of providing for "individualized" instruction. However, the specialized, personalized curriculum for mothers at Bright Prospects and the separate bilingual program for Hmong students at Ashmont resemble markedly the rather traditional school curriculum. A similar phenomenon occurs at Central Catholic where the seventh track students engage with a curriculum that is quite parallel to the first track. In other words, "individualized" programs may be much less differentiated than the language of education implies. Further permutations on "individualized" associate it with choice. At Camarena's public schools, "individualism" is structured by student and parent choice, whereas in the Catholic schools, it is structured by close monitoring and school guidance. Although all students select "individually" tailored programs, choice operates quite differently in the two sectors, creating quite different school experiences and outcomes. Moreover, as Sanders reminds, even when choice is institutionalized, teachers often describe elective courses to preclude their election by students whom they perceive as undesirable or unmotivated.

"Practical knowledge" and "high-status knowledge" embody similar complexity and ambiguity. Sanders reports that at Progressive High School, only Advanced Placement and gifted courses are considered "high-status." Such courses are "high-status" at Hanson's Suburban High as well, but the knowledge the courses embody is strictly instrumental. It is the "practical knowledge" of preparing for the Scholastic Aptitude Test. Moreover, Suburban High's technical orientation resembles strongly the "practical knowledge" Hemmings and Metz found at Quincy High, which prepared working-class students for working-class life. At both schools, students memorize facts, learn basic academic skills, and follow rules and routines. Yet, if these socially-different schools both promote "practical knowledge," Urban High offers its poor, minority, upper-track students an abstract, almost elitist, "high-status" curriculum. As these examples suggest, careful descriptions of the language of education document the intricacies with which practitioners characterize curriculum. They challenge more easily remembered formulae, such as the assumption that lower-track classes correspond necessarily to "lower status knowledge," lower teacher expectations, and lower-class students.

The studies in this volume also document the variety of functions that school participants attribute, often implicitly, to the differentiated curriculum. In some schools, such as Catholic Central, it acted as a bridge to take lower-track students to a higher track. In others, such as Ashmont, it functioned as a gate, blocking entrance to higher tracks, higher-status knowledge and, possibly, to higher education. In still other locales, curriculum differentiation provided compensation (Hemmings and Metz's Grant High School), reconciliation (Central Catholic), capitulation (Camarena's public schools), or accommodation (Hemmings and Metz's Quincy High School). Even that most common term of differentiation, "tracking," is multivocal and multifunctional. As we suggested above, sometimes curriculum is organized by "ability," sometimes by "effort," and sometimes by "interest" and projected post-secondary destinations. In some places, tracking sets students on different paths; in others, it clearly marks and monitors the paths.

We expect readers will notice other terms in these case studies. We hope the chapters will also prompt analysis of the words that inform the schools in which readers work. Readers' analyses may be guided by three, admittedly broad conclusions which can be drawn from this volume. First, curriculum differentiation occurs in every formal school context, even those which claim not to track. Second, the practice is complex and contextualized — paradoxical, we have said. And, third, acknowledgement and serious discussion of differentiating practices, rather than denying or over-simplifying them, is crucial. Tracing the twists and turns of our discourse is one way to think about the complex subtleties of curriculum differentiation and about language's power to shape, as well as to reflect, instructional practice.

## POLICY ISSUES

Finally, the chapters indicate the policy value of detailed studies of single schools, even of single classrooms, and of their careful comparison. Curriculum policy of late is written on a grand scale, about *the* knowledge that equity and excellence require from *the* American high school. The studies in this collection remind that such global profundities only occur in concrete instances. To think about them requires consideration of their specific, variable enactments. And, while the studies in this volume detail the importance of structural differences and similarities — size, sector, socioeconomics, sociocultural characteristics of students — they simultaneously argue that their significance is only apprehensible with equal attention to human agency, meaning, and contexts.

Consequently, the collection acknowledges that US high schools and curriculum are formally quite similar, but also points to important informal, cultural differences between and within schools. School culture becomes a central element in the theoretical model of curriculum differentiation. It filters community norms and individual idiosyncracies, is carried into classrooms by teachers and students, and is translated in and through daily lessons. Thus, college-preparatory Ashmont provides bilingual students their own differentiated curriculum — parallel to but apart from the mainstream curriculum. But Logan High School, a working-class school in which behavior is more highly valued than academic ability, mainstreams Asian students into lower-track classes with hopes that their docility will influence their unruly American classmates. Consequently, curriculum differentiation and being a Hmong student at Ashmont and at Logan are very different realities. And, such realities matter for adequate policy. Standardizing Ashmont's and Logan's curricula, whether "high status" or not, would still prompt differentiated responses and not necessarily equitable or excellent outcomes. For example, teachers, particularly at Ashmont, might feel de-professionalized, they might teach with increased detachment, and that in turn might distance students further from schooling.

In similar fashion, the studies question policy-makers' reliance on standardized, quantifiable outcomes, or products, as the key measure of schooling's excellence and equity. They show that processes *are* products: students' and teachers' daily experiences with each other and knowledge, although so mundane as to be overlooked, are crucial outcomes. The Hmong at Ashmont may score similarly on achievement tests as those at Logan but their experiences of schooling, self, peers, place, and adults diverge. Similarly, Additional Needs students at Southmoor may discuss controversial topics, as do their regular-track counterparts, but the discussions are less frequent, are highly-controlled and, ambiguously, are guided toward both generating and closing disagreement. To disagree is not a legitimate "additional need" at Southmoor. In like fashion, Real Teaching is not "merely" a process. It *is* the daily product: a tentative outcome of teachers' and students' negotiations of instruction and knowledge that is both socially legitimate and instructionally effective. As Sanders shows at an organizational level (chapter 10), such processes of curriculum differentiation generate institutionalized products in a variety of school types and sizes: linear, elective, and loosely-coupled course sequences.

The collection of statistical data about schools is a commonplace of policy today (although when William Torrey Harris suggested it around the turn of the century the idea was radical). These studies suggest that it is time to begin structured support for an archive of case studies of schools, as Dell Hymes (1980) has proposed. Such a project hinges on taking seriously and comparing the significance of the idiosyncracies of individual schools. Detailed ethnographies provide the data and concepts with which to begin an ethnology of education which will recognize that tracking does not have the same underlying rationale, nor the same impact, across classrooms and schools. Defining metaphors — the specific words that school people and ethnographers use to capture the gestalt of a school culture's meaning system and its relationship to wider meaning systems of the community and society — may provide a fluid classificatory system for such a typology. The articles in this volume do not add up to such a typology although they begin its discussion.

Sustained debate, in which we talk and listen to each other, is difficult in a large, complex, efficiency-driven society, yet it is crucial to both understanding and enacting curriculum differentiation. The persistent oscillations in the research literature, the recurrent policy debates, and the pervasive, ambivalent, and too frequently negative versions of curriculum differentiation pose tracking as a lightning rod which grounds serious, complicated struggles over who we are and how we shall live together. Accordingly, to ask whether schools should (or should not) differentiate curriculum is the wrong question, and to look to research results for unassailable direction is a misguided expectation. To argue universal policy and standards, no matter how noble the intention, is to disregard multivocal humanity and schooling's mediating influence. Instead, curriculum differentiation, as a sociocultural and political process, deserves our serious debate. Through discourse together, we may comprehend the spectacular diversity of American culture, critique the conditions that all too frequently constrain its manifestation in schools (for all students and teachers, but particularly for those who are lower-track or lower-status), and act to value it as an affirmation and insurance of the distinctive humanity of each and all of us.

# Bibliography

Adler, Mortimer J. *The Paideia Proposal: An Educational Manifesto*. New York: Macmillan Publishing Company, 1982.

Agar, Michael. *Speaking of Ethnography*. Beverly Hills, CA: Sage, 1986.

Anyon, Jean. "Elementary Schooling and Distinctions of Social Class." *Interchange* 12 (1981): 118–132.

Apple, Michael. *Ideology and Curriculum*. London: Routledge & Kegan Paul, 1979.

———. *Education and Power*. Boston and London: Routledge and Kegan Paul, 1982.

Apple, Michael W., and Lois Weis. *Ideology and Practice in Schooling*. Philadelphia: Temple University Press, 1983.

Astin, Alexander. *Minorities in American Higher Education*. San Francisco, CA: Jossey-Bass Inc., 1982.

Au, Kathryn and J. Mason. "Social Organization Factors in Learning to Read: The Balance of Rights Hypothesis." *Reading Research Quarterly* 17 (1981): pp. 115–52.

Bacharach, Stephen. *Organizational Behavior in Schools and School Districts*. New York: Praeger, 1981.

Baldridge, J. V. and Terrence E. Deal, eds. *The Dynamics of Organizational Change in Education*. Berkeley: McCutchan Publishing Corp., 1983.

Bankston, Mary. "Organizational Reporting in a School District: State and Federal Program (Project Report No. 82–AID)." Stanford, CA: Institute for the Study of Educational Finance and Governance, 1982.

Barney, G. L. *The Meo of Xieng Khouang Province*. Waltham, MA: Brandeis University, 1961. Laos Project Paper #13.

Barnhardt, C. "Tuning-in: Athabaskan Teachers and Athabaskan Students." In *Cross-Cultural Issues in Alaskan Education*, Vol. 2. Fairbanks, AK: University of Alaska, Center for Cross-Cultural Studies, 1982.

Barr, Rebecca and Robert Dreeben. "Instruction in Classrooms." In *Review of Research in Education,* ed. David Berliner, 89 – 162. Washington, D.C.: American Educational Research Association, 1978.

Barr, Rebecca and Robert Dreeben, with N. Wiratchai. *How Schools Work*. Chicago: University of Chicago Press, 1983.

Battistoni, Richard. *Public Schooling and the Education of Democratic Citizens*. Jackson, MS: University of Mississippi Press, 1985.

Bauch, Patricia, Irene Blum, Nancy Taylor, and Linda Valli. "Methodology Used to Conduct a Field Study of Five Catholic Secondary Schools Serving Low-Income Families, 1985" [unpublished manuscript]. Washington, D.C.

Bellack, Arno. "Competing Ideologies in Research on Teaching." Uppsala, Sweden: Department of Education, Uppsala University, 1978.

Bellack, Arno, Herbert Kliebard, Ronald Hyman and Frank Smith, Jr. *The Language of the Classroom*. New York: Teachers College Press, 1966.

Bellah, Robert, Richard Madsen, William Sullivan, Ann Swidler, and Steven Tipton. *Habits of the Heart*. New York: Harper & Row, 1985.

Bennett, William J. *Our Children and Our Country: Improving America's Schools and Affirming the Common Culture*. New York: Simon and Schuster, 1988.

Bennis, Warren G., Kenneth D. Denne, and Robert Chin, eds. *The Planning of Change*. 2d ed. New York: Holt, Rinehart and Winston, Inc., 1969.

Bernstein, Basil. "On the Classification and Framing of Educational Knowledge." *Class, Codes and Control,* Vol. 3, 2d ed. Boston: Routledge & Kegan Paul, 1977.

Bigge, June. *Curriculum Based Instruction*. Mountain View, CA: Mayfield Publishing Company, 1988.

Bourdieu, Pierre and Jean-Claude Passeron. *Reproduction in Education, Society, and Culture*. Beverly Hills: Sage Publications, 1977.

Bowles, Samuel and Herbert Gintis. *Schooling in Capitalist America*. New York: Basic Books, 1976.

Boyer, Ernest L. *High School: A Report on Secondary Education*. New York: Harper & Row Publishers, 1983.

Bryk, Anthony and Mary Erina Driscoll. *The High School as Community: Contextual Influences and Consequences for Students and Teachers*. Madison, WI: National Center on Effective Secondary Schools, 1988.

Butler, Sandra. *Conspiracy of Science: The Trauma of Incest*. Volcano, CA: Volcano Press, [1978] 1985.

Callahan, R. E. *Education and the Cult of Efficiency*. Chicago: University of Chicago Press, 1969.

Camarena, Margaret. "A Comparison of the Organizational Structure of Public and Private Schools: Implications for the Education of Disadvantaged Students." Paper presented at the annual meeting of the American Educational Research Association, Washington, D.C., 1987.

Cazden, Courtney. "Classroom Discourse." In *Handbook of Research on Teaching,* 3rd ed., ed. Merlin Wittrock, 432–63. New York: Macmillan, 1986.

Children's Defense Fund. "Preventing Children Having Children." Washington, D.C.: Adolescent Pregnancy Prevention Clearinghouse, 1985.

———. "Adolescent Pregnancy: Whose Problem Is It?" Washington, D.C.: Adolescent Pregnancy Prevention Clearinghouse, 1986.

Cibulka, James G., Timothy J. O'Brien, and Donald Zewe. *Inner-City Elementary Schools: A Study*. Milwaukee, WI: Marquette University Press, 1982.

Cicourel, Aaron V. and John I. Kitsuse. *The Educational Decision Makers*. Indianapolis: The Bobbs-Merrill Company, Inc., 1963.

Cohen, Abner. "Political Anthropology: The Analysis of the Symbolism of Power Relations." *Man: The Journal of the Royal Anthropological Institute* 4 (1969): 215–35.

Cohen, Elizabeth G., Terrence E. Deal, John W. Meyer, Brian Rowan, and W. Richard Scott. "Technology and Teaming in the Elementary School." *Sociology of Education* 52 (1979):20–33.

Cohen, Michael D., James G. March and Johan P. Olsen. "A Garbage Can Model Organizational Choice." *Administrative Science Quarterly* 17 (1972): 1–25.

Coleman, James. *Equality of Educational Opportunity*. Washington, D.C.: U.S. Department of Health, Education and Welfare, 1966.

Coleman, James and Thomas Hoffer. *Public and Private High Schools: The Impact of Communities*. New York: Basic Books, 1987.

Coleman, James S., Thomas Hoffer, and Sally Kilgore. *High School Achievement: Public, Catholic and Private Schools Compared*. New York: Basic Books, 1982.

The College Board Equality Project 1983. *Academic Preparation for College: What Students Need to Know and Be Able to Do*. New York: The College Board, 1983.

Conant, James B. *The American High School Today*. New York: McGraw-Hill Book Company, 1959.

Connell, R. W., D. J. Ashenden, S. Keller and G. W. Dowsett. *Making the Difference*. Boston: George Allen & Unwin, 1982.

Cummins, Jim. "Empowering Minority Students: Framework for Intervention." *Harvard Education Review* 56 (1986): 19–37.

Cusick, Philip A. *Inside High School: The Student's World*. New York: Holt, Rinehart and Winston, Inc., 1973.

———. *The Egalitarian Ideal and the American High School: Studies of Three Schools*. New York: Longman, Inc., 1983.

Davies, Lynn. *Pupil Power: Deviance and Gender in School*. London: Falmer Press, 1984.

DeLaney, Brian. "Choices and Chances: The Matching of Students and Courses in High School." Ph.D. diss., Stanford University, 1986.

Delaney, Brian, and Michael S. Garet. "Tracking and Choice: Matching Students and Courses in High School." Paper presented at the annual meeting of the American Educational Research Association, San Francisco, CA, 1986.

Denzin, Norman K. *Sociological Methods: A Sourcebook*. Chicago, IL: Aldine Press, 1970.

Dewey, John. *The Child & The Curriculum*. Chicago: University of Chicago Press, 1956. (Orig. 1902)

———. *The Sources of A Science of Education*. NY: Liverwright, 1929.

Douglas, Mary. *Purity and Danger*. London: Routledge and Kegan Paul, 1966.

Drahmann, Theodore. "Governance and Administration in the Catholic School." Washington, D.C.: National Catholic Educational Association, 1985.

Dreeben, Robert and Rebecca Barr. "An Organizational Analysis of Curriculum and Instruction." In *The Social Organization of Schools: New Conceptualizations of the Learning Process,* ed. Maureen T. Hallinan. New York: Plenum, 1987.

*Education Week.* "Here They Come, Ready or Not." Vol. V, 34, May 14, 1986.

Edwards, A. D. and Viv Furlong. *The Language of Teaching.* London: Heinemann Education Books, 1978.

Eisner, Elliot W. *The Educational Imagination.* New York: Macmillan Publishing Co., Inc., 1979.

Erickson, Fred. "Qualitative Methods in Research on Teaching." In *Handbook of Research on Teaching,* 3rd ed., ed. Merlin Wittrock, 119–61. New York: Macmillan, 1986.

Erickson, Frederick, and Gerald Mohatt. "Cultural Organization of Participation Structures in Two Classrooms of Indian Students." In *Doing the Ethnography of Schooling,* ed. George Spindler, 132–174. New York: Holt, Rinehart and Winston, 1982.

Erickson, Lawrence G. "Negotiating School Improvements." *Journal of Staff Development* 9 (Spring 1988): 30–34.

Everhardt, Robert. *Reading, Writing, and Resistance: Adolescence and Labor in a Junior High School.* London: Routledge & Kegan Paul, 1983.

Finley, Merrilee K. "Teachers and Tracking in a Comprehensive High School." *Sociology of Education* 57 (1984): 233–243.

Fisher, C. W., N. N. Filby, R. S. Marliave, L. S. Cahen, M. M. Dishaw, J. E. Moore, and D. C. Berliner. *Teaching Behaviors Academic Learning Time and Student Achievement: Beginning Teacher Evaluation Study.* San Francisco: Far West Laboratory for Education Research and Development, 1978. Final Rep. Phase III–B.

Foucault, Michel. *The Order of Things: An Archaeology of the Human Sciences.* New York: Vintage/Random House, [1970] 1973.

———. *The History of Sexuality, Volume One, An Introduction.* New York: Vintage/Random House, 1980.

Furlong, Viv. "Anancy Goes to School: A Case Study of Pupils' Knowledge of Their Teachers." In *School Experience,* ed. Peter Woods and Michael Hammersley, 162–85. London: Croom Helm, Ltd., 1977.

Furstenberg, Frank F., Jr., J. Brooks-Gunn, and S. Philip Morgan. *Adolescent Mothers in Later Life.* Cambridge: Cambridge University Press, 1987.

Gamoran, Adam and Mark Berends. "The Effects of Stratification in Secondary Schools: Synthesis of Survey and Ethnographic Research." *Review of Educational Research* 57 (Winter 1987): 415–435.

Geddes, William Robert. *Migrants of the Mountains*. Oxford: Clarendon Press, 1976.

Geertz, Clifford. *The Interpretation of Cultures*. New York: Basic Books, 1973.

Giroux, Henry A. *Ideology, Culture, and the Process of Schooling*. Philadelphia: Temple University Press, 1981.

Goldberg, Miriam, Harry Passow and Joseph Justman. *The Effects of Ability Grouping*. New York: Teachers College Press, 1966.

Goldstein, Beth L. "Schooling for Cultural Transitions." Ph.D. diss., University of Wisconsin, Madison, 1985.

———. "The Interplay between School Culture and Status for Teachers of Immigrant Students." *Educational Foundations* 2 (1988): 52–76.

Good, Thomas and Jere Brophy. *Looking in Classrooms*. 4th ed. New York: Harper & Row.

Goodlad, John. *A Place Called School*. New York: McGraw-Hill, 1984.

Gordon, Linda. *Woman's Body, Woman's Right*. Harmondsworth: Penguin Books, 1976.

Greeley, Andrew. *Catholic High Schools and Minority Students*. New Brunswick, NJ: Transaction Books, 1982.

Greene, Maxine. "Public Education and the Public Space." *The Kettering Review* (Fall 1985): 55–60.

Gusfield, Joseph R. *Symbolic Crusade*. Urbana, IL: University of Illinois Press, [1963], 1986.

Guttmacher Institute. *Teenage Pregnancy*. New York: Alan Guttmacher Institute, 1981.

Hanson, Susan G. "The College-Preparatory Curriculum at Two High Schools in One School District." Ph.D. diss., Stanford University, 1985.

———. "The College-Preparatory Curriculum Across Schools: Access to Similar Learning Opportunities?" Paper delivered at the annual meeting of the American Educational Research Association, San Francisco, 1986.

Harding, Sandra. *The Science Question in Feminism*. Ithaca: Cornell University Press, 1986.

Hargreaves, David. *Social Relations in a Secondary School*. London: Routledge and Kegan Paul, 1967.

Harvey, Michael J. "Pupil Awareness of the Career Pathways and Choice Points in the High School." *Educational Review* 36 (1984): 53–66.

Heath, Shirley and Amanda Branscombe. " 'Intelligent Writing' in an Audience Community: Teacher, Students and Researcher." In *The Acquisition of Written Language: Response and Revision,* ed. Susan Freedman, 3–32. Norwood, NJ: Ablex, 1985.

Henriques, Julian, Wendy Hollway, Cathy Urwin, Couze Venn, and Valerie Walkerdine. *Changing the Subject*. London: Methuen, 1984.

Henry, Jules. "Attitude Organization in Elementary School Classrooms." In *Education and Culture: Anthropological Approaches,* ed. George Spindler, 192–214. New York: Holt, Rinehart and Winston, Inc., 1963.

Hirsch, E. D. *Cultural Literacy: What Every American Needs to Know*. Boston: Houghton Mifflin Co., 1987.

House, Ernest R. "Three Perspectives on Innovation." In *Improving Schools: Using What We Know,* ed. R. Lehming and M. Kane, 17 41. Beverly Hills, CA: Sage, 1981.

Howe, Florence. *Myths of Coeducation*. Bloomington, IN: Indiana University Press, 1984.

Hurlich, Marshall G. and Nancy D. Donnelly. "Markers of Hmong Identity in the United States." Paper presented at American Anthropology Association meetings, Denver, 1984.

Hymes, Dell. "Educational Ethnology." In *Language in Education,* ed. Dell Hymes, 119–25. Washington, D.C.: Center for Applied Linguistics, 1980.

Jackson, Philip. *Life in Classrooms*. New York: Holt, Rinehart and Winston, 1968.

———. *The Practice of Teaching*. New York: Teachers College Press, 1986.

Jelinek, Mariann, Linda Smircich and Paul Hirsch, eds. "Organizational Culture." *Administrative Science Quarterly* 28 (1983): 331–338.

Jencks, Christopher and Marcia Brown. "Effects of High Schools on Their Students." *Harvard Educational Review* 45 (1975): 273–324.

Kammen, Michael. *People of Paradox: A Contrapuntal Civilization*. New York: A. Knopf, 1974.

Kaplan, Cora. *Sea Changes*. London: Verso, 1986.

Keddie, Nell. "Classroom Knowledge." In *Knowledge and Control,* ed. Michael F. D. Young, 133–60. London: Collier-Macmillan, 1971.

Kleinfeld, Judith. *Eskimo School on the Andreafsky.* New York: Praeger, 1979.

Kliebard, Herbert. "Curriculum Theory as Metaphor." *Theory into Practice* 21 (1982): 11–17.

———. *The Struggle for the American Curriculum 1893–1958.* New York: Routledge & Kegan Paul, 1987.

Lee, Valerie E. "The Effect of Curriculum Tracking on the Social Distribution of Achievement in Catholic and Public Secondary Schools." Paper presented at the annual meeting of the American Educational Research Association, San Francisco, CA, 1986.

Lee, Valerie and Anthony Bryk. "Curriculum Tracking as Mediating the Social Distribution of High School Achievement." *Sociology of Education* 61 (April 1988): 78–94.

Lesko, Nancy. *Symbolizing Society: Stories, Rites and Structure in a Catholic High School.* New York: Falmer Press, 1988.

Lewis, Magda, and Roger Simon. "A Discourse Not Intended for Her: Learning and Teaching Within Patriarchy." *Harvard Educational Review* 56 (November 1986): 457–472.

Lightfoot, Sara Lawrence. *The Good High School.* New York: Basic Books, Inc., 1983.

Luker, Kristin. *Abortion: The Politics of Motherhood.* Berkeley, CA: University of California Press, 1984.

MacCannell, Dean, and Juliet Flower MacCannell. *The Time of the Sign.* Bloomington, IN: Indiana University Press, 1982.

MacDonald, Madeleine. "Socio-cultural Reproduction and Women's Education." In *Schooling for Women's Work,* ed. Rosemary Deem, 13–25. Boston: Routledge & Kegan Paul, 1980.

March, James G. and Herbert A. Simon. *Organizations.* New York: John Wiley and Sons, Inc., 1958.

McNeil, Linda. *Contradictions of Control: School Structure and School Knowledge.* New York and London: Routledge and Kegan Paul, 1986.

Mehan, Hugh. "Structuring School Structures." *Harvard Educational Review* 48 (1978): 32–46.

———. *Learning Lessons.* Cambridge, MA: Harvard University Press, 1979.

Merelman, Richard. *Making Something of Ourselves: On Culture and Politics in The United States*. Berkeley: University of California Press, 1984.

Metz, Mary H. *Classrooms and Corridors: The Crisis of Authority in Desegregated Secondary Schools*. Berkeley: University of California Press, 1978.

————. "Sources of Constructive Social Relations in an Urban Magnet School." *American Journal of Education* 91 (1983): 202–45.

————. *Different by Design: The Context and Character of Three Magnet Schools*. New York: Routledge and Kegan Paul, 1986.

————. "Real School: A Universal Drama Amid Disparate Experience." In *Educational Politics for the New Century: The Twentieth Anniversary Yearbook of the Politics of Education Association*, ed. D. Mitchell and M. E. Goetz. Philadelphia: The Falmer Press (1990).

Meyer, John W. "The Impact of Centralization of Educational Funding and Control on State and Local Organization Governance (Project Report No. 79–B20)." Stanford, CA: Institute for Research on Educational Finance and Governance, 1979.

————. "Organizational Factors Affecting Legalization in Education (Project Report No. 91–B10)." Stanford, CA: Institute for Research on Educational Finance and Governance, 1981.

Meyer, John and Brian Rowan. "Institutionalized Organizations: Formal Structure as Myth and Ceremony." In *Organizational Environments*, ed. John Meyer and W. Richard Scott, 21–44. Beverly Hills: Sage Publications, 1983.

————. "The Structure of Educational Organizations." In *Environments and Organizations*, M. Meyer and Associates, 78–109. San Francisco: Jossey-Bass, 1978.

Meyer, John and W. Richard Scott. *Organizational Environments*. Beverly Hills: Sage Publications, 1983.

Meyer, John, W. Richard Scott, and Terrence E. Deal. "Institutional and Technical Sources of Organizational Structure Explaining the Structure of Educational Organizations." In *Organizational Environments*, ed. John Meyer and W. Richard Scott, 45–70. Beverly Hills: Sage Publications, 1983.

Morgan, Edward. *Inequality in Classroom Learning: Schooling and Democratic Citizenship*. New York: Praeger, 1977.

National Catholic Education Association. *Catholic High Schools: Their Impact on Low-Income Students*. Washington, D.C.: National Catholic Educational Association, 1986.

————. *United States Catholic Elementary and Secondary Schools, 1984–1985. A Statistical Report on Schools, Enrollment, and Staffing; Special Focus on Minority and Non-Catholic Enrollment.* Washington, D.C.: National Catholic Educational Association, 1985.

The National Commission on Excellence in Education. *A Nation at Risk: The Imperative for Educational Reform.* Washington, D.C.: United States Government Printing Office, 1983.

Oakes, Jeannie. *A Question of Access: Tracking and Curriculum Differentiation in a National Sample of English and Mathematics Classes.* Los Angeles, CA: UCLA Laboratory in School and Community Education, 1981a. Technical Report No. 24, A Study of Schooling.

————. *Tracking Policies and Practices: School by School Summaries.* Los Angeles, CA: Graduate School of Education, 1981b. University of California Technical Report No. 25, A Study of Schooling.

————. "The Reproduction of Inequity: The Content of Secondary School Tracking." *The Urban Review* 4 (1982): 107–122.

————. *Keeping Track: How Schools Structure Inequality.* New Haven: Yale University Press, 1985.

Ogbu, John. *Minority Education and Caste: The American System in a Cross-Cultural Perspective.* New York: Academic Press, 1978.

————. "Variability in Minority School Performance: A Problem in Search of an Explanation." *Anthropology and Education Quarterly* 18 (December 1987): 312–335.

Ovando, Carlos J. and Virginia P. Collier. *Bilingual and ESL Classrooms.* New York: McGraw-Hill Book Company, 1985.

Page, Reba. "Perspectives and Processes: The Negotiation of Educational Meanings in High School Classes for Academically Unsuccessful Students." Ph.D. diss., University of Wisconsin, Madison, 1984.

————. "Lower-Track Classes at a College-Preparatory High School: A Caricature of Educational Encounters." In *Interpretive Ethnography of Education at Home and Abroad,* ed. George and Louise Spindler, 447–72. Hillsdale, NJ: Lawrence Erlbaum, 1987a.

————. "Teachers' Perceptions of Students: A Link Between Classrooms, School Cultures, and the Social Order." *Anthropology and Education Quarterly* 18 (1987b): 77–99.

————. "The Lower-Track Curriculum at a 'Heavenly' High School: 'Cycles of Prejudice.' " *Journal of Curriculum Studies* 21 (1989): 197–221.

————. "Games of Chance: The Lower-Track Curriculum in a College-Preparatory High School." *Curriculum Inquiry,* in press.

Parsons, Talcott. "Suggestions for a Sociological Approach to the Theory of Organizations–1." *Administrative Science Quarterly* 1 (1956): 63–85.

Patterson, Jerry L., Stewart C. Purkey and Jackson V. Parker. *Productive School Systems for a Nonrational World.* Alexandria, VA: A.S.C.D., 1986.

Peng, Samuel S., William B. Fetters, and Andrew J. Kolstad. *A Capsule Description of High School Students. High School and Beyond: A National Longitudinal Study for the 1980s.* National Center for Education Statistics, 1981.

Peterson, J. "Against 'Parenting.' " In *Mothering: Essays in Feminist Theory.* Totowa, NJ: Rowman and Allanheld, 1984.

Pomerantz, Ann. "Compliment Responses: Notes on the Cooperation of Multiple Restraints." In *Studies in the Organization of Conversational Interaction,* ed. Jim Schenkein, 79–112. New York: Academic Press, 1978.

Popkewitz, Tom, Robert Tabachnick and Gary Wehlage. *The Myth of Educational Reform: A Study of School Response to a Program of Change.* Madison, WI: University of Wisconsin Press, 1982.

Powell, Arthur G., Eleanor Farrar, and David K. Cohen. *The Shopping Mall High School: Winners and Losers in the Educational Market Place.* Boston: Houghton Mifflin, 1985.

Precourt, Walter. "Ethnohistorical Analysis of an Appalachian Settlement School." In *Doing the Ethnography of Schooling,* ed. George Spindler, 440–453. New York: Holt, Rinehart and Winston, 1982.

Rains, Prudence Mors. *Becoming an Unwed Mother.* Chicago: Aldine, 1971.

Riordan, Cornelius. "Public and Catholic Schooling: The Effects of Gender Context Policy." *American Journal of Education* 93 (August 1985): 518–39.

Rist, Ray. *The Urban School: Factory For Failure.* Cambridge, MA: MIT Press, 1973.

————. "On the Relations Among Education Research Paradigms: From Disdain to Detente." *Anthropology and Education Quarterly* 8 (1977): 42–49.

Rogoff, Barbara, Mary Gauvin, and Shari Ellis. "Development Viewed in its Cultural Context." In *Developmental Psychology,* ed. M. Bornstein and M. Lamb. Hillsdale, NJ: Lawrence Erlbaum, 1984.

Rosenbaum, James. *Making Inequality: The Hidden Curriculum of High School Tracking.* New York: Wiley/Interscience, 1976.

———. "Social Implications of Educational Grouping." In *Review of Research in Education,* ed. D. C. Berliner, 361–401. Itasca, IL: American Educational Research Association, 1980.

Rosenbaum, James and Susan Presser. "Voluntary Racial Integration in a Magnet School." *School Review* 86 (1978): 156–86.

Rosenthal, Robert and Lenore Jacobsen. *Pygmalion in the Classroom.* New York: Holt, Rinehart & Winston, 1968.

Rowan, Brian. "The Effect of Institutionalized Rules on Administrators." In *Organizational Behavior in Schools and School Districts,* ed. Samuel B. Bacharach, 43–59. New York: Praeger, 1981.

Rutter, Michael, Barbara Maughan, Peter Mortimore, and Janet Ouston. *Fifteen Thousand Hours: Secondary Schools and their Effects on Children.* Cambridge, MA: Harvard University Press, 1979.

Ryle, Gilbert. *The Concept of Mind.* Chicago: University of Chicago Press, 1949.

Sacks, Harvey. "An Initial Investigation of the Usability of Conversational Data for Doing Sociology." In *Studies in Social Interactions,* ed. David Sudnow, 31–74. New York: Free Press, 1972.

Salganik, Laura H. and Nancy Karweit. "Volunteerism and Governance in Education." *Sociology of Education* 55 (1982), 152–161.

Sanders, Nancy M. "Organizational Perspectives on Curriculum: A Sociological Study of Paths Through High School." Ph.D. diss., Stanford University, 1989.

Sanders, Nancy M. and Nancy C. Stone. *The California High School Curriculum Study: Paths Through High School.* Sacramento, CA: Department of Education, 1987.

Sarason, Seymour B. *The Culture of the School and the Problem of Change.* Boston: Allyn and Bacon, 1971.

Schwartz, Frances. "Supporting or Subverting Learning: Peer Group Patterns in Four Tracked Schools." *Anthropology and Education Quarterly* 12 (1981): 99–120.

Scott, W. Richard. *Organizations: Rational, Natural, and Open System.* Englewood Cliffs, NJ: Prentice-Hall, 1987.

———. "Introduction: From Technology to Environment." In *Organizational Environments,* ed. John W. Meyer and W. Richard Scott. Beverly Hills: Sage Publications, 1983.

Scott, W. Richard and John W. Meyer. "The Organization of Societal Sectors." In *Organizational Environments,* ed. John W. Meyer and W. Richard Scott, 129–153. Beverly Hills: Sage Publications, 1983.

———. "Environmental Linkages and Organizational Complexity: Public and Private Schools (Project Report No. 84–A16)." Stanford, CA: Institute for Research on Educational Finance and Governance, 1984.

Sedlak, Michael, Christopher Wheeler, Diana Pullin, and Philip Cusick. *Selling Students Short: Classroom Bargains and Academic Reform in the American High School.* New York: Teachers College Press, 1986.

Sizer, Theodore R. *Horace's Compromise.* Boston: Houghton Mifflin Company, 1984.

Slaughter, Diana T. and Deborah J. Johnson, ed. *Visible Now: Blacks in Private Schools.* New York: Greenwood Press, 1988.

Slavin, Robert. "Ability Grouping: A Best Evidence Synthesis." *Review of Educational Research* 57 (1987): 293–336.

Smith, John and Lons Heshisius. "Closing Down the Conversation: The End of the Quantitative-Qualitative Debate Among Educational Inquirers." *Educational Researcher* 15 (1986): 4–12.

Smith-Rosenberg, Carol. *Disorderly Conduct.* New York: Oxford University Press, 1985.

Sorensen, Aage B. and Maureen T. Hallinan. "Race Effects on Assignment to Ability Groups." In *The Social Context of Instruction,* ed. Penelope Peterson, Louise Cherry Wilkinson, and Maureen T. Hallinan. San Diego: Academic Press, 1984.

Spender, Dale. *Invisible Woman: The Schooling Scandal.* London: Writers and Readers Cooperative, 1983.

Spindler, George, ed. *Doing the Ethnography of Schooling.* New York: Holt, Rinehart & Winston, 1982.

Spindler, George and Louise Spindler, eds. *Interpretive Ethnography of Education at Home and Abroad.* Hillsdale, NJ: Lawrence Erlbaum, 1987.

Spindler, Louise and George Spindler. "Roger Harker and Schonhausen: From Familiar to Strange and Back Again." In *Doing the Ethnography of Schooling,* ed. George Spindler, 20–46. New York: Holt, Rinehart & Winston, 1982.

Stackhouse, E. Anne. "The Effects of State Centralization on Administrative and Macrotechnical Structure in Contemporary Secondary Schools (Project Report No. 82–A24)." Stanford, CA: Institute for Research on Educational Finance and Governance, 1982.

Stallings, Jean and D. Kaskowitz. *Follow-Through Classroom Observation Evaluation, 1972–73*. Menlo Park, CA: Stanford Research Institute, 1974.

Strike, Kenneth A. "Is There a Conflict Between Equity and Excellence?" *Educational Evaluation and Policy Analysis* 7 (Winter 1985): 409.

Swidler, Ann. *Organization Without Authority*. Cambridge, MA: Harvard University Press, 1979.

Talbert, Joan E. "Conditions of Public and Private School Organization and Notions of Effective Schools." In *Comparing Public and Private Schools: Institutions and Organization*, Vol. 1, ed. Thomas James and Henry Levin, 161–188. Philadelphia, PA: Palmer Press, 1988.

*Time*. "Children Having Children." December 9, 1985.

Turner, Victor. *The Ritual Process*. Chicago: Aldine, 1969.

Turner, Bryan S. *The Body and Society*. London: Basil Blackwell, 1984.

Tye, Barbara. *Multiple Realities: A Study of 13 American High Schools*. Lanham: University Press of America, 1985.

Valli, Linda. *Becoming Clerical Workers*. London: Routledge and Kegan Paul, 1986a.

———. "Tracking: Can It Benefit Low Achieving Students?" Paper presented at the annual meeting of the American Educational Research Association, San Francisco, 1986b.

Varenne, Herve. *Americans Together*. New York: Teachers College Press, 1977.

———. *American School Language: Culturally-Patterned Conflicts in a Suburban High School*. New York: Irvington Publishers, 1983.

Walkerdine, Valerie. *The Mastery of Reason*. London: Routledge and Kegan Paul, 1988.

Walker, R. and C. Adelman. "Strawberries." In *Explorations in Classroom Observations*, ed. Michael Stubbs and Sarah Delamont, 133–50. London: John Wiley, 1976.

Waller, Willard. *The Sociology of Teaching*. New York: John Wiley, 1932.

Weber, Max. *The Theory of Social and Economic Organizations*. Translated by M. Henderson and T. Parsons. Glencoe, IL: The Free Press, 1947.

Weedon, Chris. *Feminist Practice and Poststructuralist Theory*. London: Basil Blackwell, 1987.

Wehlage, Gary. "The Purposes of Generalization in Field-Study Research." In *A Study of Schooling: Field-Based Methodologies in Educational Research and Evaluation,* ed. Tom Popkewitz and Robert Tabachnick, 211–26. New York: Praeger, 1981.

Wehlage, Gary, Calvin Stone, and Herbert Kliebard. *Dropouts and Schools: Case Studies of the Dilemmas Educators Face.* Madison, WI: State of Wisconsin Governor's Employment and Training Office, 1980.

Wehlage, Gary, Robert Rutter, Gregory Smith, Nancy Lesko, and Ricardo Fernandez. *Reducing the Risk: Schools as Communities of Support.* London: Falmer Press, 1989.

Weick, Karl E. "Educational Organizations as Loosely Coupled Systems." *Administrative Sciences Quarterly 21* (March 1976): 1–18.

White, Kenneth. "The Relationship Between Socioeconomic Status and Academic Achievement." *Psychological Bulletin* 91 (1982): 461–481.

Whyte, William. *Street Corner Society.* Chicago: The University of Chicago Press, 1943.

Wilcox, Kathleen. "Differential Socialization in the Classroom: Implications for Equal Opportunity." In *Doing the Ethnography of Schooling,* ed. George Spindler, 268–309. New York: Holt, Rinehart & Winston, 1982.

Willis, Paul. *Learning to Labour: How Working Class Kids Get Working Class Jobs.* Farnborough: Saxon House, Teakfield, 1977.

Yang Dao. *Les Hmongs du Laos Face au Developement.* Vientiane, Laos: Siaosavath Publishers, 1975.

Young, Michael, ed. *Knowledge and Control.* London: Collier-Macmillian, 1971.

Zaltman, Gerald, Robert Duncan and Jonny Holbek. *Innovations and Organizations.* New York: John Wiley & Sons, 1973.

# Contributors

Carolyn Anderson is Assistant Superintendent for Niles Township High Schools (Skokie, Illinois). In her previous position at Crete-Monee School District (Crete, Illinois), she collaborated with Rebecca Barr to develop guidelines for instructional grouping. Information about the project has been presented at AERA meetings, in *Educational Foundations, Democracy in Education,* and a book from Erlbaum. Degrees include Ph.D., University of Arizona (1984); M.A.T., John Carroll University (1970); B.A., Allegheny College (1969).

Rebecca Barr is Dean of the School of Education at the National College of Education. Her research focuses on classroom instruction and the learning of children at risk. She is the author of three books and numerous articles.

Margaret Camarena began studying language, culture, and gender issues in education during her graduate training at Stanford University. During the past decade, she has worked on a number of national and statewide studies focusing on the educational needs and problems of minority students and women. Her research has ranged from studies of the effectiveness of educational programs for linguistic minority students and factors affecting Hispanic women's attrition from college to studies of effective public and private school organization. She is currently a research associate at the RAND Corporation, where she is working on a study of minority students in inner-city Catholic schools.

Beth L. Goldstein is an assistant professor in Educational Policy Studies and Evaluation at the University of Kentucky, where she teaches cross-cultural and women's studies, and qualitative research. After three years of teaching at the Chinese University of Hong Kong and the Thailand Refugee Instruction Project, she turned to research on curriculum differentiation for refugee and international students and their teachers in the U.S. Current projects include the work of teachers aides in creating differentiated curricula and curriculum within higher education.

Susan Hanson has been using qualitative approaches to evaluate state-funded educational programs for the past five years. She currently works for SRI as an evaluator of a three year staff development program focusing on technology. Previously, she worked for Far West Labs studying the California Mentor Teacher Program and a state-funded student teacher supervision program. She received her Ph.D. from Stanford University where she conducted her research on curriculum differentiation. Dr. Hanson has presented much of her research at AERA. Her research interests include curriculum equity and qualitative research methodology.

Annette Hemmings is a graduate student in the Department of Educational Policy Studies at the University of Wisconsin-Madison. She is currently completing a dissertation examining the way black students were socialized for academic achievement in two desegregated urban high schools. Before entering graduate school, Annette taught social studies to minority students enrolled in a Federally funded program designed to increase the educational attainments of disadvantaged children.

Nancy Lesko teaches courses in secondary education and curriculum at Indiana University. She examines schools from a feminist and sociology of culture perspective, with special attention to rituals such as cheerleading, prom queens, and assemblies. Her book, *Symbolizing Society: Stories, Rites and Structures in a Catholic High School,* analyzes the school culture and girls' friendships as structured by broader socio-cultural conflicts requiring organizational and student mediation. She co-authored a volume on alternative programs for students at-risk of school dropout. She is beginning a study of the construction of adolescence in middle schools, focusing on conceptions of gender and knowledge in the relationship between adolescent theory and school practice.

Mary Haywood Metz is a Professor of Educational Policy Studies at the University of Wisconsin-Madison. A sociologist, she is the author of *Classrooms and Corridors: The Crisis of Authority in Desegregated Secondary Schools* and *Different by Design: The Context and Character of Three Magnet Schools.* She is currently writing more from the data used in their article on American high schools in communities of differing social class.

Reba Page taught high school English, history, and special education classes for ten years. Now an Assistant Professor of Education at the University of California, Riverside, she studies and teaches about curriculum theory, interpretive research methods, and sociocultural foundations of education. A book about curriculum differentiation, *Ambiguous Patterns: An Ethnography of Lower-Track Classrooms,* will be published soon.

Nancy Sanders is an Assistant Professor in the division of Administration, Curriculum and Supervision in the School of Education at the University of Colorado, Denver. Her research interests are the relationships between curriculum and organizational structure of schools and the effects of curriculum structures on equity. She teaches courses in curriculum, curriculum design and evaluation, and organizational theory.

Linda Valli is Associate Professor and Director of Teacher Education at the Catholic University of America in Washington, D.C. She is the author of *Becoming Clerical Workers,* a critical social analysis of gender, schooling, and workplace relations. Her primary areas of research interest include gender issues in education, school cultures, and reflective teaching. She is presently editing a book of case studies and critiques of reflective teacher education programs.